# KEEPING THE PEACE

LAURIE POINTING

First published 2013

National Library of Australia Cataloguing-in-Publication entry:

| | |
|---|---|
| Author: | Pointing, Laurie. |
| Title: | Keeping the peace. Vol. 1 / Laurie Pointing. |
| ISBN: | 9781922109590 (pbk.) |
| Subjects: | Queensland Police Service--Anecdotes. |
| | Police--Queensland--Anecdotes. |
| Dewey Number: | 363.209943 |

Typeset in Garamond 11pt.

Cover Design by Boolarong Press

Cover Images: Babinda Police Station 1918.
Bulloo Downs Murder, Thargomindah. Bone find. Tracker Tommy Swan in foreground with Sgt Ted Warner in background. Donated by Laurie Pointing July 2012. Images identified by Lyle Pratt, July 2012.

Published by Boolarong Press, Salisbury, Brisbane, Australia.

Printed and bound by Watson Ferguson & Company, Salisbury, Brisbane, Australia.

Supported by

This book is dedicated to the memory of my late brother,

Retired Regional Superintendent,

**Albert Thomas (Tom) Pointing – QPM**

28/05/1928 – 21/03/1999

# Acknowledgements

First, I acknowledge the contribution from the following retired police: Bob Smith, Bill Larkman, George Rickertt, Neil Raward, Kevin Kruger, George Edwards, Don Braithwaite, who also supplied the 'Pioneer Policing story', Neville Travers-Jones, Ossie Cislowski and Gordon Duncan, who assisted me greatly in obtaining Ossie's story. A big thank to Jack Farrell for his contribution to the Aussie Cislowski story as well. In addition, Roslyn Mary Peters nee Kelleher, Barbara Bainbridge, widow of the late Mervyn Bainbridge, and Sergeant Bill Feldman, who supplied some interesting aspects into Merv's career, and Greg Early, who interviewed and obtained the story from the late Abe Duncan.

For their computer skills and expertise, a big thank you to Samantha O'Hanlon, Jill Norton, June Collins, Jenny Dyer, Yolanda Kahler and Kylie Plukaard from Cooloola Colour Graphics, Gympie, who assisted with photocopying and the reproduction of photographs. Thanks to Commissioner of Police Bob Atkinson (now retired) for writing one of the Forewords for the book, Mat Rigby, Media Section Police Headquarters, Brisbane, Lisa Jones, Duncan Leask and other staff of the Queensland Police Museum who assisted greatly with images from bygone years and information regarding the career paths of the retired police who contributed. Retired Sergeant Lyall Pratt, who assisted with identifying photographs from the 1965 Bulloo Downs murder investigation, and Pat O'Brian, Ross Beer and Grannie Pearce for their contribution to the Tom Pointing story.

I am extremely grateful to Geoff Barlow from the Gympie Regional Library who undertook the huge task of editing each story.

Finally, this book would not have gone to press without the generous sponsorship I received from the Queensland Police Union of Employees, Queensland Police Credit Union and Bridges Financial Services.

# Contents

# Forewords

If you ask a Queensland Police Service officer whether they have seen anything unusual during a shift, most will say no. If you ask them whether they have faced any risks, or if they have gone above and beyond the call of duty, again, most will say no.

It's only upon reflection, or upon repeated questioning, that an officer might divulge a story or two. More often than not, these stories reveal fascinating circumstances where officers have faced significant risk, or have gone out of their way to help members of the public and fellow officers, and to keep the peace.

It is some of these stories, these otherwise unrecorded accounts of courage, commitment and everyday service, that Laurie Pointing collects in this book to provide a permanent testament of the lives of members of the Queensland Police Service.

These lives are inextricably linked to the history of the Service, as the officers' experiences take place against a backdrop of an organisation in constant evolution. The officers' lives are also inevitably linked to the history of Queensland, because every event of significance, of tumult, or of community celebration involves the participation of officers of the Service.

In 2014, Queensland police celebrate 150 years of service to the Queensland community, and this collection of stories, of lives and of history encourages current officers to recognise their own roles as having pivotal importance to the future of our Service and of our State.

I encourage members of the Queensland Police Service, and members of the community, to read this book and be inspired for their own story to make a difference.

Ian Leavers

General President & CEO

Queensland Police Union

The Queensland Police Service has made a significant and unwavering contribution to this great State and I for one am extremely proud of this fact.

That's why I'm very pleased that someone of the calibre of Laurie Pointing has chosen to document this rich and eventful history through a collection of short stories.

Knowing Laurie personally, I felt it was fitting he had decided to take on this responsibility, as not only does he hold the Service in high regard, but Laurie also possesses the ability, integrity and dedication to produce a book that will stand the test of time.

Bringing history to life can at times be challenging. It's easy to become overwhelmed with the facts and lose sight of the human element that invariably is the most interesting part. That's why I find stories written by the people that were actually there at the time are always more valuable and emotionally inspiring.

Quite often, it can be too late before we realise this, and that's why it's vital we have in our midst people like Laurie Pointing who are prepared to put in the time to capture these important memories.

I highly recommend this book and hope that a diverse range of people are able to gain from it a greater understanding of and respect for the Queensland Police Service.

Jillian Steinkamp

QPCU Chairman

This book is a fine collection of police-related stories and experiences from a wide and diverse range of writers.

Laurie Pointing has encouraged, inspired and pursued the collation of these accounts in his usual persuasive and focused manner.

Laurie is an author himself, a great storyteller, and has always had an interest in the history of policing.

Sadly, much of the rich history of the Queensland Police Department and its members has been lost over time. Laurie Pointing's efforts and the contributors to this book significantly help address that gap.

The book is dedicated to Laurie's brother, the late Tom Pointing, who I had the privilege of working for when he was the Superintendent in Charge of the North Coast Region in the early 1980s.

Laurie himself had a fine and varied police career, rising to the rank of Assistant Commissioner. My most significant impressions of him in that regard were his tenacity and competence as a detective and his contribution to the Queensland Police Service as a senior officer in the post-Fitzgerald era.

The Pointing tradition continues proudly in the Police Service, being progressed by Laurie's sons, John, Brett and Glen.

On the journey of life we meet many people. Some unique. Laurie Pointing is one. I value his friendship, but regardless, few would argue that his contribution to the tapestry of our world has been rich, colourful and always interesting.

I commend this book not only to retired and serving members of the Police Service, but to members of the public in general.

Bob Atkinson<br>Commissioner of Police – Qld<br>Police Headquarters, Brisbane

# Prologue

In 2014 the Queensland Police Service will embrace 150 years of history. Its official history was written by Dr W Ross Johnston and published under the title The Long Blue Line.

The reader may be surprised to learn that the Queensland Police Service is younger by only 35 years than the original police model – The London Metropolitian Police – as established by Sir Robert Peel in 1829.

My idea for this book came after reading two publications by Marion Houldsworth, who had interviewed and recorded the stories from numerous men and women who had spent all their lives living and working in the bush. The late Professor David Myers, AM, the founder of Central Queensland University Press Outback Books, encouraged me to explore the possibility of putting together a book of short stories by retired police officers. So what you hold is the final product of Marion Houldsworth's methodology and David Myers' encouragement.

My earnest thanks go to those retired police who participated in this project. All of them have made significant contributions to policing in this State. They represent a wide range of experience, and no matter where they served, or in what capacity, they all tell their stories in their own way. They offer perspectives and opinions that may overlap, vary or be in conflict. I keep this rich mix as I have exercised a very light editing hand.

The stories cover the period 1936 through to 2004. As the book came together, I was reminded that the core purpose of policing is to keep the peace. It always has been: It always will be.

To illustrate this point I have taken just one story of pioneering policing at the turn of the 20th century. Set in Finch Hatton, we thank two local people, Blair Hunt and the late Mel Lowth, who rescued handwritten records reposing in mildewed, leather-bound station log books (1906-1913) and gave them new life in a booklet – I Beg To Report. Don Braithwaite combined those records with information taken from files held at Police Headquarters to tell a story of a worthy policeman and his style of police work over a century ago. We enjoy the quaint use of language and official salutations of those days.

I thank Commissioner Bob Atkinson for writing the introduction to this book and for his kind permission to reproduce excerpts from The Long Blue Line. These excerpts, serving as footprints in history, are scattered throughout the book in chronological order for the purpose of setting the stories against a background of Queensland policing in bygone years. The excerpt about Mr Seymour is presented more fully because he was the first Commissioner of Police for the State of Queensland.

Finally, I dedicate this book to the memory of my late brother, Tom. His story is very special to me.

While this book is the work of many hands, for any errors that might have slipped through, the responsibility is mine alone.

It gives me much pleasure to invite you to share these stories.

**Laurie Pointing**

# Pioneer Policing

Finch Hatton lies in the Pioneer Valley 80 kilometres west of Mackay. Until 1900 a mere handful of settlers lived in the valley, but the discovery of gold, rich stands of cedar and ideal soil for the growing of sugar cane soon called for a central village that was named Finch Hatton.

The real boom began in 1904 with the arrival of the railway line. A sugar mill was built in 1906, followed in 1909 by a school with 100 pupils. By 1910 the district population was 870 and two years later the township boasted a turf club, progress association and a uniformed brass band. All of a sudden it was the commercial and social hub of the valley.

This is a story of bold, vibrant growth on the outer edge of settlement. But it was an unruly, brawling community consisting of a volatile mix of hard-drinking construction workers, miners, canecutters, timbercutters, mill hands, farm labourers, railway and road navvies.

Prior to 1906 Finch Hatton was policed from Mirani, a mounted officer with pack horses visiting the settlement every few weeks as he travelled to and from the Eungella gold diggings in the Clarke Ranges to the west. In August 1906 Constable H J Kelly was stationed on a temporary basis in the township for the sugar harvest and found accommodation in the mill barracks.

In November 1906 the constable applied for a new pair of handcuffs because those on issue had been broken by a prisoner named John O'Brien. O'Brien had been arrested for drunkenness and creating a disturbance and, in the absence of a lock-up, he was chained to the ambulance building at the mill. He escaped by pulling the flooring boards up and went to Bly's blacksmith's shop and cut the handcuffs off. Kelly recaptured him after pulling him out from beneath an outhouse.

Kelly had little luck with prisoners. In January 1907 he arrested an Aborigine named Billy and "secured the prisoner to the verandah post of the ambulance building by means of a chain secured to his leg by means of a pair of handcuffs, there being no leg iron at the station". As Billy was thus secured for 21 hours, the constable thought his request to use the closet was reasonable. Kelly escorted the prisoner to the closet.

After a few minutes Billy rushed out and ran up the steep mountainside at the back of the township and escaped. He was recaptured within a few days and Constable Kelly concluded his report on the incident with the plea: "I spared no effort to retake him … I hope that you will see fit to recommend that I be dealt with leniently in this matter."

In response to a petition by the townspeople, a permanent police presence was established in 1907. Constable Hagerty was the first posting. With his wife and children he settled into a small, ramshackle house that also served as the police station, although it was a half-mile removed from the village.

At that time Hagerty had nine years' service, having been sworn in on 16 July, 1897 at the age of 24 years and three months. He was described as – 5'8 and a half inches tall with "carroty" coloured hair and red complexion. A teetotaller, during his career he earnt the sobriquet "The Red Terror". While waiting for a cell to be transported from town, he chained prisoners to a messmate log.

The following cases are selected to show the variety of matters calling for the constable's attention during 1907 –

- A boy shot dead when trying to repair a pea rifle.
- The supply of liquor to an Aborigine by a hotel licensee
- Making enquiries into two men recommended for appointment to the Commission of the Peace
- Interviewing an Aborigine suspected of being a lunatic who was frightening the wife of a station manager by demanding tucker and tobacco and talking about how many people he had killed. No further action was taken when the manager said the man was more a rogue than a lunatic and that the man would be re-employed to look after the milking cows.

During 1908 a total of 92 prisoners passed through the lock-up – an extraordinary arrest rate for a one-man station. As if Hagerty did not have enough on his plate, he was also appointed an acting Clerk of Petty Sessions. Early that year one of his reports read –

Finch Hatton Station

22 February, 1908

Relative to:- The state of the house that is rented for the police in Finch Hatton.

Sir,

I beg to report the state of discomfort of the accommodation of the barracks at this station. The house is old and full of white ants and consists of bush timber and slabs with a tin roof and back with a low roof without ceiling or lining. The wind and rain beat through the cracks in the walls so that it is difficult to keep a lamp alight. The white ants have eaten away the roof battens so the rain beats in there as well.

(The constable goes on to suggest the purchase of land and the building of a police station in the township itself.)

(Sgt) P J Hagerty

Constable 512

Another report read –

Sir,

I beg to report that my wife gave birth to twins, a male and a female, in the night of the 10th instant. Both of them died five hours later. I had them buried on Peoples' selection yesterday afternoon.

Samples of reported cases handled in 1908 are now reproduced in short form –

- Death of an Aboriginal female BLOSSOM. "She was buried by the Aborigines in the camp."
- Interview of a hotel licensee thought to be insane.
- Inspection and unfavourable report on the dirty conditions of the Terminus Hotel and the drunkenness of the licensee.
- A Chinese gardener supplying alcohol to an Aborigine.
- Charles Primrose pretending to be a detective.
- A serious assault in the barracks of Cattle Creek Mill.
- An improvement at the Terminus Hotel. "There are now enough sheets for the beds."

These cases give some idea of the scope of Constable Hagerty's duties ,but make no mention of the frequent patrols he was required to make on horseback to "show the flag" throughout his division to reassure the general populace and prevent such offences as the theft of livestock. However, 92 arrests for the year tell us that he understood that the central tenet of policing is to keep the peace. Obviously this energetic policeman made regular foot patrols of the village and kept the drunks and other troublemakers under control by kicking bums and casting miscreants into the lock-up. By doing so he permitted the decent citizenry to feel secure and to enjoy reasonably tranquil lives. After all, this was the constable's cabbage patch and his principal responsibility was to keep it clean and safe.

Arrest figures for 1909 are not available, but here are some of the cases handled by the constable:

- A man crushed by a rolling boulder when working on Eungella Range road.
- The death of a two-year-old boy wandering between moving cane trucks.
- Severe injuries sustained by a man who fell over a cliff in the scrub while on a turkey shoot.
- Investigated a report that an adopted, illegitimate, 10-year-old girl had been pinned to a table by her tongue and turned out into the bush all night. (When interviewed the "parents" denied abuse and accused the girl of stealing money and food.)

Constable Hagerty concluded his report with "The opinion of neighbours is that the child had a hard life and is not cared for. I think it a charity to have this little girl moved as soon as possible".

- An application by a woman for an old-age pension. In supporting the application the constable stated "She is of temperate habits and of good character and has a family of 12 children".
- Breach of Sunday trading at Cattle Creek Hotel.
- Constable Hagerty is caught up in a dispute between the Directors of Cattle Creek Mill and the suppliers, which led him to arrest a grower, Mr Powell, on a charge of trespass. (The following year Powell's solicitor served the constable with a District Court Summons claiming £100 damages. Hagerty asked the Department to pay for his defence as "I have no intention of paying the amount as I am not in a position to do so". When the case came to court, His Honour gave judgement for a "non-suit" without costs.)

One case in particular is worth reporting in full –

Finch Hatton Station

Mounted Police Armed Constables, with their new short magazine rifles. *Queensland Police Museum.*

15th September, 1909

Sir,

I beg to report that on Tuesday the 14th instant while at Owens Creek making inquiries, Mrs Joseph followed me from her house on to the main road. On the way down she said to me, "I am going to pull that bloody rotten stinking thing out of her house". I said to her, "You go home and don't be making trouble for yourself. This is a public road down here and if you are going to use bad language I will have to summons you for it".

She said, "I don't give a bugger for police or gaols or anything else. I will have that bugger out of that (Meaning Mrs Lisk)".

Mrs Joseph when on a public road in front of Mrs C A Lisk called out, "Come out here you stinkpot. I am not done with you yet, you dirty rotten low bugger".

I cautioned the woman, but it was of no use. She then turned her back on Mrs Lisk and, in a stooped position, kept slapping her hands one after the other on her posterior, calling out at the same time "You can kiss this you low stinkpot".

There is not the slightest doubt that this woman is a bad lot……

P J Hagerty

Constable 512

On the 6th July, 1909 Mrs Hagerty gave birth to a male child who was named Robert Phillip Hagerty.

During that same year the constable made several reports regarding the state of his accommodation and applying for a second man at the station.

During the year 1910 a total of 148 persons were arrested, not counting three lunatics. By then the township boasted three hotels, two billiard rooms, two public houses, seven stores, two sawmills, two butcher shops, two saddlers, three blacksmiths and wheelwrights and was on the circus circuit.

The family occupied a new home and police station in July 1910, but there was no indication that the constable be given assistance. All his endeavours to gain additional staff, although strongly supported by Sub-Inspector Garraway of Mackay, came to nothing.

Overwhelmed by his workload, the final straw came when he was called upon to carry out a canvass of the Roll. On 19th August, in some desperation, he wrote a strong application (all his paperwork was handwritten) setting out his plight. This report found its way to Commissioner Cahill, who directed Chief Inspector Urquhart to examine the situation.

(Frederick Charles Urquhart was an outstanding police officer, explorer and author. He led a native police contingent in hostile engagements and was speared in the groin and wounded by a tomahawk. He was first to arrive at the wreck of the Quetta in 1890. He served as Police Commissioner 1917-1921 before going on to become the Administrator of the Northern Territory.)

This was Mr. Urquhart's report to Commissioner Cahill on 12 October, 1910 –

Sir,

I have the honour to report and recommend to your favourable notice Constable Hagerty of Finch Hatton who I think is an exceptionally good man. In a rough place among a very rough class of people he has made 71 arrests singlehanded this year and is most highly spoken of by the respected portion of the community. He has stood and stood well as the solitary champion of law and order in a very rough place and he badly needs assistance. I strongly recommend that a young, physically strong constable be sent to Finch Hatton to assist him as soon as possible.

I have the honour to be

Sir,

Your obedient servant

(F C Urquhart)

Chief Inspector

Constable King was transferred to Finch Hatton as additional strength that same month. He held a Silver Police Medal for Merit in recognition of his daring in stopping a bolting horse harnessed to a sulky in Albert Street, Brisbane.

The benefits of an additional man were realised in 1911 when arrests dropped by 45 to 103. When the railway station was broken into and an attempt made to break open the safe, Hagerty and King performed well by locating and arresting the two offenders in Pinnacle.

During the same year applications were received for new hotels in Finch Hatton, Netherdale, Pinnacle and Gargett. Hagerty objected to every one, but it is recorded that the incidence of sly-grog selling increased.

Also in the same year the mill workers, farm labourers and canecutters went on strike and set up strike camps near Mt Dalrymple school and on Cattle Creek near Pinnacle. Althought there were confrontations between the strikers and the farmers as well as a few incidents of violence, the two policemen kept the situation under control.

During 1911 an interesting incident occurred when a man being pestered with bandicoots about his camp set a trap for them by loading a gun and placing the muzzle a few inches off the ground with the trigger cocked and a string from the trigger back around a twig and then to the front of the muzzle with a piece of bread attached. In the dark a friend walked along the track and tripped the trap and the charge went through the side of his leg.

In August 1911 Mary Hagerty, the daughter of Mr and Mrs Hagerty, was confined in the Mackay Hospital for over a month with diphtheria, and as ordered by the doctor they were obliged to send her south for some months.

In the year 1912 the arrest figures for Finch Hatton station fell by 50% to 52. The boisterous village had been tamed. Events for the year included –

- The bakehouse burnt down, but the baker's cart was saved.
- The girl previously mentioned as being ill-used by her foster parents walked 12 miles to seek refuge at the police station following constant mistreatment. She was taken in at the station and, asking for an instruction as to what was to be done, Constable Hagerty pointedly emphasised that he had already furnished four reports about the girl's welfare. The constable reported his concern about a blind Aborigine named Jimmy who often went from house to house for food. In seeking instructions Constable Hagerty commented, "I think that it would be a charity to have this man placed in a home for Aborigines".
- Another child of Mr and Mrs Hagerty was stricken with diphtheria and was confined to the isolation hospital at Mackay. The Pioneer Shire Inspector visited the station and fumigated the bedroom that the child occupied.

Constable Hagerty was transferred from Finch Hatton to Stewarts Creek in February 1913, his replacement being Constable J T Paton. The following year Constable King was transferred back to Brisbane. The absence of Constable Hagerty's firm hand was evidenced in a report by the Mackay Daily Mercury on 27th March, 1914:

> On a night recently while the officer was away at tea a game of "two up" was commenced in the centre of the main street, which was followed by a disturbance, and when the policeman put in an appearance he got knocked about with the result that he had to call upon a local Justice of the Peace to assist him "In the King's name" to effect an arrest.

During his service Peter Hagerty was posted to 18 different stations. His final appointment was to south Brisbane and he rose to the rank of Sub-Inspector. In retirement he settled in Manly where he died in 1954. His son, Robert, who was born in Finch Hatton on 12th July, 1909, became the third generation of the family to be a Queensland police officer.

As to old Finch Hatton, although now respectable, it is a tad down at heel. Its glory days are behind it. The railway lines have been torn up; the sugar mill has gone. But for one day every year it becomes a boom town once again as the venue for the Pioneer Valley show. This year (2011) some 17,000 patrons passed through the gates.

Should you attend the best one-day country show with the most beautiful setting in Australia, pray listen for the echoes of Finch Hatton's colourful past and spare a kind thought for a gallant Constable Hagerty cleaning up a raw boom town single-handedly by kicking bums and throwing miscreants in the clink.

Queensland's first Commissioner of Police was David Thompson Seymour, who held the post for 31 years. This record has not been, and is never likely to be, broken.

SEYMOUR, David Thompson

Born 5 November, 1831 at Ballymore Castle, Ireland, son of Thomas Seymour, gentleman; educated at Ennis College; entered army 1856, lieutenant 1858, to Sydney 1859; arrived in Brisbane 1861 in command of the first detachment in Queensland after separation; aide-de-camp and private secretary to Governor 1861; Acting Commissioner of Police January 1864 and confirmed in office in July 1864 (after retiring from the army); leave of absence 1894 (during insolvency); retired 30 June 1895 on £700 pension; foundation member of Queensland Turf Club and on committee for over 30 years, also on committee of Queensland Club; died London, 31 January, 1916.

(Australian Dictionary of Biography, vol 6 p 112; Bob Good, 'Our First Commissioner', Queensland Police Journal, August 1985, 16-17. W Ross Johnston, The Long Blue Line p 11.

In 1866 Commissioner Seymour wrote: "I regret to have to mention that during the past year bushranging has made its appearance. Five bushrangers have been captured, but the 'Wild Scotsman', James McPherson, has hitherto baffled all attempts to arrest him."

*The Long Blue Line,* W Ross Johnston, 1992 (p 54)

# Bob Smith

During September 1970, I was transferred to the Criminal Investigation Branch, Biloela in Central Queensland. Stan Thorne was the recently appointed sergeant first class of police in charge and the staff consisted of one sergeant first class, one sergeant second class, approximately seven or eight uniformed constables and one detective. There was one civilian member – a young female who attended to the telephone, front-counter inquiries and typing of reports. Biloela at the time was within the Rockhampton Police District.

The Police Commissioner at the time, Ray Whitrod, had introduced a system where police personnel who had been stationed at one establishment for a period of 10 years and longer were to be relocated, and Senior Constable Bob Smith of Burleigh Heads station was one such officer. He was transferred and arrived at Biloela during October 1970.

At this particular time there was no designated Police Prosecution Corps in our State and usually a sergeant at a headquarter stations would be selected to perform this role for an indefinite period of time. Prior to Stan Thorne's arrival, committal proceedings in the Magistrate's Court at Biloela were conducted by a sergeant, acting as police prosecutor, from Rockhampton. Stan took over this role as well as the management of the station and once Bob Smith settled into his duties, Stan handed him the responsibility of the unofficial police prosecutor.

Bob performed this responsibility professionally and was later transferred to Brisbane, becoming one of the original prosecutors when the Police Prosecution Corps was formed in Brisbane in 1972 under the leadership of Inspector Stan Hambrecht.

When I transferred to the Prosecution Corps, Brisbane, in January 1979, Bob was a senior officer with the Legal and Training Section at Police Headquarters. He retired at age 55 years with the rank of superintendent. Bob was a most competent officer, well respected by staff, both his superiors and subordinates. He was always available to assist others with a problem and his research ability with regards the criminal law was greatly appreciated, not only by police prosecutors, but by the vast majority of the legal profession.

Bob's departure from the department at the height of his career was a huge loss as, over the years, he had gained considerable knowledge and research expertise in both police prosecutions and legal and training.

**Laurie Pointing**

# Bob Smith

I was born at the Lady Bowen Hospital, Wickham Terrace, Brisbane on 6 July, 1929, and was named Robin Alexander Smith. I was educated at the Junction Park State School, Annerley, Brisbane. We lived at Gowrie Street, Annerley on which the school had an alignment.

Having successfully completed the Scholarship Examination, I went to the Industrial Boys High School in George Street, Brisbane. This was next to the Queensland University when it was then located in George Street. In 1942, after two years at college, I sat for my Junior Examination. Trade subjects did not count towards Junior Examination as only the academic subjects were counted; nevertheless, I managed to scrape through and I looked around for an apprenticeship in a trade.

Electrical places were difficult to find and I was indentured to sheetmetal work. I did my trade in Stanley Street, South Brisbane, where the new Mater Private Hospital is now located. My boss made café and hotel equipment. We made pie ovens and urns and soda fountains for most of the cafes in Brisbane. We also did a lot of work in Ipswich and Toowoomba.

The American Liberty Ships came into the Brisbane River and moored near the Fish Markets. I did a fair bit of work on the air-conditioning pipes on these vessels and, on one occasion, I worked on an American destroyer. I managed to get some cigarettes for my father and my lunches.

It took five years to finish my apprenticeship, which I did successfully. I had to attend the Central Technical College, or TAFE as it is now called, five nights a week in my final year, along with the fellows doing engineering at the university. Once I obtained my trade certificate my pay was £5/10/0 [$11] a week as a tradesman. We got plenty of overtime and so I made a few bob when we were not on strike.

The Metal Trades Union was frequently on strike, sometimes for weeks at a time. I met a few mates of mine down the coast over Christmas holidays in 1951 and we decided to give metalwork a miss. Two of my friends became engineroom artificers in the Navy. They were made petty officers in 90 days and were working 40 hours a week and were being paid £15 [$30] a week.

Victor O'Brien was a senior constable at the Annerley Police Station. He played bowls with my father. He told me he was earning over £25 [$50] a week with penalty rates and overtime, working an extra day a week. He got an application to join the police force and took me to see the doctor who had private rooms next to the police station.

I had lived in Annerley all of my life and only had one job. Inquiries into my background did not take long. I was accepted as a probationary at the Police Depot, Petrie Terrace in a relatively short time. After the eight-week training I was sworn in as a constable of police on 17 March, 1952 and allotted Registered No. 5371. This was later changed to 0458.

On the day of swearing in, a group of probationary constables in full uniform of the day and blue stripes down the trousers (King's Colours), under the control of a training constable attached to the Police Department Training Establishment, marched to the Treasury Building, North Quay.

The Treasury Building contained, among other government departments, Police Headquarters. The Commissioner of Police was absent and the Police Force (now known as the Police Service) was under the superintendence of the Deputy Commissioner, Mr Patrick Glynn.

The probationaries were assembled in a meeting room, each of whom was in possession of a copy of the Holy Bible. They repeated the Oath of Service and were sworn in as constables in the Queensland Police Force by the Deputy Commissioner. Each member received a set of numbers and an identity card. This completed the swearing in, as opposed to the ceremonial occasion that it has become today.

The group were then marched back to the Police Depot where they attended the Depot Stores and were issued with the rest of their uniform, handcuffs and baton, a copy of the Government printers' Criminal Code, Traffic

Act of 1949, Police Act and Rules, and Vagrants, Gaming and Other Offences Act. The new members could purchase copies of the other statutes.

A very important publication was the Queensland Policeman's Manual, which contained instructions on how to carry out all of a policeman's duties and investigations, called "General Instructions". These instructions formed the basis of police qualifying examinations, which consisted of two parts, i.e. law and police duties. The "manual" remained out of print for years, which made it necessary for many constables and higher ranks to seriously study the police station copy and attend lectures on subjects to have any chance at the exams held each year.

Having obtained their books, et cetera, the new constables were given their assignments. A few were transferred to a country station while the rest were sent to Roma Street Police Station, City Headquarters, where most of them appeared on the roster for "Beat Duty". Some were transferred to Woolloongabba Police Station, the South Coast Headquarters, also for beat duty. The South Coast Police District encompassed the whole of the present-day Gold Coast and Logan Police Districts, extending as far south as Coolangatta and including places like Beenleigh and Rathdowney. The inspector in charge of the district and his support staff was housed at the Woolloongabba Police Station and his second-in-charge, a sub-inspector of police, was attached to the Southport Police Station.

Although single police were required to reside in barracks at the Police Depot, Woolloongabba or Fortitude Valley Police Station, they were permitted to reside out of barracks if no accommodation was available. As the South Brisbane Police Station at Gray Street was closed in early 1952 and moved to Woolloongabba, most of the new constables who had been assigned to the "Woolloongabba" were permitted to reside out of barracks in private accommodation.

Before their respective movement, they were provided with a "route". A police officer could not move to a new position without this document, which showed from wherever he came, "time and date of departure" and "time and date of arrival" at the new location.

I was sent first to Roma Street where I rode dispatches for about 10 days, after which time I was then sent to Woolloongabba and then to Annerley, relieving for about six weeks, and then to Burleigh Heads, relieving for three months.

The accommodation was very poor at Burleigh Heads, as it was at most South Coast district stations. I relieved at many suburban stations in the South Coast district, i.e. Annerley, Moorooka, Kangaroo Point, sleeping in the cells there; East Brisbane, Woolloongabba Inspector's Office, and South Coast Area Office in uniform – no plain-clothes duty except with the Bodgie Squad for about a month. I also relieved at Beenleigh, Beaudesert and Burleigh Heads. I also walked the beat at Woolloongabba every time I returned from relieving duty.

In early 1952, an endeavour was being made to recruit constables for the forthcoming "royal tour" of the then Princess Elizabeth and her new husband, the Duke of Edinburgh. However, while in Kenya en route to Australia, the Princess's father, King George IV, died and the tour was postponed. The Princess later came to Australia, as Queen Elizabeth, in 1954.

Queen's Escort, Queen St, Brisbane, 1954. *Telegraph Roman Newspaper.*

The police uniform had been changed in 1951. The tunic was open at the collar with lapels and numbers attached to the epaulet at the shoulder. The shirt was blue with two collars, attached by studs, and a navy-blue tie. The tunic was not worn in summer and the long-sleeved shirt with epaulet and numbers at the shoulder was worn. Upon the death of King George IV, the blue stripes down the trouser leg were removed and the Queen's Crown substituted for the King's Crown on the buttons.

Brisbane Police wore navy-blue uniform with white helmet or cap, while country police wore a similar uniform in khaki serge with slouch hat or cap. In summer months the serge could be changed to drill material. Black or brown boots, as applicable, were worn. Uniforms were "off the rack"; however, in recent years they were made from measurement forms.

Firearms were issued from the Firearms Section, after an approved application, if there were any available. Usually such a firearm was a well-worn, recently seized weapon of any calibre from .22 to .45, with 20 rounds of ammunition. Unless a holster came with the firearm, the constable had to purchase his own. Upon approval, a constable could purchase his own firearm and ammunition. Firearms had to be worn concealed, whether in uniform or plain-clothes. Plain-clothes police were to be dressed in suits with a hat. Very often they were seen dressed in a dustcoat to protect their clothing, which they had to purchase themselves from a clothing allowance.

Beat duty was performed from each Headquarter Station in three shifts each day, i.e. 6am to 2pm, 2pm to 10pm and 10pm to 6am. The Traffic Beats were from 7am to 3pm and 3pm to 11pm. Traffic Police performed these beats directing traffic at all of the major intersections where motor traffic and trams needed controlling, and this continued until traffic lights were installed around Brisbane.

Constables on beat duty and "reserve duty" at Headquarter Stations were also assigned to control traffic at school crossings on main roads in the am and pm to enable the children to get to the school grounds safely. To save removing police from the beats, reserve constables were used to deal with emergencies. They travelled to the scene of the incident by tramcar upon which they rode free, or by car attached to the station.

The cars in 1952 were black or navy-blue Chevrolets, Buicks or Dodge sedans, all of which were very second-hand, until the Holden sedan came to replace such vehicles. The "night cars", which were under the control of the Criminal Investigation Branch CIB in the city; the North Coast Area Office – CIB Fortitude Valley, and South Coast Area Office – CIB Woolloongabba, were usually Chevrolet sedans, wireless equipped with a two-way radio, which took up most of the boot space.

An arrested person was conveyed to the City Watch-house by the arresting officer in a taxi cab, which he hailed as it passed him in the street. The cab driver was paid his fares by the Watch-house sergeant. Most arrests by beat police were for drunkenness, disorderly conduct, ie fighting or language offences. An occasional vagrant was detected and arrested.

Attached to Headquarter Stations was a Uniform Inquiry Section, where uniformed police were sent detailed correspondence from other stations, which required a person residing in the area to be interviewed by police regarding the incident to which the correspondent related. Summonses were also served and warrants (usually for "non-payment of fines") were executed. Police who had reports to write could do so on the station typewriter – usually a well-worn machine – or on his own typewriter, which he had purchased as a "tool of trade", and for which an annual typewriter allowance was paid.

Because of the shortage of police at that time, police worked in eight-hour shifts of 48 hours a week, with one day off each week. Overtime was paid for the extra eight hours. Penalty rates were paid for Saturday and Sunday work and night shift 10pm to 6am. Almost all police stations except Headquarter Stations did not work 24-hour shifts. Larger stations, in Coolangatta and Southport, had one-man shifts from midnight to 8am, while stations like Burleigh Heads and Beenleigh worked shifts until 2am to cover the busy periods.

Police on transfer or relieving duty at these stations travelled to take up duty via public transport, unless the member had his own motor vehicle. A member en route to any of the police stations to Coolangatta went by rail which, in those days, travelled as far as Tweed Heads. The member was collected by police vehicle, except Burleigh Heads, which only had a motorcycle outfit as a form of transport, which could not manage the member and his luggage. The member was required to take the local bus service from West Burleigh railway station to the Burleigh Heads police station, where a travel voucher would be given to the bus driver who had to forward it to the Police Headquarters, Brisbane for payment of the large sum of two shillings and six pence (25 cents).

In 1954 I rode Royal Visit Escort Duty. I was lucky as I was given two bikes to ride – a black M21BSA designed as an escort bike and used for the Royal car. I had a more powerful 650cc Golden Flash for VIP escort duty, which I did a fair bit during the tour period. I escorted the Royal cars from Kelvin Grove Barracks to Toowoomba and back, which was a few hours overtime with a bit of VIP treatment, like big intersections around Brisbane manned by police to allow us to speed through. The Army drivers had the blue lights lit on the Rolls and Humbers, which got us right of way all the way through.

In 1954 Burleigh Heads had only one form of transport – a Harley-Davidson motorcycle with sidecar, a vehicle not many police officers could handle. Because I had demonstrated the ability to handle a Harley-Davidson [they are a very heavy and powerful motorbike] and was an experienced motorcycle rider, I was given the permanent position at Burleigh Heads in 1954.

They said the officer in charge, a sergeant second class, could be a difficult man to work with, but I did not find him so.

There was a sergeant and two constables at Burleigh when I first went there to reside in barracks with the other constable. I was only there a few weeks when he got married and moved out. I had no cooking facilities and ate all my meals at the local café. There was no hot water and I had to boil an electric jug for a shave. I had a cold shower during the day after having a swim. I applied for hot water, but the Works Department refused, saying there was no place to put a hot-water system. The local laundry washed and ironed all my clothing. The bedding was also washed once a fortnight, for which the Department paid two shillings and six pence.

The Works Department condemned the barracks accommodation and I was given notice to move out; so, as I had been engaged to marry my fiancee, Fay, for about 18 months, we got accommodation in a nice flat at Burleigh and got married in April 1955. I thought I would be transferred, but that did not happen until 1970 when I was transferred to Biloela.

There was barracks accommodation at the police stations on the Gold Coast. Burleigh Heads was staffed with a sergeant second class and two constables, both of whom were single and resided in the barracks. The Burleigh Heads Police Station had originally been the courthouse and Office of Tallebudgera Petty Sessions District. The Petty Sessions District of Southport took over Tallebudgera, Currumbin and Coolangatta.

The police residence, which had the courthouse attached, was pulled apart and moved to Ocean Street, Burleigh Heads, by bullock wagon. It was then set up as a police sergeant's residence, with the courthouse as the police station and office as single men's quarters (barracks). The cells of the watch-house were established at the rear with a shower room for the police in residence (hand basin and cold shower). A bathroom with hot water and a kitchen were included in the new barracks, erected in the 1960s.

The barracks at Southport and Coolangatta had a kitchen and meal room with bathroom. The police in barracks at Burleigh Heads had a contract with a café in Burleigh to provide their meals for £4/5/0 [$8.50] per week each and their laundry was also done by the local dry-cleaning and laundry business. Accommodation for police was fairly primitive in those days.

The Harley-Davidson motorcycle outfit was kept in a garage in the yard. Fuel was obtained in 44-gallon drums and hand pumped into the machine. The vehicle had to be ridden to Brisbane for a service at the Police Depot garage, as no place was available on the South Coast.

The Burleigh Heads Police Division extended from Peerless Avenue, Mermaid Beach to the Currumbin Creek Bridge, from Tomewin on the New South Wales border to Upper Currumbin, Upper Tallebudgera under Springbrook to Reedy Creek. Farms around Tomewin and the Carigal Mountains were inaccessible by motorcycle outfit and people from these places were met by arrangement at the Murwillumbah Police Station by the Burleigh Heads police.

Pig and calf sales were held at Mudgeeraba every month and, although it was within the Nerang Police Division, police from Burleigh Heads were required to attend and protect the money and check the stock permits. All transactions were by cash in those days. The attending police were armed with their personal firearm and the police station .310 Martini-Henry rifle.

Testing for drivers' licences and the issue of these documents was carried out by police stations out of Brisbane. The drivers' licences were issued each year and cost seven shillings and six pence each until the new 10-year driver's licence system was introduced in the late 1950s. Most Government money handling, ie registration fees, was carried out by the courthouse, except at places like Burleigh Heads where this work was carried out by police, who usually were agents for the State Government Insurance Office for the issue of Third Party Insurance, et cetera.

The fire brigade at Burleigh Heads was a volunteer rural fire service in the early 1950s and the equipment, hose, ladder, pump, et cetera, was carried on a trailer towed by a utility that was owned by the local plumber. The calls were made to the police, setting off a wartime air-raid siren mounted on a telegraph pole at the council office. The Rural Fire Services for West Burleigh, Ingleside and Upper Tallebudgera were stationed at West Burleigh and were equipped with a second-hand ex-military 4 x 4 truck. The police were once required to turn out the volunteers and equipment, but this proved to be unsatisfactory as police were often also away from the police station.

Southport Police Station had a detective sergeant and two detectives, while Coolangatta had a detective sergeant and one detective. Criminal Investigations on the South Coast was very busy and the courts at both places were also kept busy.

Single men residing in barracks had to be "in" at night by 11pm. At Brisbane Police Depot, Petrie Terrace, they had to be neat and tidy in their dress and wearing a hat when leaving the depot. They had to sign in before 11pm at the senior sergeant's office unless they had previously obtained permission to be "out" after 11pm. At the Police Depot they were detached to fatigue duty, which included "emu" parade, ie cleaning the grounds of the complex and emptying the grease traps. They performed cleaning duty at the Police and Citizens Youth Club complex at Lang Park and work at the Police Club rooms and bar at Roma Street Police Station.

Four to six probationaries were also detailed daily to travel to the Mounted Police Station at Oxley. They were transported in a utility truck to the stables where they cleaned the horse stalls and complex. Occasionally they used the truck to bring back manure for police stations and residence gardens.

At Burleigh Heads, the fatigues were not very onerous. The station office, counters and quarters were covered with linoleum flooring, which had to be polished once a week. The cells, toilets and bathroom also had to be cleaned. Each Sunday the windows were cleaned and clean blotting paper installed on the counter, new nibs put in the pens and inkwell filled. The ink was made occasionally from ink powder (Stephens brand), colours blue-black and red. The advent of ballpoint pens did away with this duty, although such pens were not freely available. Most police supplied their own.

Once a year the police station stores were provided and often things like soap and toilet paper were frequently reduced owing to budgetry restraints. Typewriter ribbons, coloured pencils and pens were not freely available and electric light bulbs were restricted to 60 watts. Towards the end of the budget period, bulbs had to be ordered from the Public Works, which would take up to two weeks to provide a bulb. Budgets were very strictly enforced in those days.

Each traffic offence had to be reported and forwarded to the District Headquarters for adjudication. Eventually, "parking" tickets and then "traffic offence notices" became available, mainly for breaches of the Regulations. Offences against the Act still had to be reported.

In those days, extra police were sent to the South Coast to boost the staff during the Christmas and school holidays when the population increased by thousands. The extra police were lodged at hotels and guesthouses. At Burleigh Heads the Esplanade Guest House was available for those police sent there. Road accidents, pub fights and New Year's Eve celebrations provided most of the work over this period. A solo motorcycle was provided for traffic duty. The Pacific Highway, which transversed the whole South Coast police district, had many road accidents, minor and serious, which kept police very busy over the holiday periods.

Families filled the council camping areas, usually for the six-week school holiday period in December. Easter holiday period was also very busy for police on the South Coast.

Members of the Education Section conducted police education at the Police Depot. Probationary police spent about three to six months being educated in crime and police duties. A few probationaries who sat for the final examinations after showing promise to the lecturers in a shorter period of training were sworn in after a period of six weeks. Police had to study and educate themselves, and after four years and six months they could attend lectures provided by the Police Union, in order to sit for the Police Qualifying

Examinations: constable first class at five years' service; sergeant second class at 10 years' service; a pass in this examination awarded the grade of senior constable. The senior constable was enabled to apply for a vacancy for sergeant second class and so on to sergeant first class and senior sergeant when advertised in the Police Gazette, which was published each Saturday.

The Police Gazette listed transfers, promotions, vacancies and wanted persons. All apprehensions, offences and arresting officers were also listed. Photographs of wanted persons also came with details of offences, descriptions of offenders and stolen property, and was also distributed. "Pawn Shops" also included a description of stolen property and was distributed to second-hand shops by police, who had to inspect the second-hand register kept by the proprietor of the shop to identify any items similar to those described in the "Pawn Shops".

In 1970, an inspector of police from Brisbane, together with an inspector from Southport, came to see me and informed me that I could not sit at Burleigh Heads forever and, as I had shown no indication that I was willing to move, I was going to be transferred. I, fortunately, had kept a copy of all my applications, which I produced to them. I had applied for every vacancy for sergeant second class and one-man station, no matter where that had been gazetted. This was from my promotion to senior constable 1962, which was quite a pile, and I said to them that they could not say that I had shown no inclination to move from Burleigh Heads but, rather, the Department had shown no indication that it wanted me to move. All it had to do was promote me. They tell me the Commissioner was affronted by my reply.

They gave me a choice of three places – Normanton, Charters Towers or Biloela. They indicated that I should go and ask my wife which one she wanted. They indicated that Inspector Cronau, who was in charge of the 'Gabba at the time, wanted me to go to the Criminal Investigation Branch, as I had been involved in so many criminal arrests and had two favourable records for them. The Commissioner wanted me to go to Biloela, so I had no choice after all.

Fay and I went to Burleigh for holidays while I was stationed at Biloela and I went to the police station to say hello to the fellows. Burleigh Heads had grown some, as there was a sergeant first class in charge and nine uniform men. Bill Von Blankensee was in charge and he showed me the Gazette with vacancies for a number of sergeants second class at the new Prosecution Corps, which was being formed, so I sat at his typewriter and applied.

During April 1972, I was not promoted; however, I was transferred to the Prosecution Corps, Brisbane, and I was instructed to move before the end of April or early May as I had been enrolled in the sergeant's course, Chelmer

College, in May. So, it was a bit of a rush, but all was managed and I also did the Breathalyser Course shortly after that and I did fairly well in both courses.

I seemed to do all right at prosecuting defended drink-driving cases as well. Eugene Murphy and I were sent relieving to Legal and Training Section, to join Ben Robertson in writing prosecutors' lectures. I also had to do a number of prosecutions while I was at Legal and Training. So, I would do some committals in the morning and go to Legal and Training in the afternoon. I passed the sergeant first class exam the year after I was promoted to sergeant second class. I was a senior constable still when I went to Prosecution Corps and remained so for six months or more.

I was doing a murder committal before a very senior magistrate and I was wearing the new summer uniform with short-sleeve shirt and no tie. The magistrate said to me at the morning-tea adjournment, "How long have you been prosecuting, Sergeant?" I replied, "About six months or more, Your Worship, and I am not a sergeant". He said, "Well, it seems to me that you have ample experience, and you should inform your principal officer that I feel a little insulted, as I feel Mr Sturgess does, to have a senior constable present the prosecution's case in short sleeves and no tie".

Des Sturgess made some reply about it didn't worry him, but I had known Des since we went to Junction Park School. I went back to the office for the luncheon adjournment and I was ringing the Scientific Section trying to get one of their fellows to get me a statement and appear in Court at 2pm, when Inspector Stan Hambrecht, the boss, took the 'phone off me and told them in no uncertain terms to get their "arse into gear" and got me the statement right away. Then he got stuck into the detectives forwarding the case for presenting an incomplete brief for prosecution and he would be checking all their briefs in future.

He then said to me, "I agree with your magistrate. You should be a sergeant and I told him that you would be within days. I also told him you would be in the official blue uniform whatever it is, but it would not be shorts and thongs". I was promoted before the end of that week and received an envelope with sergeant's stripes with instructions to have them sewn on to my shirts forthwith. Just to be difficult, I wore senior constable stripes for the next few days.

I was at Prosecutions from when I commenced in the month of June 1972. There were a number of former detectives who had previously prosecuted and were promoted in uniform. There was also a number of Traffic Branch Prosecutors who continued as such doing traffic prosecutions.

I was promoted through the ranks up to senior sergeant at Legal and Training. I still prosecuted if required at Brisbane and in the country, and I relieved at Wynnum, Holland Park, Children's Court and Inala courthouses. I lectured frequently at Chelmer College and the Police Academy to all ranks. I successfully completed the Commissioned Officers' Course and, on 24 December, 1981, I was promoted to Inspector in charge of the Police Prosecutions Corps, Brisbane. If there was a shortage of staff I would do some prosecuting, and I had to appear for the Commission in prosecutions against police officers before the Magistrate's Court and Police Disciplinary matters before the Tribunal and appeals against promotions. On three occasions I appeared for the Commissioner before the District Court in appeals against the decision of the Commissioner.

On another occasion I appeared before the District Court in a case against a detective for a serious breach of discipline and he claimed bias against the Commissioner and the Tribunal, so I gave him the option of selecting the Tribunal and he selected the union representative and a commissioned officer and a judge of the District Court. The judge asked me if I thought I should stand down also, but I refused and suggested the detective give evidence to prove bias by me, which I knew he could not do as I had never worked with him and did not know him.

Counsel appearing for him declined to call evidence of bias so I remained in my position. Next thing, after I disclosed particulars of the case and that I was calling interstate witnesses, he went off sick and resigned because of mental problems. We did not get him to court.

I presented a number of interesting cases during my times at Prosecutions and I enjoyed the work very much.

I was promoted to superintendent in charge of Legal and Training on 21 December, 1984, which gave me responsibility of Prosecutions, Legal and Training, Manual Section and Exams Branch. Getting books in law and statutes for the legal library proved difficult and I had to kick a few tables to get any attention. With Graham Weeks – another Legal and Training Officer – I managed to get a vote from the Treasury Department for funds to purchase books and this enabled us to set up a substantial legal library. The difficulty then was getting prosecutors who had a legal problem to use the library. The magistrates were very grateful for case law provided by prosecutors.

I was working very long hours on work for Assistant Commissioner, Legal and Training, as well as my own work, and my wife, Fay, said it was showing up in my health. I applied for retirement as from 17 March, 1986.

The Minister and the Commissioner tried to talk me out of it and the Deputy suggested I would be promoted again before the end of the year, but Fay was very pleased I was retiring. She started planning overseas trips for us. So I retired, after 34 years of continuous service. I had almost 20 years' service when I was promoted to sergeant second class; however, my promotions through the ranks from that time through to my retirement were fairly rapid. I felt, ultimately, that my career in the Queensland Police Service was both successful and personally rewarding.

(1) Although police usually conducted their own prosecutions, until 1904 private lawyers were sometimes engaged to prosecute. However, they were paid only when the prosecution was successful.

In the early days of the Criminal Investigation Branch members appeared in plain-clothes when on ordinary duty, but wore uniforms when giving evidence in court.

*The Long Blue Line,* W Ross Johnston, 1992 (p 139)

The first successful prosecution in Queensland of computer fraud took place in 1980.

*The Long Blue Line,* W Ross Johnston, 1992 (p 348)

One of the longest and most complex investigations in Queensland history involved an alleged conspiracy to defraud the public through land sales at Russell Island. From 1972 Detective Sergeant Vince Mahoney spent years on the investigation, which led to eight people being charged. The District Court trial lasted 20 months at a cost of $1.5 million. Upon a juror being declared unfit, the jury was discharged. No retrial was ordered.

*The Long Blue Line,* W Ross Johnston, 1992, (p 348)

# Bill Larkman

I first met Bill Larkman in 1980 when he was a senior constable of police stationed at Ipswich where he was performing general duties. I then encountered Bill again in late 1982 early 1983 when he was the Officer in Charge of Police at Taroom in south-west Queensland. Taroom was my old stamping ground, having worked in that district during my teenage years as a "ringer" and bush worker until I joined the Queensland Police Service from that bush town during the month of September 1958.

As a country police officer Bill was highly regarded and respected by the local people and performed his many duties professionally. In the year 1990 I was fortunate to be the Superintendent in Charge of the large Cairns police district, which included Thursday Island. On my arrival there I found that Bill was the sergeant first class of police and second in charge of the Thursday Island police division. On Thursday Island he resided in an old police residence in John Street and had the best view from any police residence in Queensland. From his front veranda you looked out over the ocean and on a clear day could see the mainland.

Bill possesses an easygoing personality that enabled him to converse with people of all walks of life and nationalities. In 1996 he transferred to Bundaberg, where he retired in 2004.

**Laurie Pointing**

# Bill Larkman

It was wartime in London. Hitler was about to attempt his second blitz with doodlebug unmanned rocket bombs. Mum was at home waiting for Dad after a visit to the doctor that confirmed I was on the way and bursting to tell him the news. The knock on the door was instead a police officer, with the terrible news that Dad had collapsed and died a couple of hours earlier at work.

I was born at London on 10 May, 1944 and named William Larkman.

Our family, Mum, two brothers and myself, saw out the war through a scenario of mad dashes to the bomb shelters, evacuation to Wales and the support of family on both sides. Peace starkly presented Mum with a tough future as we grew up in a devastated London with no welfare, a chronic housing shortage and a shortage of just about everything. Strangely though, everyone was in the same boat in one form or another and I recall a very happy childhood despite the difficulties of the times.

Salvation arrived at the age of seven when Mum remarried a lifelong family friend who changed from Uncle Jack to Pop.

Pop worked all his life for British Railways in freight. Mum had done various types of factory jobs until married and again when forced back to work to support us. They applied and won a new flat on a council estate outside of London at Romford in Essex. Suddenly London gave way to rural fields, woods and country surrounds that provided us with a wonderful backdrop to advance through school, the teens and off into the workforce.

I left school and began work at the age of 15. My education standard would have been equivalent to Queensland's junior standard. I was paid £7/10/-a week ($15) as a messenger boy in the City of London, working for a stock-exchange firm. I eventually worked for three stockbrokers and enjoyed a variety of experiences, ending up as a "Red Button" in the stock exchange itself, checking and confirming all the previous day's trading.

I do not know what the trigger was that persuaded me to apply for the Metropolitan Police. It was not out of any longtime dream or lofty ideal, but I suppose the endless posters around London of a police officer pointing at whatever, similar to Lord Kitchener in World War I, with words to the effect of, "Can you meet the challenge, do you have what it takes"? Well, I decided I could and did eventually and found myself at the age of 19 in June of 1963 treading the entrance steps to Peel House to begin the standard 13-weeks training. I was made aware that on average, one applicant out of approximately 85 eventually made it through to graduation. Some strict and tough times were ahead.

The path to these steps had already indicated that I was entering into an altogether different world as I had negotiated the scrutiny of examination and acceptance. They are worth mentioning as to this day I am still unable to understand how the process revealed my secret talents and verified that I had what it took. The medical saw dozens of blokes being pursued around from room to room by white-coated personnel in some large London building to have some aspect of our anatomy "looked at". With nothing more than a Metropolitan Police towel to protect our dignity we submitted to a variety of doctors who assessed our weight, colour blindness, family sanity, feet, etc. Had they been able to see some of my relatives and the antics they got up to, the sanity book would have been slammed shut there and then.

However, the most heinous condition that one could have, which meant instant rejection, was varicose veins. The test for this was quite quaint. One simply walked into a room and stood in front of a doctor behind a large desk. On command, the dignity towel was dropped, I swung around and with my back to him bent over and touched my toes.

During this procedure I answered a couple of questions during which the doctor leered into my innermost being with me talking to him through my legs and my head upside down. I am pleased to say I was completely varicose free!

The interview process was something else – a dozens of would-be aspirants congregated in plush surroundings of furniture, fittings and pictures in a large room as we waited to be called in for oral examination. We were all nervous and kept to ourselves, but I was surprised at the number of Scots-Irish and other blokes sporting a variety of accents that indicated that we had converged on London from all over the country in the quest to wear the unmistakable bobby helmet.

A name was called and in went the first lamb to slaughter. He reappeared some 15 minutes later, clearly stunned and confused as several of us pounced on him for information. "What paper did I read? What books did I read? Have I had sex? Do I love my mother?" he exclaimed. He ended with "What a load of shit" and pushed past us back out into the world from whence he came. His information was not very revealing other than as a warning to expect "trick cyclist" questions. As others came and went I gradually got some idea what questions to expect.

I entered another plush room when my name was called and was faced by a panel of half-a-dozen men, some in high-ranking uniform and all behind a long desk and whose scrutiny I felt as soon as the toe of my shoe touched the carpet. I successfully completed the first test by closing the door without slamming it. "Larkman, isn't it?" said one of them. "Sit down," and indicated a solitary chair directly in front of them all and about 10 paces from the door. I passed the second test by getting to the chair in my nervous state without stumbling.

"Now why do you want to join the police force?"

"To meet people really, Sir, all sorts of people that is. Help them out and feel like a useful member of society. You know, feel like I am making a difference somewhere."

They all nodded and made notes.

"Looking for excitement are you?"

"Yes I suppose, to a degree, but it is more the variety that I think I want."

More notes and nodding as I began to feel I had made a good start. Some questions followed as to what sort of books I read, what newspaper I read, what sort of responsibilities I had handled and how I had coped with the discipline in the Territorial Army Parachute Regiment.

"Do you still live at home with your parents?"

"Yes, Sir."

"How do you get on with your parents?"

"Oh good, everything is normal," as I pictured my mum nagging me for the thousandth time for leaving dirty washing all over the place and the countless indiscretions that mothers seem to remember.

"You have a stepfather, how do you get on with him?"

"Terrific. I never knew my own dad as he died before I was born. I always knew Pop. That's what we call him. He was known to us as Uncle Jack as he was a longtime friend of the family and of my dad during their early football days. We have been very lucky as he has done a first-rate job of looking after us and Mum. We have never had any of the hang-up type problems that you often get with step-parents."

The interview continued on without any sort of hitch and by the time I found myself back outside the door I realised I had done OK and a lot better than I expected. I was rather vague, however, as to what hope they had of assessing me when from all indications I was still, after a lifetime, a mystery to my mum. However, the letter of acceptance eventually arrived and prompted me to do cartwheels down the back garden as Mum hung out the washing. "I dunno," she said. "What will the neighbours say, a bleedin' copper in the family."

Suffice to say I ran the gauntlet of the very rigorous training program to begin life as a constable at Battersea and Lavender Hill in November 1963. This threw me into another steep learning curve as I necessarily grew into the police culture and mindset on the way things were done. In particular, the police sense of humour itself was a mixed blend of traditional cockney and black. It soon became clear to me that a black side to humour was part of the way of staving of the efforts of dealing with life's more rotten side. Today of course it is all counselling. Humour is a strong requirement in policing and it would surface in all matters and usually without any indication. It often prompted the resort from NCOs who might witness the general whinging of constables in general: "If you can't take a joke, you shouldn't have joined."

I had heard on a number of occasions that Australia was a land of opportunity and I had for some time been giving serious thought to a future, better lifestyle for myself and my family. It was at the East Ham Police Station in mid 1966 that I said goodbye to the Metropolitan Police after almost three years' service and boarded the Qantas "City of Parramatta" with my pregnant wife and emigrated to Australia. It was without a doubt the best decision of my life.

Brisbane appealed to me. After two years of looking around, I revelled in the new surroundings. I worked in an insurance office and also had a go at my own window-cleaning business. Tragedy hit us for the first time when our first child was born with complications and, despite every effort, died when two weeks old.

Eventually the call of the police uniform became too strong and in April 1968 I was again heading for the police training establishment to start the process all over again. The Police Depot at Petrie Terrace was home to police training, in Queensland and although I had some considerable experience under my belt, I was about to enter the web of one legendary sergeant, Tom Molloy.

The old police barracks at the top end of Caxton Street could not be described as grand or distinctive. They were, however, a landmark. A three-storey brick structure with verandas running the entire length, both back and front, interrupted only by a square central turret that encased an internal stairwell. Inside was a maze of corridors, rooms, offices, bathrooms and storage space. Unlike its Pommy counterpart at Hendon, it lacked any form of historical feeling or significance; it was basic to its needs.

I entered the central foyer, suitcase in hand, to submit to the obligatory 13-weeks training. In drab olive uniform was a sergeant, apparently contemplating the varied assortments of suitcases strewn around at the base of the stairs. "Good morning, Sergeant." "Just drop your suitcase and fall in with the others outside," he said in a business-type tone. I did so and turned to leave. "Where are you from?" said the sergeant. "Here in Brisbane," I replied. "No, no, no, no, before that, where'd you come from?" he said irritably. "Oh ,London really, but lived most of my life outside there in the county of Essex." "Well, things are a lot different here – we do things a lot different. This is a fine country so don't go getting fancy ideas that you might know better, because you will soon learn that you don't," he barked. My surprise must have been obvious as I thought of the injustice of coming 1200 miles to come up against an Irish drill sergeant. "Righto, fall in and be quick about it," he shouted. I headed out to the green parade ground to join the others. I had just met Sergeant Tom Molloy.

Sergeant Tom Molloy was a legend in his own lifetime and probably every officer serving at that time could write a chapter concerning their encounters with him. I would be confident in stating that not one of these officers missed the venom of his oratory charms for which drill sergeants are renowned, or avoided the wrath of his endless list of punishment measures. Tom Molloy was very formidable and all powerful at the Police Depot. Over the next few minutes I waited, formed up in the group on the parade ground and witnessed other arrivals who went through the same warm, welcoming ritual as I had done. They came scurrying back, one at a time like rabbits, to join the muster. I wondered if I had looked like that I thought! Eventually everyone must have arrived and settled to Tom's satisfaction. He came over and quickly demonstrated his abilities.

Tom never really spoke. He had almost a constant shout, which of course is a prerequisite for any drill sergeant. He immediately sailed into us. "You are lucky enough to have me for the next 13 weeks and if you are luckier you will be walking out of that gate you just came through as a proud and much improved person wearing Her Majesty's uniform of the Queensland Police Force. But that's a long way away because you are going to have to learn to do as you are told, when you are told, and do it at the double. None of this sloping around nonsense, you're in the Queensland Police now and anyone who doesn't like the idea of a bit of discipline had better get their bags now and head off before we start. I'm here to make men of you, make police officers of you, and no doubt a few of you will not make it. You'll be out that gate some of you before we get there. It is my job to weed you out and rest assured, I know how to do it. So let's make a start. My name is Sergeant Molloy and you will address me as Sergeant. You are probationaries and will be addressed as either probationary so and so or just by your last name."

He then got us to shout out our names in turn before coming up each line and asking general questions of each and every one of us and at the same time demonstrated his shouting and insulting abilities. He stopped in front of a tall bloke in front of me. "And you are?" The recruit replied in a thick north English accent. "Oh another one, have we – were you in the police over there?" "Yes, Sarge," he replied. "Where exactly?" "Leeds, Sarge." "Sergeant! Sergeant! You will address me as Sergeant," he yelled directly into the recruit's face. "Sorry, Sergeant, force of habit." "Well you had better get into some different habits here, son. And didn't you stand to attention when a sergeant spoke to you over there?" "No, not all the time." "Well, you will bloody well stand to attention every time you talk to me. Do you understand?"

With that there was what must have been an eye-duelling contest for several seconds as I saw Tom glaring at our man from Leeds, his face just centimetres from his. The tension grew when suddenly Leeds said, "Fuck you, Sergeant, I've had enough of this shit. I don't have to put up with this, you jumped-up fucking idiot", and simply walked off the parade ground, over to the vestibule and collected his bag. He strolled out along the bitumen and gave us all a cheery wave and called a smiling "Good Luck". Whereupon he passed out of the gate, not as a proud member of the Queensland Police Force, but as a disgruntled would-be probationary who had not even seen the first round out. Tom had not said a word until Leeds disappeared out of the gate. "Right, that's the first one. He won't be the last," he bawled.

It was soon obvious to me that the Police Depot, or simply the Depot, bore little resemblance to its London counterparts. It was also readily obvious the procedures were quite different as well. The most immediate surprise was that we had no uniform, we bought our own. We had been instructed to bring two or three sets of khaki trousers and shirts plus a grey trilby hat. This outfit was complemented by the issue of brown boots. At that time the Queensland Police wore a brown uniform known as drab olive.

These outfits quickly gained us the nickname of "The Garbos", which was exactly what we looked like, the only difference being that we were obliged to treat this work gear as a prized uniform in that it was laundered, pressed and starched each day. Whenever spoken to by any senior member of the Police Service, which was everybody, we were to immediately remove our grey trilby from our head, come to attention and hold the hat over our heart. Unfortunately, as time went on the khaki gradually shrank until most of us were running around with sleeves halfway up our arms and trouser legs that looked like they had an argument with our boots! None of this was inspiring or flattering.

We were eventually introduced to the man who was virtually the commandant of this enterprise, Senior Sergeant Frank Clifford.

Frank had an unusual nasally type of voice together with a peering sort of expression as he contemplated everyone. It was quickly rumoured Frank was a psychologist and in seventh heaven with his continuous and untapped source of subjects. He was a definite square peg in the proverbial round hole.

It is important to be reminded the Queensland Police Force (QP) numbered less than 3000 men and women at this time. Queensland was still a rural State and enjoyed a wonderful laid-back way of life consistent with tropical living. Trams still rattled along, and although a reader may get the impression I compared my current surroundings unfavorably with my previous police days, it was not the situation. I had lived in Brisbane for almost two years since emigrating and was well aware of the lovely change of pace and lifestyle generally. I had previously been in a force of 20,000 officers in a city of over 11 million people. There simply was no comparison, only real and perceived similarities. I differed slightly from my other English counterparts in that they had more or less emigrated straight into the QP from the old country and perhaps had not enjoyed any adjusting period.

Tom was the consummate fire and brimstone training sergeant – he was also a man of immense compassion and charity when the situation required it. He was undoubtedly a bully in the traditional army sense and an uncompromising task master who made our lives a misery very often. No matter what future officers and standards judge, Tom was a man of the times. These times were set to change, but that was not evident then. His job was to test each and every recruit. To test his temperament and to ensure you were able to stand up to what the public had to throw at you, especially if you were alone.

Tom pushed you to the limit of exasperation and goaded you into answering back or blaming others for getting caught out at something or other. He hassled us from the first moments when he blew over the loudspeaker system at full volume at 0530 hours each working morning, bellowing "All probationaries and cadets out of bed, all probationaries and cadets out of bed". His demands boomed throughout the whole building and seemed amplified along the sleeping hallways.

He would then immediately set about a general walking inspection of the building with the intention of catching somebody still in bed. He never failed. His victim was immediately treated to a tirade of abuse, which often included ancestral comparisons and perhaps a quick runaround the Depot parameters to assist the waking-up process. Tom knew every nook and cranny of the Depot, every hiding spot, and was always there before you or just after. He never let you rest. He tormented you like a cat does a bird.

But among all this was a wonderful opportunity to exercise a healthy sense of humour. Without it, life was hell. The Depot was no place for the worrier or faint-hearted. His tactics were also designed to take you down before setting about building you up to the proud day when you became an inducted Queensland Police officer. This necessitated that you learn instant and unquestioning obedience. You queried nothing, just did as he said straight away, at the double and without grinning. You conformed. Being Irish, however, left Tom vulnerable in areas of comprehension and quick wittedness and it was not altogether difficult to have some well-meaning leg-pulling at his expense. For those of us who had been there before it was easier to roll with the punches and see the funnier side of things, and once completed the training represented a time in your life with special memories.

Tom, it seems, got a little excited with our squad because it had three ex-military men and four ex-English police officers. Marching and drill was a major component of his discipline, and because he had such a wealth of previously trained men he no doubt imagined that ours would be the finest turned-out squad that ever trod the Depot turf and bitumen. We had other ideas. He put three former coppers at the front of one end of the squad and three former military boys at the other end. Whenever we about turned or faced off there would always be an experienced trio leading the way and bringing up the rear.

After a few days of drill we arranged among us that whenever we were in the lead we would take slightly slower and shorter paces, whereas on the about turn, the military leaders would take longer and more brisker strides. The result was predictable. We would just fall into a rhythm at about halfway with Tom all enthusiasm and encouragement. But when we took the lead we would bunch up and run into the back of each other with our slower steps. This would just sort itself out after an irritated outburst from Tom, which again transformed into satisfaction until the about turn again, by which time everyone was stretching out with gaps opening up everywhere with blokes hop-stepping to catch up. 'No, No, No," yelled Tom. "What's the matter with you all today. Are you all daft?" And so it went for a few days without Tom twigging what was going on. At first he blamed the two female probationaries for throwing everyone out. "Women have never been able to march properly," he informed us.

Then he found a volunteer who had been a drummer in a band and had him rigged up with a drum to beat time. In the end the novelty wore off and we decided to give Tom what he wanted and we set about marching properly. "Now you're getting it," he enthused. "There's never been a squad I couldn't drill."

One more surprise awaited us towards the end of the training course, a rowboat aptitude test. To this day I have never fathomed the origin of this desired skill as most river or water experiences take place in flooded torrential rivers in which a boat without an engine is rendered almost useless. However, we presented ourselves under the Story Bridge at the Water Police base, resplendent in our starched and pressed garbos' uniforms.

We were sent out in pairs in the gentle currents of the Brisbane River to complete a general circuit to simply demonstrate that we could handle a rowboat. Once accomplished, we were instructed via the bank through Tom's megaphone voice to hand our oars over for the next man to demonstrate his nautical skills. Nobody failed: It was just a strange interlude that had most of us baffled as to the purpose of it all.

But the three months or so training flew by until Swearing-in Day was upon us: 7 August, 1968.

This was a procedure I enjoyed and unfortunately one not then practised by my London counterparts. It involved a great deal of drill and marching practice, which also included the presence of the Police Pipe Band, always a stirring initiative. For me, there has always been something special about being part of a musical parade or marching with a band. This occasion was no different and was a wonderful finale. We were in new and full uniform for the first time, our garbo outfits gone for ever. Tom marched us on in front of our families and friends, forming a parade facing the Police Depot entrance. Our parade was overseen by a special guest in the form of Mr Joh Bjelke-Petersen, who was then Premier elect and was performing his first official function before himself being sworn in later that day by the Governor. Also in attendance was the Police Commissioner, Frank Bischof, who overviewed the proceedings.

We were then called upon to declare the Oath of Allegiance and service, which was followed by a short march forward to a desk at which sat a commissioned officer. A smart salute preceded the actual signing of the Oath of Service before executing a smart about turn and rejoining the parade. We were then marched off with Tom leading and the pipes swirling. I would have to admit to feeling quite proud and 10-foot tall. We were in. I became Constable W, Larkman Registered No. 7727.

Morning tea followed as did an amazing transformation. Tom immediately changed from the ogre of the past weeks into a workmate. He treated us as men and equals and spent time talking to all of us. Tom, despite his techniques, held a position of great affection among those of us who experienced them.

Althought I felt the training itself was deficient the discipline, juvenile and menial tasks demeaning, I accepted it all as part of the system of the day. I was equally grateful for my previous army training and police service, which I felt more than made up for what was a very moderate preparation for such an important job. However, once out and in among it all again, I soon appreciated that Queensland and the QP was by far and away a much better place to be a police officer than London.

## Woolloongabba Police Station

Woolloongabba Police Station was my first official station. The transformation to the Queensland way of doing things did not happen immediately upon leaving the Depot. There were still some surprises in store.

Woolloongabba, or simply the Gabba, was an old area of Brisbane set in the shadow of the cricket ground and about 100m from the actual Gabba Junction. This was a five-ways intersection accommodating five major roads and all carried tramlines. An office, set high up on wooden stumps, took up the middle of the intersection. This was in effect the tram inspectors' control point from which they monitored the running of the trams.

It was a unique sort of construction and was a visual pivot point of the whole main area. Directly opposite the station was a timber yard that once again reinforced the big country town image that was then Brisbane. Backing this yard was the vast railway goods yard that was also a main feature of the area. Our building was so close to the cricket ground it appeared to be part of it, set in grounds and semi-parkland that led directly to the outer-oval area.

We also catered for the Boggo Road Goal. I had lived at Stones Corner for almost two years so was somewhat familiar with the area in general, which was a bonus. The station itself was somewhat quaint in appearance and not entirely what one would expect. As a police station it seemed somewhat of an architectural misfit. It was two storeys and the entrance was immediately off the footpath. It was a solid structure, and like many buildings of its age had been altered and modified to the point where it lacked any obvious planned layout.

One of my first tasks was to arrange the ownership of a new typewriter for myself and I obtained an official order for the purchase of one from the Government Store. This was an arrangement by which government employees such as myself could purchase what was seen as an essential piece of equipment totally tax free and virtually at cost. I headed uptown and took possession of a brand-new Olympia for $68. I was all ready to go, new uniform, new typewriter, new station, new career and I could let my hair grow again and look normal!

I arrived for my first shift to start at 10pm to find I would be walking a beat by myself. No real on the job training or assistance to break the ice so to speak. It was straight into it solo. Although surprised this did not faze me a great deal as I had done it before and I basically knew the area. I wondered, however, how some of my counterparts were going to fare. I was made aware that a sergeant named Joe would be keeping tabs on me. He told me he expected me to be at a certain location at a certain time so that he could give me a booking.

At this point I had my first inkling concerning alcohol consumption within the service as it was obvious Joe, although starting work at the same time as me, was a little under the weather. He pressed upon me that he did not want to see me back there in the meantime unless something positive was happening. I was also made aware that I had to get permission for just about everything, even a return to the station for a call of nature or typing of a report, while any telephone call was to be vetted by the telephone operator, who in times of doubt would refer the matter higher.

Just for the record, single officers planning matrimony were obliged to submit a report requesting permission to marry and to submit full details of his intended bride. The woman and her family would then be subject to an internal police investigation as to the suitability of the spouse. I never heard of an officer actually being refused permission, but my understanding was that any suspect spouse prompted a swift transfer to somewhere remote.

This either resulted in love being halted in its tracks or the officer simply resigned. Single officers were very vulnerable and many at that time found themselves on a train with an overnight transfer if they managed to misbehave or otherwise have any sort of personal difficulties or traits that may need correction! As I left the station I noticed a couple of the station staff were busy moving desks and idly wondered why.

I headed back to be at the station right on the dot of my allotted meal break. I now discovered the purpose of the earlier furniture movement. Desks had been simply pushed together and on top of them slept the counter officer. He was snoring without concern in full view of anyone who might attend the station and call at the counter. Most of the lights had been turned off. Over by the telephone switchboard slept the operator on another makeshift bed. He had shown the foresight to position his pillow so that his head was right next to the telephone cords and switchboard, so that in the event of a call he did not have to get up. He simply rolled into a position that allowed him to plug the lines in.

I thought it prudent to let the senior sergeant know I was in having a meal, only to find him at his desk fast asleep, so I proceeded on upstairs to the meal room where I sat in solitary wonder, musing at the preparedness of the QP. Just before leaving, the whole place suddenly came to life. A couple of detectives appeared as if by magic. A very sleepy Sergeant Joe also materialised out of nowhere and the senior sergeant and his staff were up and about. "I wonder what's happening" I thought as I trooped downstairs, which seemed to be the general direction of everyone who had suddenly become mobile. The answer was soon coming.

The milkman had arrived with the customary free crate of milk, followed shortly after by the newspapers. With that, Joe announced to the senior sergeant, "I'll go and get the pies, Senior," and he departed at a rate far superior to anything witnessed so far. Although it seemed obvious to me, I stood there wondering as to what was actually happening. I said to the senior sergeant, "I have had my meal, Senior. I'll head back out". "No, no, not yet, you've got to have your pie and bottle of milk. You can't go until you have had them. The sergeant will be back in a jiff with the pies." And so unfolded what unbeknown to me had been a ritual for many years within the QP. Eventually I learnt this procedure was followed on night work at the City, Fortitude Valley and every provincial city in Queensland.

The senior sergeant dished out a bottle of milk to everyone, always with the question "Do you want a bottle of milk?" If you said no, your consignment immediately disappeared into the depths of the senior sergeant's Gladstone bag. I soon learnt to always say yes and take it home if I did not want to drink it there and then. If you did this, you had to make sure you brought the empty bottle back the next night.

The scenario unfolded further as everyone opened one of the free daily papers that had been delivered during the early hours of the morning and began scouring various items of news. We were halfway through all the "Look at this" or "Fuck me, have you read about so and so yet?" and various other comments as the blokes came across various articles of interest until the pies turned up. The milk ritual was repeated as the senior sergeant asked each of us if we wanted a pie. Anyone not wanting one saw his pie also swallowed up by the jaws of the senior's Gladstone bag. And so it was, my first tradition revealed in the QP. I contentedly returned to my rounds and ended what was really a boring shift and not unexpectedly I did not see Joe again until we were heading for home at shift's end looking more the worse for wear than when he started.

These first few days also revealed what seemed to be a standard item of equipment – the Gladstone bag. Everyone seemed to have one. It was the backpack or briefcase of the day and sat well with the brown uniform. That and the white tropical helmet were the police trademarks of the times. The image of a police officer riding the front of a tram with his Gladstone bag and white helmet was part of the culture, and I was surprised to see the bag in such numbers as they had all but disappeared from the English scene. The white helmet was a sensible item of equipment and I quite enjoyed wearing it, as it was very comfortable. It was also quite distinctive, particularly when performing traffic duty. Both items were to disappear almost overnight a few years later when blue uniforms were introduced.

My first week of night duty at Woolloongabba Police Station was quite a learning curve. The pace of things was certainly slower than what I had once been used to and the ready friendship of workmates was also a marked bonus. The awe really started at the senior sergeant level and gradually grew from there to God status when dealing with the sub-inspector and inspector. The sergeants and senior constables enjoyed a "Don't argue with me, do as you are told" level of authority and they usually had a considerable number of years' service by that time. On average it took a constable 10 years to become a senior constable and from about 17 to 19 to become a sergeant. So although they were classified as workmates, you were never in any doubt you were the subordinate and the seniority system of service was very much to the fore.

A mid-1968 snapshot of the QPS indicates that there were no section houses for single police officers or any form of rent assistance. The Queensland Housing Commission earmarked a certain number of premises, usually flats, to police families in mainly provincial towns. Police accommodation did exist in Brisbane in a small way, usually in the form of a police residence within the grounds of a suburban police station for the benefit of the officer in charge. Some one-time police stations that had been decommissioned were given over to police residences for the lucky few. Residences outside of Brisbane were provided for country station staff, and in cases like major cities such as Bundaberg, Townsville or Cairns, senior officers or essential positions (watch-house keeper) enjoyed departmental residences. Many country stations combined a police office as part of a residence.

Unmarried officers were not allowed to share any private accommodation with the opposite sex. Living in sin as it was termed was not tolerated. Dismissal was possible, but the Department had a more hands-on method of dealing with anyone who upset them in this fashion. It was not uncommon to learn that an officer had been "railroaded", given a 24 or 48-hour immediate transfer, usually far north or out west where he could expect to serve out an average two-year penance. Officers also had to seek written permission if they intended to take leave and travel outside of their police district and to supply details of their intended travel.

Very few female police officers existed, most of whom were stationed at the three main Brisbane stations, The City, Woolloongabba and Fortitude Valley. Large provincial centres usually had one. Recruits had to be 5'8" (1.73cm), of good eyesight (no glasses) and hearing and be of sound and capable physical condition, free of any debilitating problems such as asthma. A male officer had to be clean shaven, although a moustache was permitted, but not to descend below the upper lip. No long hair or sideburns. Any departure from these requirements brought a swift rebuke from either the senior sergeant or inspector in terms that left no doubt that corrective action was quickly required. Conformity was the order of the times.

We wore a brown uniform known as drab olive with brown boots and three different types of headgear. Most work was done on foot and bicycles were nonexistent. Police utilised trams and buses if they were obliged to travel any distance as they travelled free, en route to a traffic point or school crossing. Police cars were not prolific and existed in the form of a variety of makes, models and colours. Signs were that Ford Falcons and Cortinas were being increased, but again mainly at the three large Brisbane stations and provincial cities. Many suburban stations not yet issued with a Cortina operated with a motorbike with sidecar, or in some cases with a Morris Mini! Police cars looked more like taxis with the illuminated sign on the top, but with an adhesive police badge, affectionately known as "the pineapple", stuck to both front doors.

The breathalyser was still only being talked about and trialled and personal police radios were still about three years away. Traffic control throughout Brisbane at both rush-hour periods was almost totally done manually, and many intersections had a traffic policeman for over 12 hours on weekdays. All reports were typed as almost every officer had his own typewriter, the maintenance of which was a tax deduction. Reports were done usually in three to seven copies, which meant copious amounts of carbon paper and a hefty wastage of paper and forms generally, as typing errors were not accepted. Likewise handguns were an optional item.

Although every station had an issue of firearms, officers were allowed to gain approval to purchase their own handgun, usually in the form of a small automatic. Firearms were not worn on display and most were carried in shoulder or ankle holsters or simply stuck in a waistband out of sight. Many officers simply put them in a car glove box if they were on motorised patrol. Otherwise, the only measure of protection issued was a baton. Not many officers bothered with it as it was a fairly lightweight affair, more resembling a chair leg than a piece of defence equipment.

All officers were issued with the relevant government acts plus a thick green book titled General Instructions, known throughout the service as “G.I.s”. This was our bible of all the do’s and don’ts about our profession and outlined all official procedures, disciplines and treatment of government property. What was not in it was not worth worrying about. Alongside this to me were a number of acts, the three most prominent being the Queensland Criminal Code, Vagrants, Gaming and Other Offences Act and The Traffic Act. These three pieces of legislation were our bread and butter authority and contained direction on just about any offence known to man. The whole force revolved around them and, collectively with the G.I.s, they governed the whole study, prosecution and promotion processes. Naturally these publications had to be kept up to date and every month or so an officer would be issued with pages of amendments.

We would spend hours sometimes cutting and pasting slips of paper in among various sections of the books where changes had been made to some aspect of the act. We ruled through and deleted lines of print and somehow had to write in the new wording to the relative section. Sometimes whole new sections had to be included, and it was not long before many of these acts became almost impossible to decipher as it was not uncommon that some sections were altered time and time again. Newly sworn-in officers always inherited a nightmare in that the acts they were issued with came straight out of stores and many months of associated amendments were issued with them, a vast backlog to attend to straight away.

Complementing this procedure was the weekly circulation of Commissioner’s Circulars, Weekly Wanted Lists and the fortnightly Queensland Police Gazette. The Commissioners’ Circulars were updating directives in regard to law or internal procedures brought about by the ever-evolving changes or influences upon life generally. Legal interpretations were clarified and any internal practices, good or bad, were commented upon. The Weekly Wanted List was a current circulation of serious offences committed throughout the whole State, and in some cases interstate, and contained a synopsis of what had happened, with names of suspects and/or photos or descriptions of persons wanted for interviews.

It was a general "be on the lookout for these villains" publication. The last publication, the Queensland Police Gazette, was the one seized upon first by everyone. It contained all the promotions, retirements, transfers and, more importantly, position vacancies within the service, and also updated the Weekly Wanted List by publishing the names of those since arrested or interviewed in relation to previously circulated lists. It was read almost from cover to cover and was our main artery in keeping abreast of colleagues, where they were and what they might be up to. This publication complemented the once a year issue of The Seniority List. This listed everyone in the force by name, rank, number, date sworn in and date that an officer achieved his current rank. It was not alphabetical, but started off with the Commissioner and went down through each rank with the names listed in strict seniority. Everyone in The Job knew exactly where he fitted into the pecking order of promotion. My situation at the time did not warrant any excitement as it was at the very bottom at the back!

Again, all these publications and circulars had to be read by everyone and cross-referenced with previous issues, much in the same way as the amendments to the acts. Those closing in on promotion usually elected to update The Seniority List against the Police Gazette and happily strike a line through a name above him with a notation in red of being either retired, promoted or dismissed. It was akin to punters studying the horse-racing page. The circulars were also directed to all members of the station to "Note and Return" before they were filed.

Promotion for all except to commissioned rank was by way of promotional exams, conducted twice a year over two days. The first day was for law, the second day for police duties. Law was exactly that and honed in on your knowledge of specific sections of a variety of acts and legislation, with the regular requirement of being able to quote legal definitions and whole sections. Duties were questions of various scenarios and how you would deal with them and what section of law or act you would apply to justify your actions. Most questions would surround bread and butter issues commonly faced by police in an effort to ensure that we kept abreast of our powers.

Occasionally an obscure question would be thrown in such as your saluting obligations to a commissioned officer while sitting on a horse! General ranks consisted of, starting from the bottom, constable, constable first class (one stripe), senior constable (two stripes), sergeant second class (three stripes), sergeant first class (three stripes surrounded by laurel leaves) and senior sergeant (crown surrounded by laurel leaves). Each of these ranks had a stipulated number of officers under their charge that increased at each higher level. In this way, officers graduating through the service learnt to manage a gradually increasing number of officers under them.

I began another shift that week by being told I was on reserve and to just hang about the station in case I was needed. I typed off a couple of files before relaxing back with a magazine. Typing reports in those days was a trial in itself. As stated earlier just about everything had to be done with between three to seven copies, which meant seven sheets of paper and six sheets of carbon paper, a formidable wad for any typewriter.

Not many of us (with the exception of cadets who were actually taught to type) were competent typists, but generally we became more proficient, albeit with two fingers as the years progressed. The sight of a single finger pecking at a keyboard was common, which, combined with the inevitable number of mistakes, made report writing a chore. Any mistake had to be corrected seven times and any mistake not spotted before the report was presented for submission to the senior sergeant resulted in a single red pen line across the front copy and you were obliged to do the whole lot again.

However, I was work free when the sub-inspector found me and asked if I was an approved driver. Once I confirmed I was, he tossed me a set of car keys and said, “Good, you can be my driver for the night”. I got my gear and headed for the car-park area of the station yard where I found a huge black Rambler sedan. At the time I owned a manual VW Beetle, and although I had by then driven the odd police car I had never had any experience on a car such as this. It was automatic, very powerful and had power brakes. I got in and familiarised myself as best I could with everything before the sub arrived and indicated for us to go. I negotiated the first obstacle easily enough thanks to the automatic gears, a driveway out of the station that inclined up to the footpath level and across it. I halted at the kerbside to check for traffic and saw traffic just about to start off from my left at the Gabba intersection.

I had plenty of time if I hurried a little so I gave the accelerator slightly more push. The result was like the start of the Bathurst 1000. The Rambler leapt from the stationary position like a shot out of a gun. Although startled I tried to appear relaxed and in control. Unfortunately the car was still accelerating as I made a right turn to gain the opposite lanes. The tyres were screaming in protest in a fashion that would have attracted a hoon ticket from any self-respecting traffic cop. The sub-inspector was pinned against his door throughout the turn. He calmly readjusted himself when the screeching stopped and we were straightened up heading towards the Vulture Street traffic lights.

I came to the lights and stopped with a jerk as I experienced for the first time the capabilities of power brakes. The sub once again jerked forward suddenly and flapped back into his seat. Things were not going well. "Turn left here, we'll head down Vulture Street to the west end," he said. I duly turned left and was doing a very comfortable 60kph and starting to feel relaxed approaching another set of lights that were green. It looked as if I would sail through the lights when they changed. I was caught at a distance where you would maintain or slightly increase speed and safely go through on an amber light. I began to squeeze the accelerator when my instincts told me I had a commissioned officer with me and should do everything correctly. I applied the brakes firmly and the effect was immediate.

We stopped on a sixpence, about 15m short of the stop line, tyres screaming even louder than before with the sub-inspector fighting frantically to stay in his seat. He ended up almost on his knees with his fingers clutching at any possible hand-hold on the dashboard. He just about had everything under control when the sudden stop backlash occurred and he lost his grip and was jolted back on to his seat. He was lying back on the generous seat with his legs bent under him from the knees down. The back of the seat forced his head forward and his cap was knocked off and covered his face. At any other time you would probably have roared with laughter, thankful there had been no danger and relief at your own stupidity. I blurted out an apology as the sub retrieved himself and returned his frame to composed dignity. I thought I would be sacked and waited for the verbal blast that was surely coming.

"Not used to power brakes are you, son?" he said. "No," I said, "I have never driven anything like this before." "Thought so," he countered, "just take it easy and allow yourself a bit of extra space in the traffic. Put the brakes on gradually next time." "Yes, Sir," I said. Thankfully we completed an extensive patrol throughout Bulimba, Morningside, south Brisbane, Highgate Hill, West End and just about all over the south side without any further mishap. We got back to the Gabba OK. The sub good-naturedly said, "Well you didn't kill me, you got me back in one piece".

Another shift saw myself and another relatively new constable directed to catch the tram to Melbourne Street and take up with Sergeant Horrocks to do the South and West End areas. We did so and duly arrived at the Melbourne and Grey streets intersection where Sergeant Bob Horrocks was waiting for us. Bob was an elderly sergeant, obviously not far off retirement. Rheumy-eyed and silver-haired, he was the classic old-timer who had seen it all. "Righto, drop your meal and other gear off at the meal room and come back here," he said as he pointed vaguely up Grey Street towards the William Jolly Bridge. We walked in the general direction, but could only find a few shops and business premises, some of which were vacant and boarded up. They looked almost derelict.

After a short while we went back to Bob and explained we could not find any meal room. "Can't find it, what's wrong with you. Don't know what they teach you these days. Couldn't find your arse in two grabs some of you." We traipsed back to where we had just been and he stopped outside one of the empty shops that was boarded up. "Here it is, plain as day. Can't find it," he huffed. We stood there, still unsure what he was talking about. With that, we followed him down a narrow alley beside the shop into a back garden-type area. It was overgrown and littered with countless newspapers, bottles and tins.

Bob ignored all this and led us through an unlocked back door into the shop proper. This was it, a large shop area surrounded by cupboards and workbenches. There were no lights. The front window was painted over from the inside and there was a large table in the middle and an assortment of chairs. It was an absolute dump. "Right, leave your stuff here and let's get you blokes on the go," said Bob.

We were given our beats and meal times before Bob went his own way. I found this area more interesting than the Gabba, probably because of the river and eyesight closeness to the city itself. Being night duty, however, and almost 11pm, my initial impressions of the location appeared quiet and contradicted the hive of activity I was to experience later on different shifts. The approaches to the old Victoria Bridge and the stretch along Stanley Street up to almost Vulture Street was, I later found out, the ultimate den of iniquity.

It is an area now long done away with. It now includes the present-day museum, arts centre and the extensive South Bank. Back then though, it was a run-down section that was not suburban, but mainly industrial and shops. It was also of course the interstate railway station area, which generated a fair bit of activity. A string of hotels ran almost the length of Stanley Street, starting with the Manhattan on the corner with Melbourne Street. The infamous Manhattan Walk was a small park that separated two hotels and I was soon to realise this section of town was probably the main feeder station for Watch-house customers across the river. It was then the main Aboriginal area of Brisbane, with all its associated squalor and friction.

But for now I was content to stroll the Montague Street commercial area and to generally find my way around and take it all in. Just up from the main intersection towards the bridge was a London leftover – a blue police telephone box, almost identical. This became a regular central point where we would wait with a drunk for a cab to do the short ride over the river to the Watchhouse and also a place to get out of the rain. This now seems an absurd situation, taking drunks or arrested persons to the Watch-house by cab if a paddy wagon was not available.

One would simply guide one's customer to the police box, ring up the Gabba, which would then arrange a taxi. You placed your customer in the back, got in with him and would then be driven to the Watch-house. The cabbie would accompany us in and present a chit to the Watch-house Keeper for the cost of the fare and would then be paid out of a tin money box from under the counter. The cabbie would then be let out to continue his public duties!

I found quite a few well-known business premises on my rounds, the best of which were Peter's and Paul's ice-cream depots, which operated 24 hours a day. In here I had my first contact with a microwave oven as it was customary for workers there, police and any other associated delivery person having business there to enjoy the benefits of their canteen. This canteen housed numerous vending machines that took no money for their own products. I enjoyed many an ice cream or magically heated meal while passing the time with men dressed in white industrial clothes and boots. The river was another attraction with the lights of the city and the Treasury building being reflected on its placid surface.

No-one had told me about the area under the William Jolly Bridge. It was the night-time doss spot for all the vagrants, Aborigines and associated drunks who gravitated there after the pubs closed. There were over two dozen of them there, most asleep, huddled together at this cold time of year. Some were battling on with the odd flagon or port bottle. This interrupted my little jaunt to the point where I was at a loss to know exactly what to do about it. I did not know then that this function was universally well known.

I traced my way back to the police box and advised the Gabba as to what I had found. "Are they playing up at all?" asked the voice at the other end of the phone. "No," I said. "Well just leave them there, they will all be gone when the sun gets up", and with that the phone went click. Obviously the telephone operator found it too difficult to keep himself propped up on his makeshift bed in an uncomfortable position to explain everything to me. It was, I learnt, the procedure to simply clear the place out from time to time using the "drunks' van" in order to run a general check as to who was about. Otherwise they were left in relative peace. Sure enough, when I did my first 6am shift there I headed off to the bridge to find it completely clear of vagrant bodies. I never discovered where they evaporated to during the day, but for now it was back to the alleged meal room for a few sandwiches. I half expected to see my meal devoured by rats, but surprisingly everything were intact.

Stretched out on the table, snoring robustly, was Bob. Three bottles of milk had been delivered, so I simply sat at the table with Bob in the middle and ate my food as quietly as possible and left without disturbing him.

After a week of night work I was sent to do 10 days at the annual Brisbane Ekka, which was again a new and enjoyable experience. It had a holiday atmosphere about it all and was my first contact with country folk. Being a city type all my life I found the whole concept of the Ekka fascinating. The police office was a small, wooden, double-room structure just inside the main gate. We simply reported in and were given a section of the grounds to patrol and instructed to pop back in from time to time. In reality you went anywhere and everywhere. Lost kids and broken-down elderly people who found it all too much were the main source of business.

Otherwise it was a fairly straightforward patrol, and just being there. A few roughs, drunks or pickpockets in Sideshow Alley were common during the evening and the boys at the Cattleman's Bar needed an eye kept on them. But basically lost kids and messages took up most of the action.

Paul's and Peter's Ice Cream delivered continuous supplies of ice creams to the police office, predominantly as a means of assisting us to look after the always present waiting room full of missing kids. Some were happy to just sit and wait, but many would cry the whole time. Policewomen were often on hand during the day shifts to play mother hen. Whenever a kid looked like overfretting you simply took him to the upright canvas freezer and let him or her pick an ice cream. The average was two ice creams before one of the parents turned up. I had never had so many ice creams in my life as I did during that Ekka. We were also given a meal voucher by the RNA Association for use at any of the catering outlets.

It did not take long for the best food to become identified and it was very rare indeed not be sharing a full roast meal in the best dining hall with several other police. On top of that was the joy of casually wandering around and talking to the country people who had come from all over Queensland. It was also an education for someone like me who found it difficult to comprehend at that time the size of their properties and the work and logistics involved in their lives. It was not unusual to strike up a regular friendship with some of them, and during the evening and later hours you would often find yourself lazing back among the straw with either a cup of coffee or a beer. It was a common sight to see police knocking off at about 10pm or later with cow or horse manure stuck over them.

My one claim to fame at my first exhibition was to impress the senior sergeant on People's Day with my microphone skills. Every so often the police would broadcast across the whole grounds details of missing children who could not be pacified or who had been there too long. This was usually done by one of the policewomen. However, the senior sergeant foolishly asked me to do it and gave me a piece of paper with written details. I read through the announcement in the usual manner, intrigued by the sound of my own voice booming out over all the sounds of the exhibition. One of the kids, a little boy who I had just given an ice cream to and who I had won over a bit, was bawling his eyes out again and was looking at me at the microphone just outside the office. I beckoned him over and he came, still crying. I held the mike up to him and he bawled straight into it and his sounds went right around the grounds. "Anyone who recognises that cry may be pleased to come to the police office and collect it. Any child not collected within 20 minutes will be put up for adoption," I announced, entering into the general fun of things.

I don't think the senior sergeant had ever moved as fast in 20 years as he bolted out of his chair towards me. He snatched away the mike that I had fortunately by now turned off. "Piss off out of here," he snarled. "We don't need smart arses like you getting us all into trouble." He continued to eye me with a jaundiced look for the rest of the day, which spoke the unwritten message that he did not want me anywhere near his office. Needless to say my ice-cream intake for that day reduced considerably.

Back at the Gabba after the Ekka I experienced first-hand the delights of South Brisbane and the hotels of Stanley Street. Manhattan Walk looked like a huge outdoor recovery ward for drunks. They lay everywhere. Although there was a fair number of Europeans, the majority of people were Aborigines. It was obviously their adopted section of Brisbane. Fights erupted and were quelled in a flash, and although a very boisterous atmosphere, there was not any serious trouble. It was mainly just drunkenness. Some brawls went the whole hog with broken noses, cuts and some being rendered unconscious. I met Elly Bennett a few times there, a well-known and somewhat famous Aboriginal boxer. He could be stroppy with the drink sometimes, but usually was OK if handled with a bit of tact.

The drunks' van did continuous rounds the whole of the late shift after dark. If it turned up at one of the hotels and I was nearby I would be expected to go in and assist to fill the wagon. Ninety-nine per cent of the time it was straightforward. The burly sergeant simply walked in, walked around the bars, checked everyone and decided who had had enough by a light tap on the shoulder. He then stood at the door and called out those who he had selected. With a bit of feigned argument sometimes they just got up and went outside and got into the open paddy wagon. Occasionally we had a struggle with an odd one or two, but generally it was all done quite civilly. Once in a while there would be a sort of mini revolt and it would be a bit of a free-for-all between the police and the drunks. This usually entailed the addition of extra paddy wagons and a continued clean-up of all the pubs to bring them under control.

Some of them, usually the women, would run away and a game of "catch me if you can" would take place. One Aboriginal woman had her own idea of fun and was well known for her antics. She was often the lure for a standard police joke if any rookie police officer was present. "Go and get hold of her and get her in the van," ordered the sergeant to one of the constables who had only a few more weeks' service than I did. None of the old stagers moved to help, but stood watching in some obvious anticipation. I went forward to give a hand whereupon the sergeant motioned me back saying, "No, no, hang on, he'll be all right". With that our keen hero carried out his order and took hold of his runaway and was getting her organised to come back to the van. Without warning she jumped at him, wrapping her legs around him and they both fell to the ground with her on top. She then delightfully urinated over the officer, holding on to to him until she was finished.

The sergeant and the other blokes who had seen it all before thought it quite hilarious. Our wet-stained hero came back to the van with his grinning prisoner. "I wish you wouldn't do that, Lizzie," said the sergeant as she let herself into the van. "You want to watch her in future, lad," he said to the constable, "she only does that to coppers she fancies."

The drunks' van usually continued on for about another half-hour, or two more runs after closing time, to clean up the area. This entailed doing a walk-through search of all the bushes in Manhattan Walk and pulling out all those who could not make it to the William Jolly Bridge. The drunks' van crews seemed to know most of the nooks, crannies and hiding places and it was amazing just how many extra bodies we loaded up from an apparently empty scene.

While my few weeks at the Gabba were relatively uneventful, I witnessed one incident that passed into history. I was driving a night-duty patrol car on Sunday, 1st September, 1968 with Joe who, as usual, was fast asleep, snoring up against his passenger-door pillar. Having a sleeping partner like this always made the shift a chore, but that was the way things were. I drove aimlessly around in search of a bit of action and upon reaching a point at Highgate Hill I was able to look out and over the city of Brisbane and beyond, always an enjoyable sight. What made tonight different were flames licking the night sky at North Quay. The Supreme Court was ablaze and it presented a dramatic sight. I looked at Joe and told him there was a big fire in the city. "Nothing to do with us, not our area," he said without opening his eyes and promptly resumed his sleep.

I had nothing else to do and no doubt became mesmerised by the pyrotechnic display unfolding in such dramatic fashion. I began making my way down towards William Jolly Bridge. Joe was still asleep as I got there so I decided to go the whole hog. I crossed the bridge and made my way on to North Quay and slowly made my way past the fire. I was down to just a crawl as I looked up at the dancing flames and all the associated reflections given off from other windows and the wet streets from the fire brigade.

It was a most enthralling sight. The flames were right up in the roof and the lovely old building was obviously a goner. The sound of an arriving fire tender woke Joe up with a start and he found himself surrounded by a sea of rotating lights, flames and action everywhere. He must have thought he was in hell. "What the fuck's going on here, where are we?" he said, looking alarmed. "Look, Sarge, the Supreme Court, it's burning like mad. You don't see too many fires like this," I said. "Get out of here," he yelled, "piss off back to the Gabba." He could not have been less interested, so I simply made my way back across the Victoria Bridge, by which time Joe was back in the land of Nod.

I enjoyed some excitement before my notification of transfer came through to Townsville and I was happy at the thought of going north to something in life completely different. "Something completely different" materialised in the form of a simple traffic accident at the corner of Ipswich Road and Vulture Street one evening. It was but a minute from the front door of the Gabba Police Station and was nothing remarkable as we waited at the scene for the arrival of a tow truck to clear the intersection.

Everything had been taken care of, with just the formality of clearing the road to be done. Standing around, generally checking the damage to the remaining vehicle, I was suddenly interrupted by my workmate, Senior Constable "Dinger" Bell. Without warning he yelled "Run", grabbed my tunic by the shoulder and propelled me towards the footpath. "Run," he again shouted. Now overtaking me and obviously keen to get to the pavement, he was dragging me by my tunic as I endeavoured to match the rate of his headlong propulsion. At the same time I became aware of the awful sound of squealing tyres desperately broadcasting their protest and warning of disaster.

Disaster struck in the shape of a Mini sedan as it sped almost unchecked down the slight incline towards us and struck the already disabled vehicle waiting to be cleared.

I glanced backwards and sideways in some horror as I watched the Mini rise up from the rear and pirouette over the stationary car and slightly change direction towards us. My strides became noticeably more urgent and longer. The sound of grating metal and splintering glass cascading along the bitumen between our racing feet bore testimony to the race we were running. Our desperate athletics took us out of harm's way as the Mini began a slide, circling on its roof past us and down towards the Gabba intersection. A man could be clearly seen upside down at the steering wheel as the sound of tearing metal continued.

After what seemed an age it spun to a stop and suddenly everything seemed eerily quiet, until the screaming commenced from inside the Mini. Instantly galvanised, we ran the few steps back to find the young man, a school teacher, covered in blood and obviously in panic. He was trapped fast, and although not a pretty sight, appeared fairly well intact. Fortunately the tow truck for the first accident arrived and with it, and the combined help of several male pedestrians, we were able to right the Mini in a controlled and gentle manoeuvre. Once it was established that the driver was not seriously hurt we set about reporting a second accident in the space of a few minutes and gradually sorted things out.

It had been an electrifying experience and one that stays indelible upon a memory. "Dinger" Bell had without doubt galvanised me to safety and prevented probable serious injury to myself. But once over it was simply a case of walking back to the station, typing up the report and having a laugh about it. In hindsight we must have looked highly comical with our gooseneck strutting at high speed as we fled to safety.

## Townsville

Townsville beckoned and a new chapter was about to unfold for me. This chapter really started a career full of change, locations and experiences that would be hard to match in any other profession. Internal changes gradually took the Queensland Police from its somewhat old-fashioned past and on into a modernising future. The new Police Academy became a reality, with emphasis on higher education standards, and alcohol consumption within the force was more directly addressed now, being almost eliminated. I saw much of the State of Queensland, eventually serving at Fortitude Valley and Hamilton police stations, Brisbane, being a founder member of the Queensland Police Dogs, the first in Australia. Transfers to the Brisbane suburban police stations of Stafford and Ipswich followed and promotion to Sergeant took me to Taroom for six years as Officer in Charge. I became the last Sergeant First Class of police at Thursday Island before that rank was disbanded as a result of the Fitzgerald Inquiry. My last 12 years with the service were spent at Bundaberg.

I look back on a career not perfect, with probably many instances I would now do differently. Interestingly I witnessed pre- and -post Fitzgerald and the huge overhaul that resulted. This change was inevitable, essential and in the main successful. Not all the resulting changes have been right, particularly regionalisation, the promotion system, rank structure and the performance of the commissioned ranks in general. In particular, the current promotion system is more deceitful, dishonest and open to corrupt influence than the old seniority system ever was. But these things are all ongoing challenges for the future and, hardly affect my satisfaction and pleasure of almost 40 years' proud service as a police officer.

## Dog Squad

It was not long after joining the London Metropolitan Police that I knew I wanted to become a police-dog handler. I do not know why – other than that aspect of police duty was something that strongly appealed to me.

I was understandably miffed when joining the Queensland Police some years later to learn that there were no police dogs, or in Australia for that matter. So once ensconced in my first permanent posting to Townsville I began what was to become a four-year campaign for their introduction. I began submitting reports with articles, statistics and incidents relating to police dogs and never lost an opportunity to highlight how in various incidents that occurred from time to time, the outcome could have been beneficially influenced by the use of a police dog. I was a managerial pest as any change within the QP was akin to plaiting sawdust! Fortunately, shortly after I began this campaign Commissioner Ray Whitrod was appointed, a man who, although controversial, was a reformist and a disciple for change.

Once back in Brisbane I secured the help of a fellow police officer, Vic Belbin, who kept a wonderfully trained Doberman, which was quite a competent tracker. Apparently Vic's father had been associated with dog training and had passed these skills on. With the added interest of a Courier Mail reporter we set up actual tracking and search situations and used Vic's dog to track and find the reporter. He came up trumps every time and led eventually to two very good articles in the Courier Mail espousing the benefits of police dogs. Together with two good books that I submitted, which focused on police dogs, I was hopeful that some positive result was not far away.

As things stood at the time (1968-1972) the German shepherd or Alsatian dog was universally frowned upon throughout Australia. Breeding imports were banned in just about every shire in Queensland. The breed had been inbred almost to a point where it bore only fleeting resemblance to its European cousin, and any dog attack that took place in a community was nearly always credited against the German shepherd, regardless of the amount of that breeding content present. It was further maligned as it was contested that the German shepherd had over time bred with the dingo, resulting in a super breed of a cunning and vicious canine.

The Australian German shepherd of that time tended to have long and lanky legs, a straight back and generally lent more towards a small wolf in appearance. Broadly, however, it was still a very attractive breed, having much in its favour, especially when trained and cared for by German shepherd devotees. Only the RAAF used trained guard dogs and handlers as part of their air-base security.

This photo was taken at the Roma Street Railway Station in mid 1974 to promote the patrolling of trains to address the assaults and wilful damage being inflicted. Left to right; Const.1/c Bill Larkman, Sgt. Cec Austin, Const. Dave Laird and Const.1/c Charlie Degnan. Dave and Charlie were the two first dog handlers trained by the RAAF in 1972. *Queensland Police Museum.*

At last in 1972 two officers were selected to train as dog handlers at the RAAF Base at Amberley. They were Constables Charlie Degnan and Dave Laird. I was galled to the point of severe frustration at not being one of them, but took comfort from the fact that my efforts had at least led in part to their establishment and that hopefully in the future, as the unit grew, I would have my chance. The Queensland Police Dog Section was at least up and running. Memory does not allow me to state what success or impact was achieved by these first two teams. What I do know is that an administrative attitude was apparent that seemed to suggest "You have got your dogs, now get on with it". It certainly was not a case as to how good or bad the dogs were as each of the handlers gave 101 per cent, much of it in their own time. Things were done on the cheap and our two officers were not overwhelmed by support or interest and battled on more or less on their own.

At the end of 1973, right out of the blue, two more officers were selected to become dog handlers and would be sent to Wellington in New Zealand for over three months to complete a full police-dog training course. This time I was one of them and would be teaming up with a newly promoted sergeant, Cec Austin. I was, of course, elated, but at the same time felt concerned for the two existing handlers as they could justifiably feel that they and the RAAF had been rejected and that their own futures would be somewhat vague. We were duly scheduled to fly out at the very beginning of February 1974.

In between that time, of course, we experienced the 1974 January and Australia Day floods that crippled Brisbane in such dramatic fashion. There was also the serious consideration of leaving a wife and four very young children behind, always an unknown for families facing such a situation for the first time. We considered that actually going to New Zealand was of a secondary importance compared to the career opportunity given to me and the fact that it had been a longtime dream. I felt it was destiny and we decided to go for it. Cec also had a young family, and although somewhat older and senior to me, no doubt wrestled with the same considerations. We flew out together from Brisbane and saw from the air the still-receding evidence of destruction and scars being left by the massive floods.

We arrived in Wellington and were immediately treated to the fine hospitality and friendship of our Kiwi counterparts. The police training centre was at a place called Trentham and was previously a wartime army base that had been modified to a police training centre. Cec and I were to share a double barracks room together. We soon found out that we were not the only special outside trainees on the course, as also attending was an officer from Fiji, Situveni Bulli, and two New Zealand Customs officers, John and Jeff. Like us, Situveni was to have a German shepherd, but the Customs boys were to train two beautiful black Labradors, which were to become their first drug-detection dogs. Completing the intake were several New Zealand police officers, all of whom were complete novices like us. The training was overseen by the officer in charge, Senior Sergeant Trevor Beatson, who was blessed to have under him Sgt Alan Symes. Alan was unique among dog trainers, being one of those rare individuals who seemed capable of getting into the minds and understanding of another species. He was brilliant, great to work with, a natural and probably the hands-on brains of the show. It did not take long to realise that Beatson ran a first-class show. We had a day or two before the course started and we were shown around Wellington and its police headquarters, plus we had an introduction and welcome from their very cordial commissioner. Naturally we were keen to meet our dogs.

The New Zealand Police were pulling out all stops and keenly aware that their reputation was on the line. They were anxious for us to succeed and of course hoping that the QP would build their own successful dog section from the foundations they were about to teach us. The dogs they had chosen for us were just terrific. Cec was to be teamed with a four-year-old, pure-bred, ex-operational police dog named Lex.

Lex was predominately black, but with additional tonal greys. He had proved himself an outstanding dog and the Auckland Dog Section from where he had come had fought tooth and nail to keep him, and indeed opposed him going to Australia as he was one in a hundred. The reasoning behind Cec having a proven dog instead of a novice was that he would be able to produce results for us almost straight away. Lex was a brilliant tracker, a scorcher at man work and crowd control. He was, in short, a magic dog.

I was teamed with a donated dog named Sam and was impressed with him from first sight. He was a 12-month-old, pure-bred ginger dog with a white chest and an almost black saddle. He was beautifully proportioned with a magnificent head. Symes spoke to me and gave me a rundown on what he felt were the dog's characteristics and temperament. "The one thing you must always be with this dog is the boss; he is a tough dog, a hard dog, so don't go soft with him. He has a great heart and will work all day for you." As usual, time was to prove that he was spot on.

The course itself was excellent and was pretty full-on and included classroom work and discussion. Everyone was given a thesis topic to work on throughout the course. Mine was to present a thesis on how to train and establish a team of explosive and other specialist detecting dogs within an operational police-dog unit. One of the New Zealanders was given the task of researching the Kuri, the native New Zealand dog, similar to our dingo. The result was quite surprising as his research and presentation took the subject into new territory that resulted in much interest by the New Zealand Natural History Museum.

We were outdoors over 90 per cent of the time in rain or shine and conducted training in all areas and situations imaginable, including everything from patrolling in the city centre to tracking on mountain slopes in sheep farms. I had no trouble with obedience, agility, man work and crowd-control training. Off-the-lead wind searching was also OK, but I struggled with tracking. This was disappointing because tracking is the main requirement that justifies a police dog.

Becoming frustrated with the difficulties did not help, especially when other men on the course seemed to be advancing well in this area. I was trying too hard and at the same time thought too much about what the dog was doing. In short, I was not reading my dog. It was very late in the course that the penny dropped and things came together, but I had run out of time to cement the lessons learnt and still had some catching up to do. I finished the course quite well, but was not as experienced or established in tracking as I and the training staff would like to have been. Cec, on the other hand, had a dog that was just a natural and almost achieved 100 per cent on anything he stuck his nose to. I found this annoying sometimes and it helped compound my problems and dent my confidence.

However, this aspect did in fact have its beneficial side, because with all the ongoing difficulties I had in grasping tracking and the more intense one-on-one training I received because of it, I did in fact at the end of the day learn and understand more about the subject in comparison to someone who sailed straight through it. Because of this, not only was I able to sort my own problems out, but was able to become a better instructor myself in the future when we began training our own dogs and handlers.

Before leaving New Zealand, Senior Sergeant Beatson took me aside and told me how I had worried him for a while, but that he was totally confident that I had the ability to identify problems and sort them out. Although he would have liked me to be stronger in the area of tracking, he had no doubts that we would succeed well. Many months later when he visited Australia and conducted a progress assessment he was happy to tell me that his comments had been vindicated.

Both Cec and I had managed to bring our wives and families out towards the end of the training, which was great. In all the time that we had been away not one person from the police hierarchy had been in touch with me or my wife to check to make sure everything was OK. It was the first time I had been away from home like this and had found it much more difficult than I had envisioned. Thankfully the boss at Hamilton Station and a couple of our closer friends there had kept in contact. At the end of our training, Cec went off to Auckland and I went off to Christchurch where we spent a week working with those respective dog units on their regular shifts. Cec and I flew home in mid-May 1974 with two superb and valuable dogs, a gift from the New Zealand Police and the first imported purebred German shepherds.

The first couple of days back were spent with family, seeing the Commissioner and the inevitable media interest. It was decreed that we would now be assigned to CI Branch who had their major city office at Petrie Terrace, just down from the Depot. Why we became part of CI Branch I shall never know as they had no real interest or understanding of us. We were given a dog office on the top floor at the Depot as all training was now done at the new Oxley Police Academy. It was a taste of things to come, as completing the training was the easy part and now it was down to the real business and the melding of our new unit into the fabric of the QP generally.

There was so much to do and so many things to start simultaneously. Unfortunately, we had to wait quite a while for dog-training equipment such as jumps, scaling wall, overhead walking plank, hoops and small trestles to be made and delivered, despite the fact that the plans had been forwarded weeks before from New Zealand. It was a bit of an indictment when I made a full set of my own from demolition timber and had them all up and running before we as a unit got our official ones. The effort was well worthwhile as I set up my own obedience course on vacant government land immediately next to my garden fence at the old Pinkenba Police Station, and I would put Sam over them at the beginning and end of every shift.

One immediate difficulty was that of the four dogs, two had been trained somewhat differently from the other two, and probably without at first realising it, there was an unspoken rivalry starting up, as from the word go it was obvious that two different camps on training philosophy existed. I later realised that although the RAAF and New Zealand Police systems were similar in most things, there was in fact a wide difference in the application of the respective dog units. RAAF dogs were predominately a guard-dog function and worked the majority of their service on and within a large air base. Attack work was very high on their agenda.

Our dogs worked within the community and tracking was their priority. Added to this was that we were still obliged to use RAAF Amberley as our fortnightly dog, training base, which in hindsight was not a good idea. After apparently being snubbed, the RAAF boys had to tolerate two new blokes turning up with their "You Beaut" dogs with the inevitable comparisons. This was further aggravated by the situation that the officer in charge of the RAAF dogs was responsible for our assessment. Being as we two new handlers were relatively green and still finding our way, it was no surprise that we did not assess too well to begin with, and that unfairly some of their methods and standards were applied to us.

Dog-handler mateship and diplomacy could not address all of these difficulties. It was an awkward situation and we had much to be grateful for from the RAAF, but they had some methods that conflicted with ours and vice versa, and it was time to consider going our own way. We now had our own officer in charge with Cec and we had a rough idea as to what directions we needed to go in. We got on well. I was one of those young, up-and-at-them ideas men who wanted to do everything in a day, whereas Cec was more the steady-as-we-go type, so things fell round about in the middle.

One important aspect was to get the rest of the force to understand and appreciate what a dog unit could do and explain in basic terms how a dog works. To this end, we began lectures at the academy and set about having a suitably worded section included within our General Instructions Manual. The unit was initially Brisbane-based, but could, of course, be sent to anywhere within a reasonable radius such as Stanthorpe, Darling Downs or the Sunshine Coast. We also had the dogs perform a short flight in one of our air-wing aircraft in order to confirm that they would fly all right and perhaps extend the range to provincial locations.

Many basics had to be established and this new police addition made familiar to all serving officers. Some early successes would, of course, be a natural promotion, but these were going to be hard to come by until such times as the police force was educated enough to request us on a second-nature basis. Between the four handlers, we worked mainly late shifts as a single-officer patrol, covering both the north and south sides of Brisbane. Two-officer patrols were sometimes possible and we tried to conduct a training track or search at least once in a shift.

We would check with each other as to availability before laying a track or hiding some article, usually within an industrial or other commercial area. Once done, a fellow handler would arrive and receive the basic information one could usually expect from a witness in order to establish a possible starting point. The commencement point of any track or search was always the most difficult. This required the dog to be cast around on a 10m line attached to a tracking harness and, with the appropriate commands, it would be set to work to sniff out the scent of the imaginary offender. Once indicated, the dog would move straight into his "let's go" mode, often taking his handler with him, and once a strong, invisible track had been located the end result was usually successful.

Of course, as we progressed we undertook to make tracks more complex and upgraded the overall difficulty. All handlers more or less kept a good ear out across the general police radio in an attempt to identify what might be a suitable dog job. Any recent break-in, recently abandoned stolen car or any incident whereby a suspect had decamped on foot would send us speedily in that direction in the hope that we could get there early enough before any such scene became hopelessly contaminated.

I had a couple of early successes. One Sunday afternoon I heard that Senior Constable Joe Griffiths at Banyo Station was attending a factory break-in and he later advised VKR that he needed assistance to search large industrial premises as indications were that two offenders might still be inside. I contacted Joe direct and told him I would be there within minutes. Upon arrival, we found Joe was duly keeping the premises under surveillance.

We quickly found the entry point and gained entry ourselves. Inside were mountains of stacked pallets going up 15 feet or more almost to the ceiling. We had a visual look around, but nothing obvious was apparent, so I did what became usual practice and shouted out that I was a police officer with a dog, that we were about to search the premises and that the dog would be set free. I also announced I would wait a minute for any person within to make themselves known to me. That time elapsed without any development, so I put Sam to work with the appropriate command.

It was copybook stuff. Sam did a circuit of the inside of the warehouse, obviously working and tail up. He completed this run and on coming back to me took off down a wide centre space and began going up and down. He then gave a strong indication as his head came up, going from side to side and sniffing the air. "There's something here, Joe," I said. Sam then swivelled around on his back legs, still checking the air before he gave three or four small front-leg jumps to get his head higher. Then he zeroed in on one particular pallet and began circling it, again trying to get higher by reaching up against it with his front paws. He then started barking enthusiastically.

I climbed up to the top of an adjoining pallet and looked across to see two males lying down. "Are you coming down by your own steam or do we have to come up and drag you down," I said to them. 'We're not coming down with that dog down there," said one of them. I shouted down to Joe what I had found and climbed down. I secured Sam and called upon the offenders to come down, which they did. Joe took them into custody and later gave them over to the Criminal Investigation Branch.

Joe was absolutely tickled pink about the dog and how he had found them so quickly. He was quietly impressed that Sam had found them when at no time could he have seen them. I explained to him facts surrounding scent and how it is made up and how the dog had gone from initial ground-scent searching to that of wind or airborne scent. I did not tell him that he had just witnessed our first success and that I was more tickled pink than he was. After that, Joe was a great advocate for police dogs, telling everyone about it and suggesting that they call us first before doing a search themselves. He rang me up from time to time to see how we were going and I got the impression he had unofficially adopted Sam.

Another time I was patrolling when an emergency call went up for police to attend a serious disturbance at the Gresham Hotel in The Valley. I was close by and got there within a couple of minutes. A large group of people were outside the pub in a short side street. There was a lot of shouting, pushing and shoving, plus about half-a-dozen blokes shaping up and throwing punches.

The group was mainly of South Sea Islander appearance. I decided to contain things until other police, who I knew were en route, arrived, and took Sam from the caged police vehicle and approached the mob. I called upon them to behave themselves, which had the desired effect of stopping the immediate disturbance; the mob seemed less impressed by the fact that there was only me there. Sam at this stage was simply quiet by my side and although I knew he was very interested in what was going on he did not give any outward display of aggression. The offenders began to advance on me so I had Sam bark out some warning to them that the stakes were increasing slightly.

This stopped some of them, but several, and particularly one, a huge hulk of a man who felt he was a match for anyone, came on with an apparent intent to do me mischief. After unsuccessfully cautioning them twice to fall back, I doubled the length of the lead by a quick shift and re-clipping of a spring clasp and let Sam fan out in front of me. Sam bounded forward in a barking display of nastiness and I had judged the distance perfectly as he came to a restrained stop just inches in front of the main antagonist. Suddenly all bravado ceased. One of them back-pedalled quickly to join his mates again, whereas the giant in front of me seemed transfixed to the spot, unable to move.

If it is possible for a black man to turn white then this fellow did, going quite pale. Suddenly, as if electrocuted, he darted to his left and ran to the kerb where a taxi had just stopped. A woman was opening the rear door when our hero pulled her out of the way and jumped in, yelling "Let's go, come on, let's go," and the cab took off. By now I had Sam back on the short lead and was suggesting to the rest of them that they wait quietly until other police attended.

They readily agreed and stayed like that until a couple of minutes later when the "cavalry" arrived.

I put Sam away back in the vehicle feeling quite elated. In a short space of time I had gone to two incidents that had gone off text-book style and had witnessed for the first time the magical effect of Sam in full flight upon a group of alcohol-inspired louts. I was pretty pleased as it helped to make up for all the miles of non-event patrolling or going to jobs that had no result for one reason or another.

Things were going well. The huge amount of effort and personal time that we were all putting in made things worthwhile. It was becoming obvious, however, that our superiors were either not too interested or were at a loss as to how to manage this new unit. We lacked someone at commissioned level who could educate those in charge of the purse strings and to understand what was required and have some sort of progressive plan outlined for the future.

We negotiated very good contract arrangements with Borthwicks in regard to the supplying of quality dog meat and also secured the services of a reputable vet. However, some of these bills must have surprised our masters as it appeared very much to me that the "You have your dogs, just get on with it" attitude still persisted. We solved many of our difficulties ourselves and overcame obstacles that seemed too hard for higher rank. We were always gradually moving forward in spite of many needless frustrations.

The initial and primary function of the Police Dog Unit (PDU) was the patrolling of State schools in order to reduce the break-ins and damage that was then being experienced on a more or less Brisbane-wide basis. We would stop off and check quite a number of schools during a late shift and we had a few successes in locating persons who should not have been on the school grounds. Not all were suspect though. Quite a few had amorous intentions towards each other! The very nature of schools again provided ideal locations to maintain training and we would often use the odd one to search or run a track. It was wise not to use too often the same persons to lay a track or hide up somewhere so we would sometimes convince other police crews and dog handlers to assist us.

Another area that was experiencing a good deal of trouble was suburban rail lines, so train patrols were included in our responsibilities and we worked in conjunction with the Railway Squad. A lot of damage was being inflicted upon trains, with seats being slashed, windows broken and many travellers harassed by louts. This was a much more visible presence than the schools and quite well received and appreciated by the public.

I was very handy to a "suspect on premises" call at Hamilton one evening and was on scene within two minutes. Three males had broken into a house and were attempting to bolt as they realised police were on the way. I was making my way along the side of the house to block off the rear exit when a young man jumped out of a window and landed just a few feet in front of us. Sam was immediately aroused and needed little encouragement in declaring his willingness to clean his teeth on him. However, a quick suggestion that the offender stay right where he stood was made, with the result that when supporting police arrived we already had one ready for the back of the police van. Quick inquiries revealed that two other men had decamped out of the back door shortly before my first customer, and as the scene had not been contaminated in any way by other police, I decided to attempt a track.

Sam went to work straight away in a fairly confined space and we had soon hopped over some garden fences before finding ourselves heading outbound on the footpath of Kingsford Smith Drive. It was a strong track and like all dog handlers in this situation the adrenalin was working overtime, as quite frankly there is nothing more exciting than pursuing human prey. We went on for several hundred metres and across a couple of intersections without missing a beat when quickly we came to a blind corner with a high fence. Sam went straight around left and propped and started growling menacingly. In front of him were two young Maori men standing with their backs pressed to the fence and both with terrified looks on their faces as they looked with downcast eyes at Sam but faces straight ahead. It looked quite amusing really and I found it even more so when considering that a New Zealand dog had just located two New Zealand offenders! So it was three out of three and a very happy CI Branch crew who took them in for questioning.

Bikies featured in another incident at suburban Milton one night, in a small, low-set house near the brewery. Normally, motorcycle gangs tend to gather in out of the way places, away from public attention. However, here they were displaying most of their feral skills, conducting a party that had got well out of hand with music of unbelievable loudness, the foulest language at shouting level and empty bottles being thrown out on to the road. About three dozen bikes were parked in an impressive military-style line along a kerb. The house appeared to be wall-to-wall bodies with men spilling outside and the house seemed to be moving to the beat and rhythm of the music.

It was another classic stand-off as initial police contact had been rebuffed in true renegade bikie style and they were now just enjoying baiting us. I arrived with Sam to find a growing number of police waiting for the arrival of a commissioned officer. One duly arrived; an inspector who had gained a wide reputation for no nonsense and positive action when running a Fortitude

Valley-based drink-driving team known as Murphy's Marauders. He approached the house in an attempt to open a line of communication, but was jeered, threatened and insulted. A second attempt with a megaphone met with the same derision.

The inspector walked back and joined us all and announced that some strong action was required. With that he walked to the first Harley-Davidson, smashed the headlamp by kicking it out and pushed the bike on its side. The result was electric, all the party shouting ceased and the music went off. The inspector used the loudhailer again to reason with the bikies, but the derision was again repeated. The inspector invited one of the officers to kick another headlight out and push the bike over. He promptly obeyed and we turned our attention back to the party house to gauge any response. It was quick in coming. Their leader, known as the sergeant at arms, appeared to confront the inspector.

A heated conversation took place and certain threats were made and guarantees given. All bike numbers had been recorded and searched. Within a short space of time, pairs of bikies were allowed to leave after licences had been checked, until eventually all had gone and peace was restored. The house was inspected and searched and it was established that the building was a rental, soon to be re-listed for new tenants. My involvement had long ceased and I left to continue patrols with a now tame situation to be finalised by the police responsible.

The Dog Unit was moved to the control of the Brisbane Mobile Patrols, which seemed a far more sensible proposal. Although the Mobiles came under the control of a senior commissioned officer and other inspectors, it did not improve the understanding of the needs or basic application of a dog unit and we were still often left battling to have a voice heard.

The other main injection of change was that we were to set about training four new handlers of our own. It did not seem to concern anyone that we had absolutely no facilities or equipment that even vaguely compared to that of New Zealand or the RAAF. No suitably fenced enclosed training area was available, nor did we have anything that could be construed as a training headquarters. However, we set about selecting four new trainee handlers and the obtaining of four suitable dogs. We advertised for donation dogs and received encouraging responses.

Cec and I criss-crossed Brisbane, inspecting and assessing dogs, and eventually found four, one of which the Queensland Police purchased. Our next problem was where to keep them, and fortunately the RSPCA at Yeronga came to our assistance with temporary kennelling until we were able to have them go home with their intended handler. Constables Bob Clowse, John Casey, Terry Hawkins and Ken Johnstone were accepted from a good field of interested applicants. By this time the import ban on German shepherd breeding stock had been lifted and we were seeing some good results from reputable breeders.

Cec and I were to be responsible for the bulk of the training, with support and back-up from Charlie and Dave, who in the main were to continue to fly the flag patrolling. Cec and I were still subject to patrols and call-outs whenever possible. This, of course, meant quite a hefty workload for us and very often one or both of us had to abandon training and attend to a dog job if no-one else was available. We sometimes took our trainees with us, who occasionally got on the job training. In the main our training consisted of picking each other up each day and driving to some prearranged location and taking each other back at day's end. We set up our dog-training equipment such as jumps, hoops and hurdles within the grounds of the police academy. It was very time-consuming and not the most satisfactory arrangement, but it was the best we could do in the given circumstances. We did our best to imitate training locations and scenarios as experienced in New Zealand and secured the use of various establishments to facilitate searching of premises, both for persons and property.

But again, funny things happen. We had all four trainees and ourselves going through our obedience and agility paces on the academy sports oval that was also being shared by Wayne Bennett and his football gladiators, who were also training. Wayne came over and out of interest began talking to Cec and asking general questions about the dogs. He watched as they scaled walls, walked a high plank, jumped through hoops and did the basic obedience routines. "What happens if you set your dog on to an offender, but then realise you have got the wrong bloke," said Wayne to Cec. "Aaaah well, that's when a dog is better than a gun really," regaled Cec. "You can't stop a bullet, but you can always call the dog off." "Can you do that?" asked Wayne. "Yes, dead easy," said Cec, "I'll show you if you like." With that Cec explained to Wayne a brief exercise whereby he asked Wayne to simply jog off away from us and when about 80m or so away he would call upon him to stop.

He instructed Wayne, however, to ignore this and when about 100m away he would release Lex to stop him. When about halfway, he would call the dog off and Lex would come back to him. John Casey, who was standing with us, looked at me with concern and whispered, "I don't think this is a good idea".

Lex was a great man-work dog, but sometimes his keenness made him somewhat deaf (the shutters come down as we would say), and Cec would have to exercise some determined voice control in order to have Lex leave, cease the attack and return to the handler. This was sometimes the case in training as the rubber arm sleeves we used incited Lex tremendously, and although I had seen Lex perform this exercise well on a number of occasions, I had also seen times when Cec had to get very forceful in order to have Lex desist. However, on this occasion Wayne did not have and should not need a protective rubber sleeve?

Wayne duly jogged off away from us and Cec duly called upon him to stop at the prearranged distance. Wayne continued on as arranged and Lex was released. About 40m out, Cec shouted "Leave", to Lex, who promptly ignored him. Cec gave out another more emphatic "Leave" but with the same result and Lex was closing in on Wayne. A very desperate, urgent and higher-pitched "Leave" also proved ineffective and we watched in mock horror as Lex latched on to the top of Wayne's leg. Lex had a good bite and Wayne immediately went into arm-flapping gyrations and yelled out in obvious pain. Cec was hot-footing over to him, having by now successfully brought Lex under control. The dog was coming back to him with his famous "I bit that bastard as well" look and allowed himself to be leashed. Wayne was not impressed and made quite a few derogatory remarks about Lex and our dog unit in general before heading off to the nurse for some first aid.

With our first home-grown training course completed and the addition of four new handlers we gained some additional flexibility in our operability. Eight dogs and handlers eased the burden on Cec and myself and allowed some wider variety of training ploys. We remained under the control of Brisbane Mobile Patrols, under an ever-changing commissioned officer in charge. All, however, seemed uninterested in understanding what we did, our specific problems or how best to deploy us. We battled along among ourselves, submitting endless reports in an effort to get equipment and some proper dog establishment.

We were encouraged when the old Kelvin Grove Police Station residence was given over to us, kitting out the premises with all sorts of begged, borrowed or stolen items. One of the handlers moved in with his family, and although it was really inadequate, it was a start. We were also assigned our own commissioned officer to oversee our section and to hopefully carry our message to higher levels. His appointment was on the basis that he was a dog lover and was particularly interested in pig hunting and pig dogs!

We carried on with the best of intentions and spirit and everyone put in a maximum effort despite the obvious parsimonious attitude of our masters. Results were gradually coming, even if it was mainly only us who recognised it. After another year a second training course was scheduled for another four handlers which, like the first one, was conducted without any proper training facility or support location. Almost everything was done by way of contact with persons known to our squad members. The use of any training facility, be it a factory, railway yard or specific building, was begged and borrowed by us as work colleagues.

This second course coincided with serious domestic difficulties for me as almost constant evening and night shifts were taking its toll at home. Added to this, I could see my dream slipping away, caused by something totally unseen, the seniority system. Every time a training course was conducted, officers senior to me would graduate and pass me in any future promotion. Unlike Cec, I was in an untenable position whereby officers I had trained and continued to train operationally would automatically win any future promotion over me. I discussed the situation with Cec and advised him that I would seek to have a position of Dog Trainer established, without any immediate reference to promotion for myself, as a way of protecting my involvement with the dogs and maintaining some degree of influence within the section.

Cec saw the merits of it all, but my proposal was dismissed out of hand by our overseeing inspector, effectively clouding my future. The result was that some internal jockeying became evident by some to best position themselves for future promotion that must logically come.

With these serious difficulties on two fronts, it became obvious to me that some self-assessment was due and I decided to resign from the dogs and seek my return to general suburban police duties at Hamilton. I felt that if the QPS was willing to so easily squander the skills they had opportuned for me and the input I could give on their behalf, then it was time to regroup and move on. It was a difficult decision, but one I never really regretted, as like the old saying about one door closing, another far happier door eventually opened.

Cec stayed a while longer before being promoted, eventually moving out and further up the promotion ladder. Naturally, I kept an eye on and some contact with the early handlers and was very pleased when some years later, control of the unit passed to Sergeant John Casey, one of the men in our first training course. John persevered and took the unit to a truly professional status, with dog sections all over the State and, finally, the establishment of a properly built Dog Section Headquarters at Oxley, complete with a dog-breeding program to ensure sound quality of stock and the training of a variety of specialised dogs, including drugs, explosives and cadaver detection.

John Casey oversaw interstate interaction with other police dog units and maintained the connection with New Zealand. All these things may have been my dreams over 30 years previously, but the important thing was that they eventuated. I take some pride in that.

Bicycles were introduced into policing in 1896 at a cost of £13 ($26) each. This was twice the price of a police horse.

*The Long Blue Line,* W Ross Johnston, 1992 (p135-6)

# George Laidlaw Rickertt

They say that you can take the boy out of the bush, but not the bush out of the boy, and that's exactly how I would describe George Rickertt, who has never lost his country upbringing. A big man with a big heart and an easy-going manner and attitude to match. I saw quite a lot of George in my Biloela and Rockhampton days and found him to be an energetic and helpful officer who was always prepared to go that extra mile in the execution of his duty. As the officer in charge of the Rockhampton Police Garage, he shouldered a huge responsibility and performed his duties in a most competent way. George was highly respected by his subordinates and those officers, both sworn and unsworn, who came into contact with him on a daily basis. In his managerial duties he was in constant contact with members of the business community where he was highly respected.

**Laurie Pointing**

## George Laidlaw Rickertt

Born in Nanango on 5 February,1944, at Ringsfield Maternity Hospital, I was christened George Laidlaw Rickertt. My father's name was also George; my mother's name was Muriel, but she was always nicknamed Nell. Dad passed away in 1983, Mum is still going well. I have two sisters, Roby and Vicky, and a brother, David. Ringsfield is still there today, being used for an old peoples' home.

I started school at Nanango in 1949. In those days there was Prep 1, 2 and 3. There were civilian teachers and we had Miss King and Miss Ziebarth. Before I left Nanango, I can remember two nuns, Sister Mary Maninna and Sister Mary Liam. They were both very good at dishing out punishment, and if you misbehaved you copped the edge of a wooden ruler across the back of your knuckles while they were holding the end of your fingers.

I then did Grades 1 and 2, and then, during Grade 3 in 1953, we moved back to the family farm, which was between Nanango and Goomeri. The school there was called Johnston West and was a one-teacher school – the teacher taught from Grade 1 through to Grade 8. When I arrived there, the teacher's name was Norm Bothwell, who was followed by Ted Lee, then came Dennis Wengert. When the latter left, we had Bob Alexander for a short time (he was there in a relieving role), and then Noel Stephenson came. He was there until I finished in 1958.

In June 2009, I was in Nanango visiting Mum, who lives across the road from the Catholic church and school complex. I went across to the school (the two school buildings are still there) and I spoke with the lady there about past records. They still have the old original enrolment ledger, which is a book approximately 40 cm by 60 cm with a hard cover and about 20 ml. thick. All entries are handwritten in ink. The entries had your name, date of birth, when you started school, the time you were away from school, and your father's name and his occupation.

In 1954, I spent three months at a convent at Yarraman. The nuns there were a bit different; and bit more compassionate. The nun in charge of our dormitory was Sister Mary Demonfort. I recall one morning hearing her alarm clock go off and decided to go to the toilet, which was downstairs. I looked up the hallway towards her room, and there she was – stark naked. I came back from the toilet, and, by this time, she was dressed. They used to wear a leather belt around their waist with the end hanging down past their knees. I got a pretty good dust-up because I had seen her without any clothes on. I often thought since, she should maybe have had the door closed. There were 25 of us there as boarders and it was also run by nuns. I returned to the reunion there in 2008 and quite a few of the old students were also present.

I then went back to Johnston West where I completed Grade 7 (which was a scholarship back in those days). In 1959, I went to Downlands in Toowoomba, where I completed sub-Junior and then returned to work on the family farm. That was my education, as I am sure it was for a lot of the officers in the Police Service.

When I turned 17, I went to Nanango with Dad to get my driver's licence. The sergeant at the time was Brill Cronin, one of nature's gentlemen. I got my licence after a nervous hour or two. Back in those days, you had total respect for police. You would not think of misbehaving when they were around. How things have changed – for the worse. It must be very frustrating for the teachers of today. I have always thought that, when they changed the title from Police Force to Police Service, it was just like any other government department.

I spent a few years working at home and then went driving trucks and end-loaders, building cattle yards and fences, ringbarking and poisoning trees. In 1968 I worked at Alexander's Garage, the Ford dealer in Nanango. Bill Alexander still runs the garage to this day.

Once morning in 1968, Senior Constable Alan King from Nanango Police came to me at the local service station. He said he wanted to see me at the police station as he had some papers for me to sign. Instant panic, because everyone knew, no-one messed with Kingy!!

I went down to the police station and the paper I had to sign was to join the Police Force. At a later date, I had to go back to the police station to sit for an exam. At that time Harry Wayne was the sergeant there. I passed the exam and went down to the Police Depot at Petrie Terrace, Brisbane on 3 March, 1969 – what a culture shock!

I had been to Brisbane twice in my life, both times with Mum and Dad. Before I had a licence, we used to drive to Dad's sister's place at Coorparoo and get a taxi everywhere. I got lost and was late getting there – my first serve. My second serve was for not parking properly. I could hear a man with a strange accent doing a lot of loud talking (it was Tom Molloy – he had a very strong Irish accent). Before I left Nanango, Alan King said, "If you want to impress Tom Molloy, you get a short haircut". I never, ever had long hair and had to have it cut really short.

This loud voice was saying, "Come here, son". I was standing there, gawking about (typical bushy]. This voice was getting louder and from very close range, he said, "Are you deaf, son?" Then the penny dropped – he was trying to get my attention. He certainly had it after that. He said to me, "Son, take off your hat and take 10 paces forward". About five paces out, he yelled, "Stop". I was wearing the old double-breasted suit with the cuff on the trousers. One cuff was turned down (third serve). I got the lecture for being untidy. The final words, "What would your mother think?" – Pretty serious offences. Another five paces out (I had my hat back on at this time), Tom says, "OK, take your hat off". He said to the rest of the squad, "OK, all you men, this man needs a haircut". He could have knocked me down with a feather!

My intake spent four months at the depot and I was sworn in on 3 July,1969 and became Constable George Laidlaw Rickertt, Registered No. 7914.

There had been some nervous and harrowing times for me. I remember Inspector Smith, Senior Sergeant Frank Clifford, Senior Constable Fred Angus, Sergeant Tom Laurie and Sergeant Bodenhan. I think there was also Senior Constable Ryan. The police garage at the time was at the rear of the depot and I would never have dreamt on that first day that I would have spent three-parts of my service in the police garage at Rockhampton.

I can recall every Friday afternoon that Frank Clifford would come and ask questions for the last hour of the day. I can still see him today: His head was tilted slightly back with his eyes closed, thinking of the next question. I used to think, "This one is for me". Unfortunately, I never got one question right in four months!! Another thing we had to learn was a system called "Know your City". They would put you at Point A with directions on how to get to Point B. When it came to question time, they would ask you, "How would you get from Point A to Point B?" Never had a clue!

A couple of probationaries pulled out during the term. Tom Molloy sorted a couple more out. Tom had the saying, "Son, if you can't handle here, you can't handle it out in the street". After we were sworn in, Tom was like a mother hen. For years after, if you went back, he knew you by your name and he always had time for a talk. But, even then, you were on your toes!

I suppose I could mention some of the humorous things that happened. One morning we had a snap inspection of our rooms. Tom had a way of waking you up in the morning: He had a loudspeaker and would blow twice into this and say, "All probationaries and all cadets out of bed". He had a habit of running his hand on top of your locker, looking for dust. If he couldn't find any he would look under your bed and rub his fingers on the sole of his boots. Therefore, the next locker had the dust on it. That morning quite a few of us got a serve for having dirty fan lights, but that was the end of it.

Another day, a big issue arose with the incinerator at the depot. One person from each room had to take the wastebasket from the room over to this big horizontal incinerator, and Tom Molloy had specified that no aerosol cans of any sort were to go in. Tom always had the stance when supervising of hands behind his back and rocking up and down on his toes. He was a fanatic to have his uniform spotless. Back in those days, we had the drab olive uniform with brown belt and brown front on the police cap, and Tom used to polish both these items with boot polish.

This one day, he happened to be standing in front of the incinerator – about a metre away – and, of course, somebody had put an aerosol can in the incinerator. When it blew up the culprit had long gone, but Tom copped the full blast of all the ashes and burnt papers coming out of door. He did not look for the culprit, but the whole squad suffered: We had to shine his door knob and glass windows.

When Tom wanted to get somebody's attention he would say, "Come here, that man". After a while, a few of the boys could take off his Irish accent. Tom had the habit of sneaking about and you didn't know when you were going to strike him next. One day a voice said, "Come here, that man". Tom was around the corner and said, "Come here, that man who said, 'Come here, that man' ". There was a scatter around the camp then.

Back then, you were allowed to smoke, but were supposed to put the dumpers in the receptacle provided. One day, between classes, Tony Roberts and I were having a smoke on the first floor. The building was T-shaped with one section of the building facing towards Petrie Terrace. Tony had finished his smoke and had a look around to see if Tom was about. He could not see Tom so he threw the dumper out on the lawn. The dumper was about two feet from his hand when the voice roared, "Roberts". Tom was hiding around the corner behind the pillar of the building. Tony's penance was to get a bucket and pick up all the dumpers on the lawn. About an hour and an half later, Tony had about three-parts of a bucket of dumpers.

We all passed the final exam and were sworn in on the 3rd of July, 1969. Even though we kept our hair cut very short, I have a photo of where I was marching up to sign the necessary paperwork. The photo shows that the side of my head was white where the sun had never been on it. This was caused by the trim from the day before. Tom always had a saying, "Son, the hair on top of your heads is yours; the hair on the side is mine".

We were all asked to fill out a form as to where we would like to be transferred. Me, being a hunter from way back, decided on Cunnamulla. I ended up at Woolloongabba. The first advice when I got up there was to forget all you learnt at the depot and start again.

A few of the men there whom I remember were: Inspector Prendergast, Walter Fraser, Gordon Hazeldean, Sergeant Tom Roberts, and I think there was Inspector McKeivor. On the shift there, we walked the beat for two nights and drove in the car with the sergeant on the third night. Until midnight we drove the boss's Fairlane: V8 motor, power steering, heater, etc. After midnight you drove a two-door Cortina without a heater. You drove without wearing an overcoat and drove with the windows down so the inside of the windscreen would not fog up. How things have changed. When you were walking the beat you had to meet up with the shift sergeant at certain times and places. Look out if you weren't there! Before you started the day shift you had to wash the car.

Later in the year I was transferred to Rockhampton. The first I knew about being transferred was when Alan King came up to Mum and Dad's house (they had sold the farm and were, at this time, living in Nanango) and said to me, "I see you have been transferred". I replied, "I have never heard anything about that". He then produced a Courier Mail newspaper and there it was: Myself and about 50 others, all in the paper. Could you imagine the ruckus today if you found out, by means of a newspaper, that you had been transferred and had not been notified first?

I arrived in Rockhampton towards the end of October 1969, with my wife, Kay, and son, William Leo, who we were to lose in a car accident on the 31st of May, 1988. Our daughter, Allison, came along in November 1972. She is now married to Andrew Davey, and they live on a property near Alpha. Kay and I were later divorced. I later remarried and daughter, Megan, arrived in October 1987. She lives in Rockhampton and is still annoying all and sundry.

The first man I met at Rockhampton Police Station was Ernie Benson, who still lives in Rockhampton and is the president of the Retired Police Association. The first shift I worked was with Col Jensen. Unfortunately, Col passed away in 2007. Some of the officers that were there were: Abe Duncan, who was Superintendent; Senior Sergeant Bob Cartmill; Tom McGrath; Gordon Thompson; Harry Royes; Andy Anderson, who was the watch-house keeper; Frank McNamara, CI Branch; Bill McClintock, traffic; Norm Ganter; Bill Bergan; Errol Walker; Sel Castledine, radio electronics; and Jack Augustine, who was one of the inspectors. This is to name but a few.

Those first shifts I worked there were certainly a lot different from the city environment. There was none of the crap – lining up for lectures, etc – and it was more relaxed. It was only a quarter in size of the area we worked at Woolloongabba. In Rockhampton you only walked half-a-dozen blocks. It was hard to get lost in Rockhampton, as you head to Berserker Mountain for a landmark.

The shifts we worked were 6am to 2pm, 2pm until 10pm and 10pm until 6am. When you worked night shift you did seven nights, 10pm-6am. You then came back and did two shifts of 2pm-10pm and then back the following day and did 6am-2pm. Then you had four days off.

In later years they changed the shifts from 8am-4pm, 4pm-12midnight and 12midnight-8am. Night shift was seven nights, 12midnight untill 8 a.m. You had the rest of that day off and then four full days and then you started at 4pm on the fifth day. Shifts were taken in turns of driving on the street, front-counter duty, watch-house duty and some beat duty.

Watch-house duty comprised fingerprinting prisoners, keeping an eye on the house charge book when new prisoners came in and, when you had a quiet shift, it was a good opportunity to do any typing. On one shift I was working 2pm-10pm when one of the prisoners from the jail section came and told me that all the other prisoners were escaping through the roof.

I called for assistance and, just as we got inside the prison cell, the last bloke was going through the ceiling. They had kept one of the metal spoons from one of their meals and had ground the corners off the handle end of it. They had done this on the corner of the concrete on the floor, thus the end had a tip on it that made it look like a screwdriver. They removed the mesh from over the ceiling light and crawled up through the hole. Some were recaptured that night and the last three the next day. It must have been a Saturday or a Sunday as the cleaning lady working at the Depot Hill State School heard the toilet flushed and nobody came out. Constable Alan Neep attended and the three last escapees were recaptured.

In those days it was all typewriters, allocated forms and carbon paper. There were no computers (thank God). Front-counter duty comprised dealing with the public, cross-referencing gazettes, and an occasional walk down the street. There was also a large hardcover log book that contained descriptions of all stolen bicycles in the area. People would come to the counter to see if their bike had been recovered. All recovered bicycles were held in the room at the back of the station, and people were taken to the bicycle room to see if their bike was there.

I did quite a bit of relieving in the Stock Squad over the years, relieving Doug Helmore and Alex McLeod. In later years Alex left and Tim Roach took his place. I once had the opportunity to assist Laurie Pointing and some other officers to do a job out on the Bauhinia Downs Road near Moura. This was in relation to a team of men who were suspected of killing cattle for beef.

Laurie was a very confident and competent operator. One arrest was made, but not in relation to killing cattle. I imagine that team of men would have been on the ball after that. In later years I saw some of the arrests that Laurie made. He definitely had a great knowledge of the law and Police Force in general.

I think I was the only bloke in Rockhampton who had on his police file that he could ride a horse. I recall going once with Tim Roach to the Mackay area and we camped at the Sarina showgrounds. We had two of the Stock Squad horses there and they were a pair of mongrels – I suppose not enough work and handling. One would load in the horse float without trouble and then would kick all day when you closed the door; the other one always caused a lot of trouble when you were trying to load it.

This one morning it would not go on the float so it was time for a fix to the problem. I walked into the next paddock and chopped down a sapling, took the bark off it and came back to the float. Tim had a rope hooked to the halter and the rope was taken up through the float and out the side door. Tim took up the strain on the rope while I gave the horse a couple of good hard whacks across the rump with the sapling. The horse went up in the float and never caused one bit of trouble after that.

Another thing that comes to mind was a trip that I worked with Alex McLeod. We were going from Monto to Miles, an area with a lot of box-tree country. Box-tree country is usually a sandy-loamy sort of country. After a lot of rain, and when the country starts to dry out, it has a hard crust on top, but is very soupy underneath. This soupy area can be several feet deep.

We came to one section of the road in a bit of a hollow where somebody had already been bogged. They had a chainsaw and had cut up some small box-trees and packed them under their wheels. When they left, they did not remove the box-tree sections from the road and these pieces were all sticking up like a tank trap. Alec decided to drive up the gutter on the right-hand side. We were driving a J2000 Jeep, which is a fairly big and heavy machine. About halfway through, it broke through the crust and went down to the chassis on the driver's side, at the same time leaning on the rill left by the grader. We could not even open the door.

Then we started a lot of shovelling. We got all the sand from the side and underneath the vehicle and packed a pile of grass under the wheels. Alex started to drive the vehicle and down it went again. By this time the angle of the vehicle was so great that you could not even place the towel I was using to wipe the perspiration from my forehead on top of the turret. Well, the shovelling started again. By the time I finished shovelling this time, you could not see over the heap that I had shovelled out.

I said to Alec, "This is our last chance". Up the paddock a hundred yards was a stand of small pine trees. We cut some down, dragged them back to the bog, cut them into pieces and packed them under the wheels. This time we got it out. Could you imagine the ruckus today if you were caught cutting down pine trees. I might add that, in those days, there was no winch fitted to the vehicle. In later years we were issued with a come-along. You must also keep in mind that, if you have nothing to hook the winch on to, the winch is no good for you either. That little episode took us nearly three hours!

The next vehicle after the Jeep was a three-speed Toyota – nowhere near as good to drive as the Jeep. The low gear in the Toyota was too highly geared and, when you hooked the horse float on, nothing wanted to move. The fuel tank was under the seat and holds only about 12 gallons. The later Toyota had a four-speed gearbox and was a far better vehicle.

We also had a police muster at a place called Rookwood at Gongango, west of Rockhampton. It was owned by Bill and Syd Black. I was there about 10 days. After about five days, I managed to collide with a tree while chasing a cow and a calf. I could not move my right thumb, and Bill, was saying it was dislocated. I was pulling on it trying to relocate it, but to no avail. I was also a bite sore in the chest. I was smoking at the time and just had enough strength in my thumb to strike a match. I went back to Rockhampton when the 10 days were up and had an X-ray taken and found I had a broken thumb and broken sternum. That put me out of action for two weeks.

The escort of prisoners and mentally sick patients in those days was nearly always done by train. There was a special carriage that had bars on the windows and doors. There was always a good ratio of police to prisoners. We used to stay at work until 4pm and be in Brisbane by 7 or 8 o'clock the next morning.

On my first escort I thought this would be fairly good: Work the first shift and then the rest on overtime. As it worked out, the four to midnight shift was actually the end of one day, and the 12midnight on was the next day. So, you were sort of doing 16 hours straight. The prisoners were then escorted by Brisbane police. At times, if there was a car for the Rockhampton district, you could drive that home, but you weren't allowed to drive the vehicle until you had a sleep first; otherwise you caught the train.

I remember escorting a mental patient once from Rockhampton to Brisbane on the normal carriage on the train: Middle of winter, wearing an overcoat and very cold, the patient was reading a book. I noticed he was not turning pages very much. I checked the number on the page. I must have dozed off. I woke up some time later and thankfully he was still there, but I noticed that he was still reading the same page. I was well awake after that. In those days, when escorting mental patients, the escorting police officer always wore plain-clothes so as not to draw attention to the other passengers that you were a police officer and in fact on duty escorting a person suffering from mental illness.

I did one stint of relieving at Westwood, relieving Peter Vonhoff. I copped the monthly returns and the quarterly returns. I had never been away relieving before and had never even issued a driver's licence. I didn't know what I was looking for or where to look for it. Peter was around the station a little bit; otherwise I could ring Kevin Cocks at Wowan or Frank Jones in the Inspector's Office in Rockhampton. They saved my day. Talk about being thrown in the deep end and being a poor swimmer!

I always used to relieve in the police garage from time to time. Back in those days we used to work in the main station in Denham Street. We had the first four bays: The first two bays housed all the oil, tyre-changing equipment, workbench, workpit, refrigerator and office desk, and the second two bays were for washing the cars. The next two bays were used by the radio technician and, in later years, we had the next bay where the wheel-alignment equipment for the cars was set up. We moved from there down to Alma Lane where we hired the shed from Andrew Davison, and we were there until we moved over to the new complex behind the North Rockhampton Police Station.

In early 1975, the North Rockhampton Station was made a 24-hour station. Around 20-odd men were taken from Southside to Northside. I was one of them. During the night somebody – don't know who – painted a white line halfway across the bridge depicting Northside and Southside. I got the blame. The original staff at Northside Station were: Senior Sergeant Jack Kelly, Tom Young, Bill Nalder, John Trennaman, Geoff Kleidon, Brian Smith and, later on, Dave McSherry.

I was at Northside for around two years, working general traffic duties with the old radar system, inquiry duties, executing warrants and issuing summonses. Most times, when using the old radar box, I worked with Ray Casey and John Goan. John was stationed at Lakes Creek.

In early 1977 I moved into the garage full-time. When I was relieving in the garage before going to Northside, Bevan Bradshaw and Ian Lindsay were in the garage. Bevan resigned and went to the Traffic Licence Issuing Section. At a later time, Ian went into the Traffic Branch. Bevan rejoined and I transferred over and worked with him. When Bevan came back in, he came back with all his service but no rank.

I had been very slack and had not bothered sitting for an exam. Before we could progress through the ranks we had to pass our First Class Constable exams. I can thank Bevan for getting me motivated. Bevan had retired down near Maryborough and I suppose is still terrorising all the cake and ice-cream shops. I managed to pass on the third go and from then on we had to do an advanced trade course.

This involved 220 hours of attending courses at the technical college. In this course, management was compulsory. I also did Machine 1 and 2, Air-conditioning, Steering and Suspension, and Fuel Injection. We also had to do an exam to be able to inspect vehicles, in order to issue roadworthy certificates.

We also attended several tyre courses that gave us some knowledge as to tyre conditions when doing mechanical inspections. When doing mechanical inspections we worked on four basic points. They were: Tyres, brakes, steering and suspension, because on most vehicles involving accidents the vehicles could not be driven.

Between 1986 and 2004 I only ever encountered a few instances where mechanical defects had actually been the cause of the accidents. Most accidents were caused from driver error or road conditions. Back then, we were known as Technical Officers, Grades 1, 2 and 3, etc. They later changed this back to police uniform ranks and I retired as Senior Sergeant.

They were good years at the garage, because you weren't putting up with all the garbage that the general staff were enduring. Back in those days all the police vehicles were sold in Rockhampton. We were doing the roadworthy certificates and organising the paint detailing. This was not too bad but, in later years, we were doing the same work plus changing over lightbars, towbars, bullbars and spotlights, and fitting mudflaps to the vehicles.

There were four of us in the garage and, if I remember correctly, we were servicing around 75 vehicles and over 30 lawnmowers. About five or six of those lawnmowers were ride-ons. With the push mowers from the country stations they could put the mower in the boot of the car and bring it to town and have it serviced. In those days there was plenty of room in the boot. These days, with all the gear they have to carry, you will be flat out putting a hat in the boot.

We also washed all the vehicles from the area during work hours. We also did all the mechanical inspections from fatal and non-fatal accidents. Quite a few of these required a court attendance, either at the Coroner's Court or when the driver was charged with an offence. The area we covered doing mechanical inspections ranged from St Lawrence to Gladstone, Biloela area and west of Longreach.

I might make mention now of the way the vehicles changed between 1969 and when I finished in 2004. When I came to Rockhampton there were quite a few two-door Cortinas, but mainly Falcons and a few Holdens. All vehicles were on rag tyres (non-radial) and all had, manual gearboxes. There was no air-conditioning. There were no carpets in the car; just rubber floor mats. The Commodores and the Falcons had the column-change gear shift and bench seats. There were roof bars with a single blue revolving light and one little siren that had to be turned on and off manually.

In later years the cars came with air-conditioning, but for a long time the cut-off point for air-conditioned cars was around Bundaberg. There were no bullbars in any of the vehicles; this included the four-wheel drives, and no spare fuel tanks. In the Stock Squad we had to carry jerry cans. In later years the cars came from the factory fitted with air-conditioning, radial tyres, automatic transmission and other modern equipment

If I remember correctly, the earlier cars were not fitted with a laminated windscreen. For years the country stations that had four-wheel drives had twin-cab vehicles with a prisoner box on the back. These vehicles were fitted with twin fuel tanks (after market) with an electric switch to switch from tank to tank. This device was not always failsafe and quite often left the driver stranded on the road.

When I moved to the garage full-time Bevan Bradshaw was in charge. There were also Rodney Herdman, Mick Godbaz and Henry Kurz. When Bevan retired, I took over in charge until I retired in 2004. When I took over, Steve Dunbar took my place, and when I retired he took over the running of the section. This section is now manned by civilians.

In 1995 there were some changes made in the system. At this time Inspector Don McLeod took over the Brisbane Section, thus putting him totally in charge. The police garage was now being called the Transport Section. There were Transport sections in Cairns, Townsville, Rockhampton, Mt Gravatt and the main section at Alderley in Brisbane. The administration of all these sections was then controlled from Brisbane. The country sections were no longer controlled by the regional centres

Straightaway this cut the paperwork back a great deal. When Don McLeod took control, bullbars on sedans were phased out. There were no more mudflaps and towbars were only by applications. All vehicles were fitted out in Brisbane and, shortly afterwards, all vehicles were sold in Brisbane. Some of these vehicles were driven down and some put on truck transport and, in the later stages, they were all put on trucks. Eventually we saw the Workplace Health and Safety issues creeping in, but if you played by their rules they were happy.

A couple of years before I finished up Don McLeod retired and Maurice Pointer took over and, as far as I am aware, he is still there today. Nearly all of the old crew has gone, with the exception of Ian Gordon, who retired and rejoined in a civilian role. Neil Jensen is still there, helping to hold the place together. Nothing much else has changed over the years.

It is now over five years since I've finished and when I am by myself in a quiet environment I often sit and think of all the things that happened (good and bad). There were a lot more good things than bad things. When you are young, you think that you will never get old: I thought I was still bulletproof when I was 50. Now, at 65, I know most of the old fellows have gone and I am not far behind them.

We had a 30-year class reunion in 1999 and somebody had found our original identification photographs. We were a fairly smooth-looking bunch, with short hair and trim bodies. When it came back to real life, I was reminded of a pack of old dogs with the hair starting to go grey on their faces. I suppose there is not much more to say, but if I had my time over I would do the same things again, only do it better.

In 1907, 47 cars were registered and this number more than doubled the following year. Despite the steep rate of increase in car ownership, there was no provision to license drivers until 1920.

*The Long Blue Line,* W Ross Johnston, 1992 (p 172)

# Queensland Police Technical Scientific Section

The Technical Section of the Queensland Police Service was founded in 1936, some 40 years before it would become known as the Scientific Section. The department was located in the basement of Morcom House, opposite Queens Park on George Street, Brisbane, and comprised of a small chemical laboratory, darkroom and a firing range for ballistic work.

Ballistic investigations were well established in police work during this period, but the experts of the Technical Section would later increase their knowledge base and expand their scope into other phases of criminal investigations. (Ballistic investigations formed part of forensic work carried out at the section, which also involved crime-scene investigations, physical comparisons of exhibits and presentation of expert evidence in the courts.)

By the 1940s, the scope of the section had increased to include forensic chemistry, document examination, classification of handwriting, identification of marks on weapons, blood tests, ultra-violet ray and infra-red radiation, scientific photography and the preparation of plans of scenes of crime.

During these formative years equipment was scarce, with the biggest expenditure being for a comparison microscope. It wasn't until World War II, when the American Army financed the purchase of a large range of equipment, were the police scientists in the section able to conduct forensic work, which at this time related to offences committed by the occupying forces.

During the 1950s and the 1960s, a team of two in the Technical Section had grown to three, with the addition of a cadet. They were then known as forensic scientists, no longer specialising purely in ballistics. (The work of forensic scientists and ballistics formed only a small portion of their expertise.)

They were known as multi-skilled operators, proficient in crime-scene examination, including fire investigation, identification of stolen vehicles, tool marks, hair, fibres, glass fragments, paint comparisons, chemical and inflammable liquid identifications and comparisons, all aspects of physical evidence comparisons (plaster casts, physical fits, trace evidence), explosive identifications and forensic photography.

In 1960, Neil Raward was the bright-eyed, 17-year-old police cadet who had joined the staff at the Technical Section and had commenced his studies in Industrial Chemistry.

This determined young cadet would later head the Scientific Section and remain in this position for the next 20 years.

On reflection of the forensic techniques used during the 1950s and 1960s, it makes you realise the great technical advances that have been made over time. For example, at least 100mls of inflammable fluid was required for identification purposes; now all that is required is micro amounts.

Paints were compared by physical techniques, but now the scanning electron microscope is utilised, and DNA technology was not available at this point. Only very basic blood comparisons were carried out compared to today when it is possible to draw a DNA profile from a single cell.

During the 1970s, the role of the forensic scientist was more clearly defined, with the multi-skilled officer investigating all areas of crime.

(During the late 1970s, the role of the forensic scientist was more clearly defined. With the multi-skilled officers starting to specialise in select areas of forensic investigations, members of the section were only involved with ballistics and shooting-related crime put forward by the arresting officer.)

Retired Inspector Neil Raward during his career was involved in many thousands of forensic cases, and in most instances forensic evidence has provided and added to the circumstantial case that has been put forward by the arresting officer.

On a particular night in 1972, a hotel night manager was shot dead on his way home and his keys to the night safe were stolen. Neil Raward recalls numerous .22 calibre discharged cartridge cases being found at the scene. A subsequent police investigation revealed that the offending semi-automatic firearm had been illegally fitted with a silencer by a Brisbane gunsmith who then test-fired the weapon to check its working condition.

Forensic staff searched the gunsmith shop for discharged cartridge cases and approximately 10,000 cases collected. Ballistic comparisons disclosed that three discharged cartridge cases from the gunsmith shop matched those recovered from the murder scene

Soon after, when the Technical Section was renamed the Scientific Section in 1976, the era of the generalist began to decline. By 1992, the Scientific Section had relocated to Roma Street Police Headquarters and staff numbered in excess of 30, with many specialising in a very select field of forensic identification.

Technically a growing interest in forensic science has consistently grown over the years and is evident in the development of resources such as DNA testing and mobile laboratories (SMIRV).

Commenting on this scientific and important section of the Queensland Police Service, former Inspector Raward said that, "Since my retirement in the year 2000, many further developments in techniques have enabled the forensic scientists to have forensic tools available that were never, ever envisaged by the early pioneers in forensic science".

Mourilyan Police Station and police vehicle, November 1973. Reference for police cars in the 1970s. *Queensland Police Museum.*

# Neil Douglas Raward

I have known Neil Raward for many years, having first met when we were both junior officers and I was a member of the Criminal Investigation Branch, Brisbane. Through hard work, study and dedication Neil became a pioneer in Police Forensic Science, and through experience, extensive research and volumes of technical investigative work developed into a competent expert witness. An officer highly regarded and respected by the Courts, his superiors and subordinates, he contributed greatly over his long career to the professionalism and scientific arm of the Queensland Police Service.

**Laurie Pointing**

# Neil Douglas Raward

### Police Forensic Scientist

### March 1960 until January 1996

## Introduction

In the twilight years of my life it is interesting to note that one tends to reflect on past experiences, and it is to this end that I believe it was important for me to document for the benefit of those officers who now work or have worked at the Scientific Section of the Queensland Police Service to be made aware of the times at the section that preceded them. I also believe that members of the general public would also find this history interesting.

## Life before the Queensland Police Force

I was born in the Royal Brisbane Hospital on 7 September, 1942 and at the time my mother was residing in RAAF accommodation at Sandgate (which is now Eventide Retirement Village) as my father, Bert, was in the South West Pacific on active service. During the war years my family was constantly on the move, living in various service houses on the eastern seaboard. My brother, Paul, was born in 1944 and I have a sister who was born in 1948.

After the war ended, the family moved to Armidale, New South Wales, where my mother's family resided. In 1947 the family moved to a small farm in South Tweed Heads, where I resided until I joined the Queensland Police Force as a police cadet in 1959.

My schooling years were spent at Banora Point and Tweed Heads primary schools and I travelled to Murwillumbah High School for five years, where I completed my matriculation in 1959.

Childhood days had many fond memories, and as for many families in the late 40's and 50's times were tough, although we never wanted for anything, enjoying the simple things that country life would bring. Tweed Heads was a small town in which a border fence divided it from Coolangatta. The kids from Tweed Heads never really mixed with the Coolangatta kids as the border fence was a barrier that prevented the normal interaction that would exist in a non-border town.

My family were good friends with Alex Griffiths who founded the Currumbin Bird Sanctuary and I had my first job there at age 11, when I used to ride my bike from South Tweed Heads to Currumbin, a distance of eight miles in those days, where I used to clean out and replenish the numerous bird compounds, which were in the fledgling tourist attraction. The distance and the money was not a consideration as I was happy to have a source of income to buy the little extras that my family could not afford.

I had this job for 12 months, after which I landed the best job available, namely I became a skate boy at the Coolangatta Skating Rink, where I used to earn six shillings a session for strapping on skates and teaching patrons how to skate. Working four sessions of a weekend and most days and nights of the school holidays – I had at last fallen on my feet and the money I accumulated was quite astounding for a boy of my age. I continued with this job until I joined the Police Force.

As my high school days were drawing to an end I was still wondering what I was going to do for the rest of my life, as there were not many worthwhile jobs on offer in the Tweed District and I knew it would be necessary to leave home if I was going to pursue a career.

Having been bought up during the Depression years my mother always encouraged me to get a government job, as there was security no matter what economic times might lie ahead. Some of her suggestions included becoming a teacher, working for the Commonwealth Bank or the Postmaster-General or becoming a police officer.

My mother's grandfather was a New South Wales police officer and as the story goes he was actively involved in the capture of the bushranger Thunderbolt on the New England Tablelands. The prospect of becoming a police cadet certainly was at the top of my possible career list.

Now being a country kid, travelling to Sydney to become a police cadet was too big a move for me to handle as I really enjoyed the comfort and security of my family life. However, when it was suggested that Queensland also had police cadets the thought of only having to travel to Brisbane was most attractive, as I would not be far from home and I could return each weekend to be with my family and friends.

In the second half of 1959 I applied to join the Queensland Police Force as a cadet. As I was living in New South Wales I was interviewed by the sergeant from the Tweed Heads Police Station regarding my family background and other issues, and of course it was suggested that I should consider also applying to be appointed a police cadet in New South Wales, an offer which I politely declined.

In November 1959 I travelled to Brisbane to sit for my entrance exam as police cadet and also submit myself to the compulsory medical check by the Government Medical Officer. As a result, in early December I received a letter from the Police Force advising that I had been successful with my application and that I would commence as a police cadet at the Police Depot, Petrie Terrace, on Monday, 21 December, 1959.

My vision of having Christmas and New Year with my family and friends was somewhat shattered: How could the Police Force make me start my job as a cadet four days before the Christmas period, and perhaps I would have to work over the Christmas/New Year period? My comfort zones were all of a sudden coming to an end.

By the time I was required to commence as a police cadet, my father had established two fruit shops on the coast and he was thus able to drop me off at the front gates of the Police Depot on that fateful Monday morning. This was the start of my Queensland police career in which I served for almost 41 years.

## Life as a Police Cadet

Up until 1976 we have all have had the experience of our initial confrontation with Constable First Class Tom Molloy, the Police Force disciplinarian whose task it was to weed out the cadets and probationaries who he believed did not fit the mould of the type of police officer the people of Queensland expected to serve them. My first day was no different as at least half the 19 new cadets were marched down to the barber shop in Caxton Street to get the Molloy cut or face the consequences.

After being given a run-down on what was expected of us and meeting Inspector Herman Reinke and the Depot staff, those cadets who were staying at the wooden barracks at the Petrie Terrace Police Depot were marched to their new accommodation. In this instance, about eight cadets were to partake of the luxury of these run-down and dilapidated living quarters. I am only glad that my mother never ever saw the Third World standard living conditions of the accommodation in which we were expected to cohabitate or she would have taken me home immediately.

After unpacking we were taught to make the dreaded bed pack, which we were expected to pull apart each night and repack each morning. After this introduction, the new cadets were taken to their respective stations by the more senior cadets.

Life as a police cadet was one of survival, as there were many temptations that could lead to instant dismissal, not the least was being caught in licensed premises, as the legal age at that time was 21 years. Numerous cadets met the wraith of Tom Molloy and some of the instructors, which resulted in them having a very short tenure as a cadet. If you could survive as a cadet you certainly could face the rigors as a police constable.

In the middle of 1960 I had saved enough money to purchase my first motor vehicle, a British racing green, four-door, 1956 Morris Minor. The ownership of motor vehicles was a rarity among the cadets and my vehicle became a popular mode of transport for the other cadets who lived in barracks wanting to return home each weekend.

## A Police Cadet Forensic Scientist

My first posting was the Criminal Investigation Branch in George Street where I was to become a cadet in the Criminal Records Section. Doug Aitken was the Sergeant in Charge and Senior Constable Merv Tobin and Constable Norm Dwyer were his staff, together with three cadets. Being a filing clerk was not exactly the life I had visions of when applying to join the Police Force. However, I suppose I had the pleasure of reading police files and court briefs, which contained vivid descriptions of sexual offences that were occurring in the Brisbane area. This was certainly an eye-opener and an awakening to me as to the other side of life that my mother never told me about.

As a cadet I was aware that there was a forensic section as I used to see this person walking around the Criminal Investigation Branch dressed in a white laboratory coat, and I found out that he was Les Bardwell who was the Officer in Charge of the Technical and Firearms Section, which was housed across George Street from the Criminal Investigation Branch in the basement area of Morcom House.

In March 1960 I was approached by the Depot staff to ascertain if I would like a transfer to the Technical Section as the cadet in that section. Frank Wagner was commencing his probationary training and I could fill his vacancy. Life as a filing clerk was not really my niche in life and I jumped at the opportunity and hence started my career as a police forensic scientist, which I enjoyed for the next 36 years.

At the time of joining the section, Les Bardwell was the only police officer who undertook duties not only as a forensic scientist, but also that of a ballistic handwriting expert. Barry Short was a police officer who was studying to be a handwriting expert and I was the only cadet in the section.

When I commenced duties at the Technical Section, I was expected to undertake studies at the Central Technical College (now the QUT) with a view of obtaining a Diploma in Industrial Chemistry (DIC). Luckily for my matriculation I studied chemistry, physics and mathematics and as a consequence I received exemptions in these subjects for the first year of the course, which students could commence after obtaining a Junior Certificate.

The Diploma course was undertaken by all budding chemists employed in the laboratories of the breweries, milk factories, smallgoods factories and fertiliser factories, and we were commonly referred to as bucket chemists, as that was how much sample was needed to perform your tests as a chemist.

I would attend these part-time studies at least three nights a week for five years at my own expense, as at the time the Police Department never recognised police officers who undertook tertiary studies that would assist them in the undertaking of their duties. I graduated with a Diploma of Industrial Chemistry in 1965.

At the Technical Section, I was quickly involved with assisting Les Bardwell in the many facets of forensic science both in the field and in the police laboratory. I received numerous textbooks that were mandatory reading if one was to become conversant with the complexities of the field of forensics. I even commenced to learn to become a handwriting expert, but quickly realised that I could not become conversant in this field as well as other fields of forensic science that I was expected to absorb.

Constable Frank Wagner returned to the section continuing in his role as forensic scientist, and in June 1960 there were only two police officers and one police cadet servicing the State of Queensland in the field of forensic science.

Frank Wagner remained at the Technical Section for 18 months after he was sworn in and then transferred to general duties.

I continued to serve my apprenticeship as a police forensic scientist until October 1961 when I was called up to undertake my probationary training, which I successfully completed with my swearing-in as a constable of police on 16 December, 1961.

I became Constable Neil Douglas Raward, Registered Number 6649. My shoulder number was 5745.

Our squad was affectionately known as the Class of 61, as we had 60 probationaries commence the course and the complete squad graduated. To my knowledge it was the largest squad of probationaries ever to enter the Depot at that time, and as a result the Depot grounds could not handle the swearing-in ceremony because of the sheer size of the squad. The induction parade was held at the Brisbane Exhibition Grounds with the full pageantry pipe band, mounted police and traffic-police motorcyclists providing additional entertainment for the gathered crowd.

## Queensland Police Forensic Scientist Pioneers

The Technical Section of the Queensland Police Service was founded in 1936 by Constable Tom Baty, who was joined by Constable Les Bardwell in 1942, with the field of ballistics being the main source of work in those early times.

The Technical Section was located in the basement of Morcom House, opposite Queens Park on George Street, and consisted of an office, a small chemical laboratory, darkroom and a firing range for ballistic work.

Ballistic examinations were a well-established police science at the time, however, the experts of the Technical Section would later expand their knowledge base and enter into other police forensic pursuits.

By the 1940s, these pursuits included forensic chemistry, document examination, ultra-violet ray and infra-red forensic examination of exhibits, specialised photography and major crime-scene examinations.

During these early years forensic equipment was scarce, with the biggest expenditure being a comparison microscope.

It wasn't until World War II when the occupying American Army financed the purchase of a large range of equipment that the two police forensic scientists were able to conduct forensic laboratory examinations of offences committed not only by the occupying forces, but also offences committed by the local population, mainly in the metropolitan area of Brisbane.

In 1946 Tom Baty resigned from the Queensland Police Force when he was offered a position as a forensic scientist by the American Army in the post-war occupied Japan. After this time, Les Bardwell had several police officers posted to the Technical Section, however, their tenure at the section was often short-lived.

Les Bardwell retired as an Inspector in 1976, having been in charge of the Technical/Scientific Section for 30 years.

## Early Police Forensic Conditions

The Technical Section was in the cellar of Morcom House and this created some unusual problems, with rat infestation being the most critical. Being budding ballistic experts enabled us to use the rats as moving targets for our air-rifle target-practice sessions. Unfortunately, when we hit our target the rats would run away and die in the most inaccessible locations within the laboratory. The resultant stench was unbearable and not very conducive to ideal working conditions.

When the rats overtook the laboratory, the Brisbane City Council rat catchers, complete with fox terrier dogs, would pay a visit and assist with the eradication program.

In my early days as a budding handwriting expert it was very common for the rats to chew or even take exhibit cheques if they were left there overnight on the desk – a situation that could cause embarrassment when investigating police were inquiring as to your handwriting examination results.

The use of Kipps generators for the production of hydrogen sulphide (rotten-egg gas), which was used in the identification of chemical compounds, was a common form of entertainment for annoying the other occupants of the building, namely the Firearms, Photographic and Fingerprint Sections staff, as the fume cabinet in the laboratory was fairly ineffectual.

Fortunately, these conditions only existed for a short time as the CI Branch and the other sections in Morcom House relocated to the new Police Headquarters building in Makerston Street in February 1962. With this move a new and exciting era of forensic science was created.

A purpose-built forensic and ballistic laboratories were now established for the three police forensic scientists and the handwriting expert.

## Early Years as a Police Forensic Scientist

Forensic case work during the 1950s and 1960s was quite small, as were also the staff numbers, and this meant that forensic staff were required to become multi-skilled in most aspects of forensic science. The government forensic biologists specialised in blood grouping and seminal-stain identification, and the government chemists were involved with drug identifications and toxicology examinations.

As part of my training as a ballistic expert, I spent two weeks at the Lithgow Small Arms Factory in 1962, observing manufacturing techniques of the .303 cal. Lee Enfield rifle, which was then the major weapon for the army. I visited this factory on two further occasions to gain an insight into new barrelling techniques that were introduced for the 7.62mm SLR, which replaced the Lee Enfield rifle in the mid-1960s.

The police laboratory staff were called upon to provide a service in a vast array of forensic identifications and comparisons of exhibits.

Some of the forensic skills acquired included work in the following fields: A wide variety of crime-scene examinations (including fires, sexual assaults, murders, break and enters, etc), ballistics, identification of stolen vehicles, tool marks, fibres, hairs, paint and glass comparisons, chemical identifications, inflammable liquid identifications, physical evidence comparisons (plaster casts, physical fits, safe packing, trace evidence), explosive identification, forensic, photography and improvised explosive devices.

As a consequence, the knowledge base of the early police forensic scientist was across a wide spectrum of the sciences, with expert evidence being required to be given in the various courts throughout the State.

During this early era it was not uncommon to be cross-examined along these lines: "Yesterday you gave evidence on ballistics and explosives and today you are giving opinion evidence with regard to paint and hair, comparison; how can you expect to be an expert in all these fields of forensic science? Why do you expect these courts to believe your evidence, etc?"

These times were very challenging and required continual study of the various reference texts in order to maintain your knowledge. Once you established your credibility among the leading defence lawyers, life as an expert witness became much less harrowing.

## Old Forensic Techniques

On reflecting back on the forensic techniques utilised in the 1950s and 1960s, it makes one realise the great technological advances that have been made in forensic science: However, it should be added that the old technology certainly provided an insight into the very basics of the physics and chemistry that is taken for granted by the new generation of forensic scientists.

In order to prove that petrol was petrol, at least 100mls of exhibit sample was required for the comparison. First the specific gravity was compared with a known sample and then a technique known as steam distillation was employed. In this technique, the temperature was recorded when each 10mls of liquid was distilled and a graph was then drawn to compare the results with a known sample of petrol. Modern technology now allows for a sample of vapour from fire debris to be identified by the use of gas chromatography. The Scientific Section purchased a Varian 1200 gas chromatography instrument in 1972.

To determine that gelignite was an explosive substance was even a much more interesting exercise of basic forensic science. Chemical group separation was utilised to identify the ammonium and nitrate radical, together with the chemical identification of nitroglycerine. This was followed by the detonation test, whereby a small sample was placed on a steel plate and struck with a steel hammer.

If further confirmation was required, "the psychological test" was used. This involved smearing a small portion of the sample on to the forehead to ascertain if it produced a headache. Today, Customs officials at airports simply wave a wand into your luggage to detect and identify traces of explosives.

It was also necessary to test fire a detonator to confirm that it contained an explosive substance.

Elemental analysis of unknown metallic and powder exhibits were conducted using now antiquated group-separation techniques.

Modern technologies such as scanning electron microscopes are used to compare paint and other contact trace-evidence samples, as compared with antiquated microscopic and chemical techniques that were employed decades ago.

## Move to Makerston Street

February 1962 saw the opening of a new Police Headquarters building in Makerston Street. The Egg Board building had been transformed into a multi-purpose police headquarters and all the specialist areas of policing, including the Criminal Investigation Branch, Traffic Branch, Police Communications, Commissioner's Office, Special Branch, Licensing Branch, Modus Operandi Section and the Fingerprint, Photographic and Technical and Firearms Section were finally amalgamated in a four-storey building, with the second storey housing the forensic sections.

At the time the Technical Section was hailed as the most modern police forensic laboratory in Australia and it featured in a publication of Pix magazine.

## Ancillary Roles of the Police Forensic Scientist

During the 1960s and 1970s, police forensic scientists attached to the Technical Section became involved in several ancillary roles that were loosely related to their primary roles of forensic scientist.

## Police Emergency Squad

In 1967 the Police Emergency Squad was formed in Queensland. The model for this new squad was based on the New South Wales model in which the ballistic staff were considered to be the experts in the use of firearms and training that was involved with firearms and, as such, they played a major role in the formation of the Emergency Squad in that State.

Les Bardwell, accompanied by Jack Ryan, who was a leading detective, went to Sydney and studied all aspects of their squad, then returned to Queensland to implement the New South Wales model.

The ballistic experts in Queensland were Les Bardwell, Neil Raward and Owen Heness (who had recently joined the section). We were responsible for the formation and training of the Police Emergency Squad, which comprised these three officers together with 24 of the more experienced detectives from the Brisbane metropolitan area.

A range of weapons and tear gas was purchased and stored at Makerston Street, under the care of the Technical Section, which were responsible for all aspects of weapon maintenance and training.

Training was conducted on a regular basis at a range attached to the Wacol Army Base and excellent support was provided by the army for this training. Whenever there was a need for the squad to be mobilised, a member of the Technical Section would load the vehicles with the necessary equipment and proceed to the siege scene where other members of the squad who were on duty at the time would meet them.

The use of tear gas was very common in the early days of the squad and the ballistic experts were utilised to fire the tear-gas grenades or projectiles into the house that contained the offender. These were exciting times and a great camaraderie was generated among the squad members.

Following the retirement of Inspector Les Bardwell in 1976, the squad evolved into a more specialist role, with uniformed police with special skills in firearms being invited to join.

Each year the squad would train under the supervision of specialist army instructors at the Canungra Land Warfare Centre. I was selected as a member of the squad to attend the Special Air Services (SAS) Regiment in Western Australia for two weeks to train with that elite squad, and also with members of the Western Australia Emergency Squad.

With the advent of the Commonwealth Games in 1982, the Emergency Squad became a squad of full-time police officers and the role played by the ballistic expert was no longer required.

## Firearms Instructors

Members of the Technical Section were responsible for training all probationaries in the art of pistol shooting, an activity conducted at a pistol-club range housed in a disused quarry at Ashgrove. Tom Molloy would train the probationaries at the Depot with regard to the drill that was required at the range and we would teach them the refinements of target shooting. This training continued until 1972 when the new academy at Oxley opened and the Department employed police full-time at the academy, and part of their duties included firearms training.

During the 1960s, the Technical Section members were also responsible for training tellers from the various banks throughout Brisbane.

## Improvised Explosive Devices

During the late 1960s and early 1970s, there was a rise in attacks by terrorists throughout the world, and prior to this army personnel used to be responsible for assisting the police with regards to explosives and bomb-demolition activities. As the workload increased the army decided that they wanted to withdraw from this civilian activity to concentrate on the role for which they were initially employed.

As a result, selected police from all States and Territories attended a four-week improvised explosives course, which was held at Bandiana in Victoria.

This training continued for many years, and also police were required to attend refresher courses if they were retained in this role.

In 1971 Les Bardwell and I attended the first of these courses and for many years members of the Technical Section attended all scenes involving the finding of explosives and examination of suspected improvised explosive devices. I also attended two refresher courses at Bandiana. In the early 1980s, a full-time Bomb Squad was formed and the Technical Section no longer performed these duties.

## Lecturing in Forensic Science

After the academy was opened, civilian lecturers taught basic forensic science to all recruits; however, these lecturers moved on and the task was handled by the staff of the newly named Scientific Section for many years. Lectures were also given to all development classes at Chelmer College. The academy lecturing duties were discontinued in the mid-1980s when once again staff from the Scientific Section joined the Academy as lecturers.

As can be seen from the disappearance of the numerous ancillary roles that members of the Technical/Scientific Section performed over the years, the age of specialisation enabled members of the section to concentrate on the primary role for which they employed.

## Police Exhibits at Brisbane Exhibition

From when I commenced work until the late 1970s the Technical/Scientific Section was solely responsible for preparing displays for the Police Exhibit at the Brisbane Exhibition, for which funds were raised for the police youth clubs. These displays highlighted the work of the section by providing case histories and forensic comparison undertaken by members of the section. Rare types of firearms were also exhibited and one year there was also featured the armour worn by Ned Kelly when he was captured.

Members of the section certainly dreaded the arrival of the exhibition, as a great deal of time was required to prepare these displays as well as carrying out our duties as police forensic scientists.

## Travels of the Police Forensic Scientist

In the 1960s, 70's and early 80's members of the Technical/Scientific Section were required to travel throughout Queensland to attend major crime scenes and give evidence in the various courts throughout the State. Members were also on call 24 hours each day and were continually required to either attend local or interstate crime scenes at a moment's notice.

Life was trying for those with a young family as the children were deprived of their father for long periods of time, particularly when there was major crime scenes, for example in Mt Isa, which may take the members away for periods of up to a week.

In the early days air travel was very expensive and to travel to court usually meant catching a train if car travel was out of the question. For one court appearance I travelled to Cunnamulla and back by train, which could mean that the whole week was lost, as the timetables for that neck of the woods were very limited.

I often remember travelling to Townsville for a court case only to be told when the train arrived in that city at 10am that the defendant had pleaded guilty, and after a day of socialising in Townsville I was back again on the train at 4pm. At least they provided the members with a sleeper during the 36 hours in which it took to travel to Townsville. During this time if we were required to attend a major crime scene the air travel was utilised.

I also travelled to Cairns, Emerald, Longreach, Rockhampton, Mackay, Roma and Mt Isa by train. Thank goodness sanity prevailed and by the 1970s we were able to utilise air travel to these places to attend court.

Travel to Rockhampton was always a worry as we were required to stay in the police barracks, and after court had finished a long lunch was usually the order of the day, and on returning to the police station to pick up your route (a police travel document) you would be advised by the senior sergeant that you had to escort a prisoner to Brisbane, which was an overnight journey. Arrangements were made for police to meet you at the major towns on the way so that you could have a toilet break; however, this meeting was rarely forthcoming. Thank goodness I never had any prisoners escape during this time.

As a visiting police forensic scientist to the country centres of Queensland, whether in a crime-scene capacity or as an expert witness, the hospitality of the country detective was legendary. There was always the need for a quiet drink at a friendly hotel after a hard day in the office. When a country detective arrived with exhibits at our office there was always time for a social beer at the Police Club, where the visiting detectives could meet up with their city counterparts.

During this time officers in charge of the forensic sections attended police experts and technicians' conferences every two years throughout Australia.

These conferences were always a welcome break and a great chance to catch up with our interstate colleagues.

## Social Aspects of My Early Career

There was a strong camaraderie between members of the Fingerprints, Photographic and Technical Sections, particularly in the 1960s when it could be said that at times the workload was not very heavy. Members used to socialise after work when word got around that there was to be a keg on at a nearby hotel, and the vast majority of staff partook of the chance to get together. It was not unknown for poker or blackjack schools to develop during these sessions.

For many years the sections downed tools on Friday afternoons after a hard week's work and enjoyed a chance to reflect on the happenings of the proceeding week. There used to also be a chance to join other sections and enjoy each other,s company.

Each year the sections prided in their Christmas Party in which rivalry as to what section could have the best party were very competitive. On the day before Christmas each section was out early to put together the menu for the day, as well as gathering the necessary supplies of beverages.

After sharing the Christmas feast with our workmates, staff would mingle with staff from other sections. The Photographic Section was one party that members were weary of as a visit to that section would usually mean that they got a ceremonial drenching in one of their many photographic wash sinks.

Social cricket days were held with the Scientific, Photographic and Fingerprint Section challenging each other in bitter rivalry as to who had the best cricket team, with barbecues and drinks being part of the contest. Families of the players were also present for the fierce competition. From memory a trophy was also struck for the event.

While I realise that times have changed I believe there is still a place for staff to enjoy a quiet reflection over a couple of beers within the workplace, particularly if members of the sections have been stretched with their heavy workloads.

Talk about the good old days and feel sorry for the workers of the modern era who will be unable to experience them. They were harmless fun and the job still got done.

## Changing Role of the Media

During the 1950s and 1960s, crimes including murders, rapes and safe robberies were receiving extensive coverage via the print media, as television news was only in its infancy in Queensland. The Courier Mail and the Telegraph would provide full front-page spreads, together with follow-up news coverage for several days and, as a result, the public would feel assured that all possible investigative tools were being utilised to solve the crime.

Crime reporters Jim Crawford, Pat Lloyd and Brian Bolton maintained close personal relationships with the leading detectives, thus ensuring that they had a front-row seat at the scenes of all major crimes of the day, and the front page and the follow-up stories and pictures of these crimes certainly highlighted the work of the investigating police.

The names and faces of the leading police and forensic investigators were well entrenched in the minds of the public through this constant publicity of the crime, as evidenced in the appendices.

With the emergence of the electronic media and the decline of the print media, the public has suffered in not being able to read, talk about and relate to the horrific crimes of the day and the skills of the high-profile investigators who always, it seemed in the eyes of the public, brought the offenders to justice.

The electronic media coverage is usually very scant and never allows the viewing audience to have a full appreciation of the enormity of the crime. As a result, the public saw the passing of the old-style media coverage by well-known crime reporters of the criminal activity of the day.

It is unfortunate that the modern print media seems to only want to highlight the alleged misconduct of police, giving scant regard for the excellent investigative work that is still being carried out today.

## Transition of the Forensic Roles

It was not until the 1970s that the roles of the forensic scientist were more clearly defined, through the transition from the era of the multi-skilled forensic scientist to the specialist who had a particular affinity to their own field of expertise. No longer was the police forensic scientist expected to undertake forensic examinations of a cross-section of vastly different exhibits.

Previously this expertise was not available or the casework was not sufficient to allow for the employment of the forensic specialist.

In Queensland there is a new, younger breed of highly qualified forensic scientists who have an appetite to explore new fields of technology, and as a consequence, the era of the generalist is declining and being overtaken by the specialist.

In 1972 the Technical Section was renamed the Scientific Section, a title that still remains today.

With the retirement of Inspector Les Bardwell in 1976 I was promoted to Detective Sergeant and appointed Officer in Charge of the Scientific Section, a position I held for almost 20 years.

In 1985 I was appointed an inspector of police.

## Growth of the Police Forensic Role

From the very humble beginnings that I have already described, there was a steady evolution of the role that police played in the development of the forensic police expert in Queensland. During the early 1970s, crime-scene officers were trained during a six-month course to be proficient in basic aspects of forensic science. This training included photography, fingerprints and crime-scene examination techniques and, on completion of this training, the officers were deployed in various districts throughout Queensland.

Specialist forensic police and fingerprint experts were still required to conduct forensic examinations of the major crime scenes throughout the State.

In the mid 1980s, scientific and fingerprint experts were deployed at a regional level to complement the role of the crime-scene officer. This deployment meant that the Brisbane-based expert was not being required to assist local detectives in the examination of major crime scenes throughout the State.

In the early 1990s, the new Police Headquarters was opened at Roma Street, Brisbane, and within this building was a modern forensic laboratory to accommodate the increasing number of police forensic experts. Civilian forensic scientists were also being employed in the laboratory to assist in specialised tasks that were beyond the scope of the police forensic scientist.

This new era also allowed for the forensic police officer to become more specialised in the various fields of duty, eg ballistics and tool marks, identification of stolen vehicles, arson investigation, etc., and thus evolved the role of the forensic police officer from that of a generalist to a specialist in the various forensic roles that members of the Scientific Section were required to undertake.

By the mid 1990s, approximately 30 staff members were employed at the Scientific Section, together with several other members of the section who had been deployed at a regional level.

While there have been many advances in technology during the past decade, the role of the police forensic officer has stabilised as compared with the level of expanding technology that highlighted the forensic scene in the 1990s.

## Recruitment of Police Forensic Scientists

The employment and retention of police forensic scientists was a challenging task as there were no expert allowances payable to these officers. In the late 1970s, the Scientific/Technical structure was established for members of the Scientific and Photographic Sections and the Fingerprint Bureau. This structure allowed for separate pay scales, which incorporated an expert allowance, and a promotion structure to be created that recognised the individual expertise of the police expert.

The police experts at the Scientific Section were titled Scientific Officers, while the Photographic and Fingerprint staff were then know as Technical Officers.

Prior to the introduction of this structure I was appointed a plain-clothes constable in the early 1960s. I was later appointed a detective constable, and as I progressed I was appointed a detective constable first class, detective senior constable and later a detective sergeant.

Fingerprint experts were paid an allowance for their expertise, however, no such allowance was payable to members of the Technical Section. By being appointed a plain-clothes constable and later to the rank of detective members received the detective allowance together with a clothing allowance, thus compensation for the lack of remuneration in the Police Award for experts attached to the Technical Section.

This structure allowed for a career progression without the expert officers having to undertake the normal police promotional exams, thus allowing them to concentrate on improving their knowledge and expertise within the new structure. This system remained in vogue until the aftermath of the Fitzgerald Inquiry, when the new, flattened rank structure was introduced to the Police Service.

During the period from the mid 1970s, police forensic officers were recruited from newly sworn police officers who had graduated with a science degree before joining the Police Force. This was a successful means of recruiting, as positions for forensic scientists in the various government laboratories were very limited and the Police Force was the largest employer of forensic scientists within the government sector.

Many of these officers continued with their studies by obtaining their Master's Degree in Forensic Science, thus allowing for greater expertise being acquired by the police forensic scientist during this new era of career development.

## The Role of the Expert Witness

Perhaps one of the most challenging tasks for the budding police forensic scientist was to establish credibility as an expert witness. The academic qualifications and the training provided for these officers, together with the respect that police forensic scientists had gained from the legal fraternity during the 1960s and 1970s, laid foundations for these officers to be accepted by the various courts of law as expert witnesses.

The credibility of an expert witness had to be gained through experience, knowledge of the specialist area of forensic science and method of presentation of the expert evidence and, to some of the police forensic staff, this was the most challenging requirement of becoming a police forensic scientist.

Presentation of expert evidence can be very daunting, as there is always the unknown that a highly skilled defence counsel might like to surprise the witness with, and thus create a doubt that the witness might have failed in some aspects of the forensic work and observations that form part of the expert evidence package before the court.

The presentation of expert evidence requires a high degree of skill, which can only be gained with experience.

## Milestones Created by Scientific Section

During the 70's and 80's members of the police forensic community were thirsting for knowledge that would enable them to compete at an international level. The Scientific Section realised these shortfalls and in doing so conducted the first Blood Splash Identification Course, which was conducted by an internationally recognised expert from the USA, Anita Wonder. Interstate forensic police investigators were participants in this course together with other subsequent courses that were conducted by members of the section.

Australia's first Motor Vehicle Identification Course was conducted by staff attached to the Scientific Section, which once again attracted interstate involvement, and ongoing courses conducted also proved very popular, with police from New South Wales, Victoria, Northern Territory and Western Australia attending.

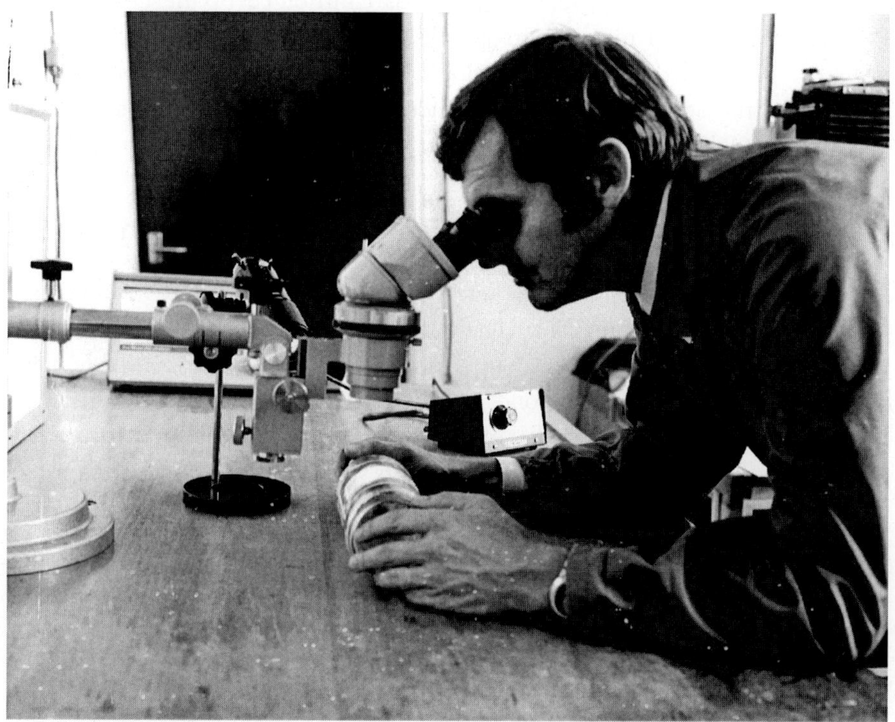

Senior Scientific Officer Grade 1 Neil Raward looks at evidence through a microscope. *Queensland Police Museum.*

During the 1970s the possession of cannabis was becoming a prevalent offence and the Government Botanist who was responsible for providing court certificates for the identification of the drug was unable to cope with sharp rises in the police workload.

An agreement was drawn up between the Police Department and the Government Botanist whereby Scientific Section staff would be trained by the Government Botanist and receive certification that would enable them to examine and certify the identification of cannabis and for this certification to be accepted by the courts. This was a landmark step that relieved the Government Botanist of what eventually became an ever-burgeoning workload for the Scientific Section.

With the advent of the scanning electron microscope (SEM) as a forensic tool, staff from the section attended training courses conducted by the QUT.

The QUT needed to upgrade their equipment and after a protracted legal agreement process the Police Department assisted with the purchase of the SEM for a considerable amount of money, thus enabling a time-sharing of this equipment, which was pro rata to the funds contributed by the Department. Police scientists spent many hours per week analysing and comparing various types of forensic exhibits, thus creating a major step forward in the forensic capacity of the section. A formal contact was signed forging the agreement between the QUT and Police Department.

## 50th Anniversary of the Technical/Scientific Section

In October 1986 the Commissioner of Police hosted a 50th Anniversary celebration (1936-1986) at Police Headquarters, with many guests being invited to attend. The first Officer in Charge of the section, former Constable Tom Baty (1936-1944), and the second Officer in Charge, retired Inspector Les Bardwell (1942-1976), attended the celebration, this being the first time that the three Officers- In -Charge of the section were able to gather at the same function and reflect on the past 50 years that the section has been operating.

I was Officer in Charge from 1976 until 1996, which meant that in the first 60 years of the section there had been only three people who were in charge as compared with more recent times in which another three personnel have headed the section during the period 1996 to 2010. Perhaps this is another indication of the changing times in the history of this section.

In 2011 the section will celebrate 75 years of service to the police and the community of Queensland.

## Formation of the Australian Forensic Science Society (Queensland Branch)

From the late 1960s members of the Technical Section were given the opportunity to attend Forensic Science Society Symposiums in other Australian States, which were held every two years. Queensland was considered to be failing in their ability to form such a society and was the subject of ridicule by our interstate colleagues.

Members of the forensic fraternity were aware of the need to form a branch of the society and in the late 1970s moves were in progress towards this end. Formation meetings were held that involved members of the Scientific Section, Health Department and the Government Chemical Laboratory, and in 1980 the Queensland Branch was formed, with forensic pathologist Dr Tony

Ansford appointed the inaugural president and I became secretary of the branch. Both of us held these positions until the early 1990s.

In 1988 during the Brisbane Expo, Queensland conducted their first Australian and New Zealand Forensic Science Symposium. Through the hard work of the organising committee this symposium was hailed as the most successful ever held. Through sponsorship, many leading forensic scientists from overseas attended, and also the first trade display was held in conjunction with the event.

From these humble beginnings the Queensland branch of the society has achieved many milestones, and I would venture to say that the Queensland branch is equal to any other branch in Australia or New Zealand.

## Some Highlights of my Forensic Career

During my 36-year career as a police forensic scientist there have been many highlights, including my first major forensic case, which became known as the Funnel Creek (wire netting) murders, south of Mackay on the Bruce Highway. Two travellers were ambushed and shot at Funnel Creek and their bodies were trussed in wire netting and weighed down with boulders and wheel rims and placed in the creek. After several days, a bloated body rose to the surface, which resulted in one of the offenders being located near Rockhampton driving the vehicle belonging to the victims. On questioning the suspect, a second body was recovered from the creek. A second suspect was later charged in New South Wales. Both men were found guilty of murder.

Another renowned case was the Weckert murders, which occurred on the same stretch of highway in the early 1970s. The Weckerts were driving from Townsville to Rockhampton when they were ambushed, shot and dumped in the bush just off the highway. An intensive search resulted in the bodies being located and several months later three youths were located in Victoria and charged and found guilty of the murders.

The Whiskey Au Go Go fire bombing, which resulted in the murder of 15 patrons of that nightclub in the early 1970s, certainly was an infamous moment in the annals of Queensland crime. Career criminals Stuart and Finch were charged and found guilty of the murders and sentenced to life imprisonment.

The murder of 18-month-old Deidre Kennedy at Ipswich in the early 1970s stirred the emotions of all Queenslanders, who were appalled at the depravity of the crime. Raymond John Carroll was charged with the murder several years later and was convicted and later acquitted on appeal. The forensic examination and comparison of a bite mark on the victim's thigh played a major role in the initial conviction of Carroll.

In the late 1990s, Carroll was charged with perjury in relation to evidence he gave in his own defence at the original murder trial. He could not be charged again with murder because of the law in relation to double jeopardy. In his second trial, advanced forensic technology enabled a more detailed examination to be made of the bite mark and, on presentation of this evidence, Carroll was convicted of perjury, which in essence reiterated that he had murdered Deidre Kennedy.

On appeal, this conviction was eventually squashed by the High Court. Since his second trial, the law in relation to double jeopardy has been repealed in Queensland. I was a witness in both these trials.

In 1983, the murdered body of a female employee of the Brampton Island Resort was found on the isolated beach on the island. A day tripper to the island, Barry Watson, was the major suspect. Seminal fluid was found on a towel that covered the body of the victim. On questioning, Watson provided a sample of his blood which, at the time, did not provide a positive link with the murder victim.

In the mid-1990s, with advancing DNA technology, the sample blood and the seminal stain were re-examined and a conclusive identification was found that linked Watson's blood and the seminal stain. Watson was later convicted of the murder and his appeal was rejected by the Appeal Court.

In 1996, after having been employed as a police forensic scientist for over 36 years and being the Officer in Charge of the Scientific Section from 1976 (20 years), I transferred to the Commissioner's Inspectorate.

During these 36 years I was involved with many thousands of forensic investigations, including several hundred murder investigations, and presented sworn expert evidence in the various courts (excluding hand-up briefs) on over 990 occasions, appearing as an expert witness in Queensland, New South Wales, Northern Territory and New Guinea.

In 1988 I was fortunate in being appointed a Fellow of the Royal Australian Chemical Institute in recognition of my services to forensic science in Queensland, an achievement that I was very proud to accept, not only for myself, but also for the dedicated and loyal staff of the Scientific Section who I worked so closely with over the preceding years.

## The Papua New Guinea Experience

Before the independence of PNG in the 1970s, Australian police assisted with the training of PNG police in the field of ballistics, handwriting and fingerprints by seconding experts for periods up to two years, to ensure that the trainee PNG police experts were able to continue in these fields after the departure of the Australian police.

With independence the system quickly fell into a shambles with no police being able to conduct ballistic or handwriting comparisons. Queensland, being the closest neighbour, was frequently called upon to assist. During December 1961 I was called upon to assist with the investigation of a shooting murder involving two expatriates, following the arrest of the suspect and the retrieval of the firearm used. I had two more trips to give evidence in the Port Moresby court. During the 15 years that we assisted I had about 10 trips to various parts of PNG to give ballistic evidence.

One particular trip of interest in which I was required to attend court after conducting a ballistic examination of a police firearm involved a Highlands police officer who fired that firearm to kill a national who ambushed their vehicle while off duty. On arriving at Mt Hagan I was advised that the town was in lockdown after being trashed by marauding nationals who were rioting in the belief that a police vehicle had struck and killed a local.

The police story was that the deceased had been flung on to their vehicle by another vehicle travelling from the opposite direction, a story that was dismissed by the locals. I was asked to examine the scene, the police vehicle and the deceased with a view to establishing the truth or otherwise of the police version.

From the examination it was established beyond all doubt that the police version was correct as there was foreign blue paint adhering to the legs of the deceased, with the police vehicle being white in colour. There was no damage to the front of the police vehicles, with the first sign of damage being in the middle of the bonnet.

I commenced to examine the exhibits at 10am and at 1pm a Coroner's Court was convened with me being the only witness. There were riot police outside the court and the court was packed with locals waiting to hear my evidence. After giving my expert opinion of my version of the sequence of events the locals were satisfied that the police were not involved and the town returned to normal. The driver of the offending vehicle was never located.

## The New Era of the Forensic Scientist

The role of the specialist has become even more refined and this has become particularly evident in the field of forensic biology with the ever-expanding advances in DNA technology.

Niche markets of specialisation are being developed in all facets of forensic science through education and advancing technology.

While the public and justice system is no doubt better served by the rapid advancements in forensic science, it is unfortunate that the young forensic scientist of today cannot take a step back in time and experience what, in my opinion, were the golden days of the frontiers of forensic science, which I was fortunate enough to be exposed to.

If I was given a chance to have my life again I would do nothing differently, as I have thoroughly enjoyed my career as a police forensic scientist, although as in most professions the good old days have long gone.

## Epilogue

After being attached to the Technical/Scientific Section for 36 years my time as a police forensic scientist was coming to an end and I transferred to the Commissioner's Inspectorate, which later became the Inspectorate and Evaluation Branch, Ethical Standards Command, in the month of January 1996.

I thoroughly enjoyed my role in this new vocation in which I was again able to travel throughout the State conducting audits of police establishments.

The highlight of my tenure at the Inspectorate involved me being chosen to lead a project team to review and recommend the re-equipping of police with new batons, handcuffs and handguns together with upgraded training programs. This long-term review, which was named Project Lighthouse, paved the way for a new era of policing in Queensland.

On 8 September, 2000 at age 58 years and three months short of being a member of the Queensland Police Service for 41 years, I retired and now live the life of a happily and contented retired police officer on the Gold Coast.

Queensland police first used photography in 1893 so as to "keep a likeness of a prisoner before release".

*The Long Blue Line,* W Ross Johnston, 1992 (p 41)

# Kevin Claude Kruger

When I first met Kevin Kruger we were both long retired and residing at Gympie and Kevin was the President of the Gympie Retired Police Association. It was about the time I had decided to collect stories from some retired police regarding their police career, and on seeing Kevin on his feet delivering a speech I decided that this is a man who can really express himself and would most probably have experienced an interesting police life. I approached him and he agreed to participate, and I am sure readers will agree with me that Kevin did in fact lead an interesting life and has put together a most interesting story.

**Laurie Pointing**

# Kevin Claude Kruger

I was born at Boonah on 9 February, 1926 and named Kevin Claude Kruger. My parents owned a little mixed farm in the Fassifern Valley called "Warrumkarie". It consisted of dairying, growing lucerne and other small crops. I attended the Fassifern Valley State School, later changed to Eaglesburg, and then to Kalbar State School. The head and only teacher at Fassifern Valley State School drove to school daily in a horse and sulky some four miles. Many years earlier my uncle, William Kruger, taught at this school for 15 years. I left school at the age of 14 after obtaining scholarship standard. That was Grade 7. Today we say Year 7. After leaving school I helped my father and brother on the farming property, where all work was performed by horses, disc ploughs and other similar machinery.

At times my father would travel to the horse sales at Toowoomba, where he would purchase saddle horses suited to the type of work in our district. Dad would rail them to Eaglesburg railway siding and we would then lead them on horseback to our property. A lot of these horses would be from down south (southern eastern States). After bringing them home it was my job to finish their education; finish breaking them in as most of them had only been handled and not ridden. I learnt a lot about horsemanship and I sustained lots of busters. Once these horses had been suitably educated to a certain standard my father would sell and trade them throughout the district.

We continued farming until 1946, when my parents sold out and purchased a similar property in the Beaudesert district called "Glenburn". I remained at home working on the property until I reached the age of 22.

I then decided to join the Queensland Police Force. I was friendly with a young lady and we were at the stage where matrimony may be considered. There was insufficient income being generated on the farm to sustain two families so I considered the Police Force might be a worthwhile occupation to follow.

Early in 1948 I journeyed to the Police Depot at Petrie Terrace, Brisbane where I made application to join. The inspector in charge was Horrie O'Brien, a huge man. One of the first things he said to me was, "Lad, you come from the Boonah area. Do you know a cattleman named Nicholas Surawski?" I replied, "Yes, he's a good friend of my father". O'Brien replied, "You would be better off if you went home and stayed on the farm". Naturally, I didn't take his advice.

Later in the year, I think it was St Patrick's Day, I kept an appointment at the Police Depot for education and medical examinations, which went quite well. I recall that there were something like 22 applicants and 11 were rejected. This may seem unusual by today's standards, but the 11 were rejected with eyesight problems, mainly colour blindness. Following the passing of these two examinations, I entered the Depot shortly afterwards to commence my training. I am not sure of the exact date we commenced our three-month training period.

We resided in barracks accommodation, which were the old wooden barracks, and each morning you would rise early and various duties were allocated to you; washing and cleaning police vehicles, sweeping leaves up around the barracks and parade grounds. Each morning you were required to fold your sheeting and blankets in a certain package and it was somewhat difficult to get right (I understand it was adopted from an old British Army tradition). Each blanket was carefully inspected by the instructing officers each morning and if not folded to their satisfaction privileges were cancelled. One morning mine did not pass inspection and leave for our room was cancelled for a week. Later in the day drill formations included rifle drill. The Depot had a series of .303 rifles and bayonets, which were used in drill practice. Then about 2pm each day we were lectured for several hours on the fundamentals of law and police duties.

There were two tennis courts in the Depot grounds and these also had to be maintained by the police probationaries. The courts were hired out for night tennis six nights a week, but never on Sunday. Probationaries were not allowed to use them. However, to country lads the sight of young girls in short tennis skirts was a welcome sight.

A few weeks after entering the Police Depot we received a visit from a salesman from a typewriter company who was well known to all the instructing police and displayed to us a variety of ancient typewriters of varying makes and models and talked to us about purchasing our own machine. The Department did not supply typewriters then and for many years afterwards. It was necessary for each individual police officer to purchase his own and we were paid a small yearly allowance to maintain this most important item of equipment. I was one of the mugs who bought a machine. A salesman from Allan & Stark also arrived at the Depot and he was given time in the lecture room to address us and display his wares in the hope of selling the new recruits new clothing. We were given instructions in "first aid" by an ambulance officer. I remember he was referred to as "Doctor Death".

To join the Queensland Police Force in 1948 your height had to be at least 5 feet 9 and a half inches in height and your weight 11 stone. I was 10 stone 4 or 5 and could not put on an ounce of weight. You were subject to a fairly thorough medical examination and the most stringent was the eyesight test. If it was shown that you were colour blind you were rejected, which was probably a good thing. To illustrate, I have a son who is colour blind and when he was about eight or nine we were down at the family property and he said to me, "Dad, that green cow down the paddock has a new calf". That's how colour appeared to him. You had to be of good character and checks on your background were carried out by the local police and reports furnished. You had to be a serving member for 12 months before you could marry. Your intended bride's background was also investigated and reports furnished. She also had to be of good character. Initially your wife was not allowed to work. When Dawn and I married at Cairns some years later I think she was one of the first to break this rule as she continued to work for some time. If you were illegitimate, (living together living in sin as it was referred to then) or gay, you were also rejected. You were not allowed to own a racehorse or a racing dog. This might bring you into conflict with gambling and tarnish the image of the Queensland Police Force.

Moving ahead to my second term with the police department, when I was stationed at Cairns a certain sub-inspector was the licensing inspector and he had friends, a man and woman who were not married but living as man and wife, and they wished to purchase a hotel. The Licensing Commission frowned upon licensees who might be "living in sin". They applied for the licence and their application was rejected on more than one occasion. Eventually this sub-inspector said to me, "Kevin, you have become pretty good on paper. I will get you to interview these people in depth and furnish a lengthy report because they are people of good character". I did as instructed and went into the matter in depth, furnishing a lengthy report in detail and eventually the licence was granted.

There was a Depot meal mess, managed by single sworn members attached to the Police Depot who also resided in barracks accommodation. These men were members of the mess committee and managed the whole procedure. The meals were very ordinary as I recall. About two nights each week you could visit the city, but first you had to obtain permission from the station sergeant. If granted, you would report to him prior to departing and were given instructions to return by 11-30pm, at which time you would again report to the station sergeant before retiring to your barracks. All departures and returns were carefully recorded in a special book for that particular intake of recruits.

When I initially passed my medical examination I was seven pounds underweight. They decided to pass me, stating that I would put on weight once I entered the Depot and started training and they would get Miss Verrell, the manageress of the mess, to cook me special meals. I don't know if she did or not: I thought I ate the same meals as everyone else.

My entrance into the Police Depot was a few months prior to the 1949 Royal visit by King George VI and Queen Elizabeth I (later The Queen Mother). The Police Department had purchased a dozen or more horses from western Queensland and they were taken to the Remount section at Oxley. Some of them had been ridden, some not. Three of us trainees were selected and taken to Oxley daily for several weeks in the mess truck, where we were engaged in breaking in these horses, handling and riding them. They were to be used in ceremonial duties for the Royal visit. Then I developed an illness that went through the Depot and affected five of the recruits. The medical profession didn't know what it was. At first they thought it was scarlet fever and we were admitted to the Royal Brisbane Hospital. There was no special isolation ward in that period, however, there were pavilions scattered around the grounds like pavilions at a state school. One particular building with a roof and no sides, with seats around the exterior for children and adult patients to sit on as they moved around in the sun, was positioned in the hospital grounds and this building was selected for use as a hospital ward. They did a few alterations, put canvas sides on it and fixed it up a bit, and the five recruits were hospitalised in this makeshift ward. At first we were treated for scarlet fever, but they diagnosed that we had a fever virtually unknown at that time. They named it "glandular fever".

You suffered from a very sore throat, a debilitating sickness that caused dizziness and vomiting. It was not a good illness to have. From memory, two of the other recruits were police cadets. One I particularly remember was Vince Stedman. I cannot remember the names of the other three. Vince made the Police Force his career and retired as a commissioned officer. We certainly had a reasonable time there. Harry Reineke was the senior sergeant in charge of the Educational Section at the Depot and he was a strong disciplinarian. He would come out and see us and say, "You boys will have to keep up with your studies". He brought out a pile of books; a Policeman's Manual each and the other lectures, one to 59, which the old-timers will remember. He was preparing to leave them with us when the sister in charge of this makeshift ward said to him, "Senior Sergeant, you know these books can't be taken out of this ward when these men leave. They will have to be destroyed".

That was a bit of a blow to Harry, but nevertheless they were the instructions of that time. Following my discharge from the isolation ward, the doctors who treated us for glandular fever were of the opinion that I had a bad set of tonsils that needed to be removed, so I was again admitted to hospital and my tonsils were removed. I can tell you that it is not a pleasant operation recuperating afterwards. Your throat is very, very sore. I had formed a close relationship with a fourth-year nurse at the hospital. The night following my operation she came to visit and my throat was that sore I was not in a good shape. When she came to my bed and started talking to me, I said, "Will you please go away. I just can't talk to anyone". That was the end of what might have been a beautiful friendship.

After my discharge I was given leave of about seven or 10 days and I went home to the family property at Beaudesert to recuperate. I was only home for a short time when I received a telephone call from Senior Sergeant Woodbury at the Depot. He seemed to have taken me under his wing a bit and was always trying to help me. I was one person who needed some help too. He said, "Young fellow, I know you are on sick leave, but there is an exam in a couple of days. It has been brought forward because of this railway strike and the Department is very short of police. You don't have to come down; you are still on sick leave, but it is open to you if you would like to sit for the examination".

I thought about it for a while and realised that with my trips to Oxley breaking in those young horses and my hospitalisation I had missed quite a lot of educational lessons and drill instructions, I was not that concerned about the drill side of things, but the educational instructions were a concern. However, I decided to return to Brisbane and sit for the examination, which I duly passed. I was not the first in the exam, but I certainly wasn't the last either. The following day we were walked to the Treasury Building to be sworn in as constables. The Police Commissioner I think it was had us take the "Oath of Office".

I was sworn in as a constable of police on 2 July, 1948 and became Constable Kruger, Registered. No. 4565.

To complicate matters, our shoulder number was different to our registered number. From the Treasury Building we were sent to a photographer in Queen Street where we had our photographs taken.

The Police Commissioner, other senior police and some sections of the Department were housed in the Treasury building. The Treasury building was located in Queen Street at the intersection with George Street, next to Victoria Park. There was a large statue of Queen Victoria in this park. The CI Branch headquarters was an old church building with limited space, further down George Street.

During my probationary period certain probationaries would be selected and I was one of them to perform night duty, 10pm to 6am with the night CI Branch patrol car. I still remember the crew: Jack Hayes was the driver, Ben McNichol was the detective sergeant and Norm Gulbransen was the rear gunner. My duty was to position myself in the rear seat and take notations of wanted persons, stolen vehicles and other important matters. I remember one night we stopped at one of the brothels and then all alighted and one of them said to me: "You can come in too and sit in the foyer and read a magazine." They appeared to know the "Madam" and while I was sitting alone a girl approached me and said, "Would you like one on the house, love, or would you like a cup of coffee?" I replied, "I'll have a cup of coffee, thank you".

A rather humorous incident occurred shortly after we had our official photographs taken. I had teamed up with one of my fellow constables, Bill Green, and we caught a tram to return to the Police Depot. At the intersection with Counter Street there had been a nose-to-tail accident between about four trams. Even though it was not a serious accident, it required a police investigation. The tram drivers were milling around and they looked over to me and my fellow constable who said, "Well, you're the senior man and I suppose you'll have to take it". I removed my brand-new notebook from my pocket, licked my indelible lead pencil (There were no issue biros in those days) and then a traffic policeman rode up on his motorbike and said "Oh, a bit of a prang, lads. Not too much damage", or words to that effect. I replied "No". This traffic policeman then said, "How long have you fellows been in the job?" I said, "About 10 minutes". He replied, "Would you like me to take it?" "I would be very relieved if you did," was my answer. That was the first job I dodged.

On the afternoon of 2 July, 1948 we were assembled in the lecture room and our transfers were announced. Six of us were transferred to Cairns, six to Townsville and two to Mackay. There were about 14 in my intake. My new station was Townsville. We were then given leave until the evening of the fourth of July when we were to arrange our departure from Brisbane. Next stop was the Depot uniform store. We only had one uniform, the one we wore when sworn in. You were not issued with new uniforms, but second-hand ones were available. If you were lucky enough to find uniforms that fitted, you were subsequently issued with them. It was only a couple of years earlier that a new-style uniform had been issued to Queensland Police. Old-style uniforms buttoned up to the neck, and you did not wear a tie. The availability of the new-style uniforms were extremely scarce.

I had a quick trip home to Beaudesert to visit the family and returned to the Depot on the afternoon of the fourth and departed for North Queensland that same evening. I think the northern rail was called the "Mail Train" and it travelled up the coast to Rockhampton, Mackay, Townsville and Cairns. Most of the carriages were of the old Pullman's type, with a pathway down the centre and bunk beds on either side. It was my first long-distance train journey and was an experience. We certainly had some high jinks on the way. About halfway through the journey we learnt that the Police Commissioner, Mr C J Carroll, was also on that particular train, which came as a bit of a surprise to us. We arrived at Townsville about 7 o'clock in the morning, a couple of days later. In those days a police officer always visited the railway station and checked on all trains departing and arriving at all destinations throughout the State. On arrival at Townsville, we approached the policeman at the railway station and, after informing him of our identity, asked directions to the police station. He said, "What are you fellows doing here?" We told him we had been transferred to Townsville and he just shook his head. We wended our way to the police station, which was a bit of a task as we had quite a bit of luggage. There was no thought of hailing a taxi. We would probably have needed several and found it more convenient to walk.

We arrived at the Townsville station just before the senior sergeant, Sam Adderman, was about to finish his night shift. He looked at us, shook his head and said, "I don't know what we are going to do with you. We didn't know you were bloody well coming. I suppose you must be a bit hungry. Leave your gear here and wander down town and have a bit of breakfast and come back about 11 o'clock". There was a station sergeant at the Townsville station and part of his duties was to look after the newly arrived constables and supply them with barracks accommodation, beds, sheets and blankets. He took us upstairs to the single men's barracks and at that time there were about 28-30 men occupying this accommodation. We were allocated a bed and supplied with our laundry - well-worn sheets and blankets. They were definitely second-hand as the sheets were covered with rust marks. We had to make do with what we were issued and not complain.

It was a standard instruction at Townsville that each night a certain number of men were kept in barracks in case of an emergency. Even if you had just completed a day's shift you would be refused a few hours leave if it was your turn to stay in. One constable, who shall remain nameless, was leaving the barracks one night without permission and while climbing down a mango tree, slipped, fell and broke his right arm. We had to convince the senior sergeant that he tripped and fell getting out of the bath.

We were introduced to the single-men's mess, which was controlled by a mess committee. I think the going rate was four shillings a meal, or maybe it was four shillings a day: I am not sure now, but it wasn't much money that you had to pay for your meals, which were quite good. The day following our arrival was a "rest day" and then we were allocated to beat duties under the supervision of a sergeant who allocated our positions and we patrolled Flinders Street. I performed this type of duty for several months and during this period there was quite a number of police being sworn in and transferred to Townsville. It was the first major increase of staff at police districts following World War II. The police strength at Townsville would have been in the high 40s and the only communication was the telephone. There were four motor vehicles attached to Townsville police station, being one for the inspector in charge, one for the CI Branch, a general duties vehicle and an almost new, white-coloured Dodge sedan allocated to the Traffic Branch.

One night at Townsville I was performing night duty with Sergeant Alf Schubel and about 1am we visited the railway station. Things were fairly quiet and the sergeant was feeling tired. We saw this empty railway carriage, so hopped in and before long we were both asleep. I awoke to find that we were rattling along in the train carriage as the train was in motion. I didn't know where we were or what we were going to do, so I awoke the sergeant and he didn't have any more of an idea than I had. Then the train started to slow down and eventually stopped. It was a mixed-goods train and we were at Stuart, the first railway station on the western line and about five miles from the Townsville Police Station. It was a bit of an effort getting back to town without the Department knowing. We couldn't telephone from the railway station for the patrol car to pick us up, but eventually we arrived back and the incident had a happy ending.

Mount Isa Police Station, October 1972. *Queensland Police Museum.*

After a few months I became the senior man in charge of some shifts, with staff junior to myself under my supervision. I would have to periodically give them a booking and ensure that they were performing their duty in the best interests of the Department. It was quite a feather in my cap so to speak. After about six months, I learnt that a constable was required to perform relieving duty at Charters Towers, so I spoke to the senior sergeant and it was arranged that I would perform this duty. On the following Sunday night, I boarded the train for Charters Towers, 87 miles west of Townsville. I arrived there at eight the next night and was met at the railway station by the local plain-clothes officer, Phil Barnett, who introduced himself to me.

I said, "There are quite a few people here tonight. What's doing?" He replied, "There's nothing doing, they're just up here to see what the new policeman looks like". I relieved at Charters Towers for some months and after some time it was notified that a nearby two-man station, Queenton, was to be closed, with the sergeant and constable to be transferred to the main station. The senior sergeant, Chas P Doherty, said, "Would you like to be here permanently, lad?" I was getting fond of the town at that stage and jumped at the idea. I was officially transferred to Charters Towers in the month of March 1949, and the only time I went back to Townsville after that were for a few court hearings and other departmental matters.

The Charters Towers Police Station was situated in the middle of the main street, which was Gill Street. It was an imposing brick building with an open veranda on the ground level and the single-men's barracks on the first floor. Half of the ground floor was police office space and the other half and half the first floor was the senior sergeant's residence. The barracks were well ventilated and the whole atmosphere was good. The sheets and blankets were virtually new. They were superior to the linen and blankets at Townsville.

Charters Towers had one motor vehicle, a Chevrolet utility, with a police strength of about 12 uniform police and one CI Branch member. Once again, the only means of communication was the telephone, and when a message was circulated regarding a stolen vehicle or a wanted or missing person, police at Townsville would telephone the particulars to Mingella, a one-man station between Townsville and Charters Towers. Charters Towers would then telephone it through to Pentland and they would then pass it on to the next station and that's how it was done. Two-way radios in police stations and motor vehicles had not been introduced in that era.

The senior sergeant was also the protector of aborigines and there were 257 on his books, mostly from outlying cattle stations. They would come to town two or three times each year and would call at the police station to draw cash from their banked wages and were issued with vouchers for clothing. They camped in the grounds of the watch-house stockade. Both Townsville and Charters Towers had a police stockade. They were built of hardwood mill timber and were about 10 to 12 feet high, the one at Townsville being considerably larger than the one at Charters Towers. Each contained a large quantity of wood and these people would always have a raging fire blazing. The Townsville stockade contained the watch-house and was situated some distance from the old Townsville police station, but I cannot recall the name of the street. Charters Towers stockade was in Hodgensen Street, about three streets from the main street, Gill Street.

Each station was allocated a telephone budget and from memory there was no limit on the number of local calls you made, but trunk-line or long-distance calls were a different matter. To make a long-distance call you first had to seek permission from your superior, and then you entered the particulars in a book stating the telephone number you called and the reason for the call. At the end of the month, when the account was received at the headquarter station, it was checked by the office staff and, if they were not satisfied with a particular long-distance call, you received a "please explain".

The police duties at Charters Towers were fairly routine; office work, answering the telephone, sending and receiving messages, attending to complaints from the public, fires, dead bodies and the escort of prisoners. We visited the railway station at the departure time of all trains and were there to meet trains arriving. There were two pushbikes at the station with thorn-proof tyres, which were not always in good working condition. The men disliked riding them so the police vehicle was frequently used to visit the railway station.

The escort of mental patients from the Charters Towers Hospital was another duty we performed. Normally we would escort them to Townsville by rail and Townsville would supply the escort to Brisbane, again by rail. More often than not, because of staff shortages, the police officer from Charters Towers would undertake the whole journey. I undertook about six escorts with mentally sick patients from Charters Towers to Sandy Gallop Mental Hospital at Ipswich, which took about two and a half days. You undertook these escorts dressed in plain clothes. Should the patient be a female you were accompanied by a nurse attached to the hospital. Then you had to return to your home station; another two and a half days. Ordinary prisoners were escorted by rail to Townsville and then to Stuart Creek Prison at Townsville.

Police were also charged with the safe keeping of concealable firearms forfeited to the Crown. They would eventually be forwarded to the Firearms Section, Brisbane. If suitable, some of these firearms would later be issued to new constables. Forfeited forearms were usually taken to Brisbane by the constable or sergeant escorting a prisoner.

During my tour of duty at Charters Towers both my parents developed serious health problems and I considered it my duty to be closer to home in case their health problems became worse. I applied for a transfer and was transferred to Roma Street in the month of August 1950. In that era I would have been one of the few constables who had not been initially transferred to Roma Street immediately after being sworn in. I performed relieving duty at a number of suburban stations, Rosalie, Bardon, Torwood and Indooroopilly. I had some leave due so went on leave and visited my family at Beaudesert, and one day I received a telephone call from a good mate of mine at Roma Street, Ted Lowe. He was the roster clerk and he informed me of my transfer to Bulimba.

I was quite pleased about this transfer and as I had a few weeks' recreational leave to go I took the family car and drove up to meet the boys at Bulimba. Bulimba was what they called a suburban station, with a sergeant first class in charge and three constables. The single-men's quarters were under the police station and the station itself was a couple of rooms built on to the police residence. The single constable was required to be in residence every night by midnight, whether on duty or not, and it was his function to attend to all incoming telephone calls between midnight and when the station opened for business the next morning. My accommodation was a single room with a cold shower. Shortly after my arrival at Bulimba, I made application for hot water to be installed. I was considered by the inspector in charge at Woolloongabba to be a nuisance for wanting hot water. I made several suggestions as to what could be installed, however, the Public Works at that stage would not hear of electricity to heat water as it was considered to be too dangerous. After several reports they did install gas and I was then able to have a hot shower. I ate my meals at the Balmoral Hotel.

The sergeant in charge, Michael Talty, was a real character. He came from the Emerald Isle and over the years we became great mates. I recall asking him one day, "Sergeant, why do you hate the English?" He replied, "Well, I'm buggered if I know. Me father hated them and that's good enough for me". He would often want you to go and "Blow the froth of a few", as he called it. His favourite drink was double rum with a beer chaser. Michael was a brother of Hugh Talty, who was the Police Union Secretary for many years.

I worked at Bulimba for a few years and during my time there our police transport was a motorbike and sidecar. I could ride a motorbike, but had to become accustomed to a sidecar. There was a bit of an old trotting track off Wynnum Road and Vince Collins, one of the other constables, took me to the track and gave me a couple of lessons and that was how I became proficient in the handling of a motorbike and sidecar.

Vince and his wife, Pat, occupied a fairly new police residence next-door to the police station and they had a son about 18 months old who was just learning to run about outside. I was invited over one evening for a meal and they both commented that Johnnie was becoming a bit of a handful. I said, "He will be different when he gets a couple of brothers or sisters". They both commented that one child was enough and were not going to have any more children. I received 12 Christmas cards over the following years and each year they added the name of another child. They eventually had a family of 13 children. In due course, Vince was promoted and transferred as the sergeant in charge of Landsborough Police Division and the police residence would not accommodate his family. He had to rent the residence next-door. Vince passed away just a few years ago and his lifetime story was a feature in the "obituary" section of the Courier Mail.

Part of my duties as the single constable was cleaning the office and the police station yard, as well as the police motorbike and sidecar. There was a vacant allotment next-door to the police station and one day the sergeant detailed me and Bill McCann, a fairly knowledgeable constable, to clean this block up a bit. He said, "Don't you fellows come in uniform tomorrow. Wear plain clothes and you can spend the day cleaning up that block". We were working away, not very hard, when along came a couple of fellows. We didn't know them and they didn't know us. One of them said, "You fellows doing a bit of time?" Bill said, "Yes, we got 48 hours". One of these men replied "When do you finish?" "Five o'clock this evening," said Bill. He then gave us 10 bob ($1) and said, "Here, when you finish, go over to the pub and have a couple of beers".

One day I received a telephone call to go and see the sergeant in charge of the Inspector's Office at Woolloongabba. "Lad, you are going to Beaudesert, you have a temporary transfer." I said, "What's a temporary transfer?" He replied, "It's not permanent". A temporary transfer was a device used by the Department to avoid paying relieving staff travelling allowance, which at that time was about one shilling and three pence a day (15 cents). Pat Crotty from Beaudesert had taken long service and I was selected to relieve, which was a bit of a windfall I suppose as it was almost my home town. Accommodation for me was nil, as another constable occupied the only accommodation available. The single-men's quarters there consisted of a room built on to the police watch-house cell. Prior to my arrival, the sergeant, Tom Holding, had obtained a bed from somewhere and put it in the corner of the courthouse. And that is where I slept for the next eight or 10 months. The police station and courthouse were under the same roof, with a veranda constructed all round the building.

Beaudesert Police Division was a bit of a breeze really, a farming community with very little crime. Transport was again a motorbike and sidecar and during the winter months the weather was freezing cold. Of a morning you would sit on the steps waiting for rays of sunshine to warm yourself up a bit. After Pat Crotty returned from his six months long service leave, the other constable went on leave and my relieving period was extended for a further three months.

While at Beaudesert there was a fellow relieving at the courthouse as the Clerk of the Court and I got to know him pretty well. I knew him as "Robbo" and one day I was telling him of a situation that occurred at Bulimba when another constable and I went to an incident. We knocked on the door, and fortunately for us, after we knocked we took a step or two backwards. As we did so, the blade of an axe came through the wooden door. The offender was somewhat mentally unbalanced. We arrested and charged him and he was subsequently convicted and fined £20 ($40).

Robbo told me that I was entitled to a moiety of that fine. I didn't know what he meant by "moiety", so he explained it to me and encouraged me to furnish a report requesting moiety payment of the £40. I did furnish a report and back it came from the inspector's office with no other comment than "refused". I furnished a further couple of reports and they all came back "refused", but I was persistent and finally they referred my report to the Justice Department, who duly paid me £10 ($20).

Not long after I returned to my home station of Bulimba, I received notification of my transfer to Camooweal. It was years later that I realised that Camooweal was my punishment for applying for the moiety of that fine.

My parents at this time were in declining health and medical opinion was that there was little hope of improvement. Paddy Glynn, an Irishman, was the Commissioner of Police at the time so I made an appointment to see him at his office in the old Treasury building to see if my transfer could be cancelled. He greeted me with "What do you want, lad?" I explained to him my reasons and he replied, "Why have you changed your mind?" I said, "What do you mean, changed my mind". He then said, "Years ago when you joined this job, you put in an application to serve at a country station". "My parents are now in poor health and I don't want to go too far away from them," I said. "Camooweal is too far away should anything happen, but I am prepared to serve anywhere within reasonable distance from my home town."

Commissioner Glynn then remarked, "That's out of the question, lad. But you will love it out there. They have street lights, bitumen roads and buses". I was very doubtful about what he said, but you couldn't call the Commissioner of Police a bloody liar. He wasn't wrong though. There was a bitumen road extending from Mt Isa to Darwin in the Northern Territory and, as it passed through the centre of Camooweal, it became Camooweal's main street. There were buses that travelled from Mt Isa through the township to Darwin twice weekly as well. With regards street lighting, there were three street lights and the hospital had the only lighting due to a a generating plant. Of a moonlight night or full moon, the authorities didn't bother purchasing spare power from the hospital, but of a dark night they would and the town would be blessed with three street lights.

I made preparations for my departure to Camooweal. I did own a motor vehicle, but owing to the state of the roads back then (May 1954) I deemed it advisable to leave that vehicle at my parents' home at Beaudesert and travel by train. I caught the train at Roma Street, Brisbane, travelled to Townsville and then boarded the train to Mt Isa, which was the end of the line. This journey took several days.

When proceeding on transfer, you had to have a route listing the various items of government property issued to you and in your possession. I had a large tin trunk that contained my books. Among other things, there were two volumes of the Queensland Policeman's Manual and a set of lectures numbered from one to 59, which you just about needed a packhorse to carry.

I arrived at Mt Isa and was met at the railway station by my old mate Ted Lowe, who was then a constable, but rose to commissioned rank as he progressed through his service. After attending to matters we had a few drinks and Ted informed me that it had been arranged for me to travel to Camooweal the next day with the stock inspector, who had business to attend to in that district. The Police Department was still doing things on the cheap and they continued to do so for many years afterwards. A bed was specially rigged up for me at the Mt Isa Police Station that night, which served the purpose just for one night.

When I arrived at Camooweal the situation there was beyond belief. The courthouse and police station were under the one roof and the building was nothing more than a corrugated iron and slab structure, unlined and unsealed, and white ants had eaten out parts of the floorboards. The courthouse Bench was a raised section surrounded by bush timber. My bed was situated in one corner of this building and there was no running water connected.

A water tank was situated on one side of this building with a tap, but the tank was empty for a long time because it does not rain very often at Camooweal. The only bathing facility was a water tank on a high stand about 500 yards from the police station, which was filled by pumping water into it from a bore. The water was mainly used for watering the troop horses. The tank stand was enclosed with galvanised iron for walls and this is where you enjoyed your cold showers, both in summer and winter. I partook of my meals at the one and only hotel and, considering the remoteness of the place, they were not too bad. The toilet was a battered shed, about 500 yards down in the horse paddock. It was surrounded with galvanised iron sheeting, commencing about 12 inches from the ground. During the cold months the wind whistled around your feet and bare legs when nature came a calling. There was no toilet paper and newspapers were fairly scarce, so you had to scrounge whatever paper you could.

I had a rather humorous old sergeant who was the officer in charge of the station. Fred Dornbusch was his name. His wife would not let him smoke inside the house and after tea each night he would walk outside and join me for a talk. We would usually sit on the courthouse steps. His wife had three or four little pug dogs and periodically the females would be on heat, which attracted quite a number of male dogs. The sergeant would not hunt them away, but be friendly to them. He would play with them and once he gained their confidence would produce this tin wax match tin with a serrated part for striking the matches. This he would rub on their backside and then quickly dab their behind with a pad he had soaked in mineral turpentine. The dogs would run some trial races leaving the scene. They never came back again.

The evenings at Camooweal were reasonably long as it did not get dark until fairly late and, while sitting on the steps of the courthouse, the sergeant would look towards the Northern Territory border and remark, "See those clouds of dust. It looks like a big mob coming in from the Territory. I would say about 1500 head and they will probably arrive here in about three or four days". It took me a little while to realise that he was always right and I used to wonder how he came to those predictions. However, I soon realised that he was an Assistant Stock Inspector by virtue of his office and had copies of all the waybills and travelling stock permits and knew of all stock movements coming into the State.

Old Fred smoked a pipe and had many good yarns to tell. At one time he was a "mounted trooper" in the Gilbert River area and on one occasion was investigating complaints of cattle duffing accompanied by a station manager from a nearby cattle station. Fred called at a certain property when an armed man emerged from a dwelling and shot Fred's companion. He died instantly. Fred was not armed and was lucky not to suffer the same fate as the station manager.

Just prior to my arrival at Camooweal the annual rodeo was held and an additional constable from Mt Isa was detailed to assist the local police. I do not recall the full details, but during the course of the couple of days that the rodeo was held a local identity was assaulted by the two constables and they were eventually dismissed from the Police Force. I think the local identity assaulted was one of the "Freckletons". Apparently the man assaulted received some serious injuries and, as a result, police in Camooweal for a long time afterwards were not highly thought of. I found the people there to be anti-police.

Bill Maloney was a detective stationed at Mt Isa. He was from a local Camooweal family and was on duty at this particular rodeo and apparently witnessed the assault. He gave evidence at the court proceedings. His son, John Maloney, followed him into the Police Force and is now the mayor at Mt Isa.

Later on in my career, when stationed at Torwood Police Station, Brisbane, I was called to an accident one night in Milton Road, not far from the police station. A local fellow had not long purchased a brand-new car, which he drove home and parked on the roadway outside his home and was inside having a cup of tea with some of his mates who had come over to have a look at his new car. His vehicle had only clocked up 13 miles. They were sitting there enjoying their cup of tea when an inbound vehicle collided with the rear of his brand-new car. That car was driven by a young John Maloney. Breathalysers had not been introduced at that stage and after investigations I considered the driver was affected by liquor so I arrested him on a charge of "drink driving". The Government Medical Officer also shared my view and gave evidence accordingly. I thought I had a good case, however, young Maloney engaged a barrister by the name of Brewer and I cannot recall the defence he used, but the magistrate found for the defence and dismissed the charge. I seem to recall the barrister was Bob Brewer, who specialised in drink-driving legislation.

As I mentioned previously, the Bench at the Camooweal courthouse was a raised platform with railings around this raised section. On these railings were hung the stock saddles and pack saddles. Should Court need to be convened we would first have to shift all the saddles and other gear that may have been thrown across these railings. There were two general stores in the town; one owned by people named Cronin and the other by the Freckleton family. These people did not like each other and never spoke a civil word between them. Both the males were Justices of the Peace and should they be required to convene Court they would be accompanied to the courthouse by their numerous dogs. We normally witnessed a dog fight prior to Court commencing.

A lot of our duties there during the droving season were out at the clearing dip and holding paddock on the Northern Territory side at the border, assisting the stock inspector, inspecting the mobs of cattle travelling in from the Territory. We just had to be there in case of any disputes between drovers and possibly station owners. At that time the big road trains – huge prime movers and trailers – were taking over and traditional droving was being phased out. A lot of the big grazing properties in the Northern Territory were owned by Vestey, an English company. Lord Vestey had arrived from England to overview the start of this new type of cattle transportation and he stopped in Camooweal for a short period of time and invited me for lunch. I suppose he would have been a man about 38-40 years of age at that time. I enjoyed his company and found him to be a rather pleasant gentleman.

During the droving season the local butcher shop closed because he got no trade. As the mobs came through, the drovers killed their own beef while waiting for their cattle to be inspected by the stock inspector. The ringers and the crew of droving camps preferred corned meat of any description and in particular corned brisket. Other cuts of meat were not highly prized by the drovers and townspeople would go out and get their meat requirements for free. No charge at all.

The troop horses were not used to any great extent. There was a Land Rover attached to the Camooweal Police Station and most of the out-of-town inquiries could be attended to by using this vehicle. An interesting incident occurred while I was there, involving an off-duty Northern Territory police officer who was returning to the Territory after recreation leave. He was driving his private Land Rover when he got a puncture at Camooweal. He had used up his spare tyres, so he called at the police station seeking assistance and asked if we had a spare tyre we could lend him. We pointed out to him that our one and only spare tyre was being used on our police vehicle. He was highly amused and informed us that the Northern Territory Police Department issued all police vehicles with four spare tyres.

In the month of August 1954 I resigned from the Queensland Police Force. I just did not fit in to the lifestyle there. I found the town to be anti-police, and the remoteness and the conditions I was living under were getting me down. I decided Camooweal was a place I didn't want to be in any longer. In addition to this Dawn was living in Brisbane and we were getting fairly friendly and it looked certain that marriage would eventuate.

I owned an old Imperial typewriter and seeing I would be paying my own freight back to Brisbane I decided I would not need a typewriter. Frank Martin with his brother were the co-owners of the Camooweal Hotel so I used a bit of salesmanship on Frank and convinced him he needed a typewriter to type out the menu to make them more professional. He subsequently purchased my typewriter for the sum of £15.

After returning to Brisbane I obtained employment as a salesman and fairly quickly realised that I had done the wrong thing by myself by resigning, so I rejoined and was sworn in on 20 December, 1954.

I was only at Roma Street for a few weeks when I was notified of my transfer to Cairns. At that time the town was a lovely place and an ideal tropical location. The population was about 15,000-17,000. I owned a little Ford Prefect utility and as the road to Cairns was not an all-year road I didn't want to drive that long distance in such a small vehicle over those rough roads. I had an uncle who was employed by a shipping company and he undertook to ship my car to Cairns on the Elsana, which was a freight-passenger boat that ran between Brisbane and Thursday Island, stopping at various ports on the way up. There were cyclones around as the Elsana was entering Trinity Bay and the weather was very rough. Where some of us were standing on the police station veranda you could see the waves breaking over the bow of the boat. My vehicle was anchored down in the front of the boat and you could see the waves washing right over the top of the car. I thought to myself that it would be a rust bucket, but as it turned out it wasn't.

A blacktracker by the name of Major Butcher was on staff at Cairns and it was arranged for Major to spend several days hosing the vehicle thoroughly with fresh water. Not that I kept the vehicle for any length of time, but a few years later it was still being driven around Cairns and there wasn't a spot of rust in it.

The police station in many respects was similar to Townsville, a wooden building with office space on the ground floor and single-men's barrack ,accommodation on the top floor, consisting of about four rooms. I occupied a room with four others. I remember Col Burridge in the bed next to me and two other constables, Gerry Williams and Graham Bergermister. Another man I remember was Terry Carroll, who was keeping company with the daughter of Jack Mahoney, the district police inspector. They later married. It's remarkable what you remember about some people, even after many years. Col Burridge had this hobby of purchasing fountain pens. Every pay day he would go into town and buy himself a fountain pen. He owned more fountain pens than you could use in a lifetime.

The Inspector drove a Custom Ford, the CI Branch had a vehicle and I think the uniform section had two vehicles, plus a motorcycle for traffic duty. At that time the Cairns police district was the largest in the State with a total of 42 police stations, which included Thursday Island. There was a fair amount of relieving duty and the overall police strength at Cairns, the headquarter station, was in the high 60s or low 70s. I did not do much relieving and at one stage the second inspector, Jim Cooke, said to me: "Lad, we will have to send a man relieving to Thursday Island for about three months. I think we will send you." I replied, "Inspector, I wouldn't like that at the moment, I am getting married in a few weeks time". He replied, "Well we better forget about Thursday Island then".

To marry you had to have at least 12 months' service and furnish a report setting out the full name and date of your intended spouse and her background and character would be investigated. If it was found that she had incurred some conviction, or her character or that of her family was not beyond reproach, permission would be refused.

There were no policing problems with the Aboriginal or Islander people, who were generally well behaved. Motels were unknown in Queensland in that era and tourists and visitors obtained accommodation either at hotels or boarding houses. My wife, Dawn, was working for the Queensland Tourist Bureau and I believed may have been one of the first married women who defied the rule that married women resign from their place of employment once they married. There were three tourist boats that made regular trips from the south to Cairns. They were the Kaninbla, Manunda and the Mandorra. There are now three suburbs at Cairns named after the boats.

When these tourist boats arrived in Cairns all passengers had to leave and go ashore so the boat could be refurbished and the linen washed. It was Dawn's responsibility as an employee of the Tourist Bureau to book accommodation for the passengers for several days at hotels and boarding houses.

My original tour of duty at Cairns was working in the inspector's office and this type of work was to my liking. One time I was chosen by the inspector to perform a special job. Six American destroyer ships had berthed in Cairns and the inspector supplied me with his car, with the instructions to take the six captains sightseeing to wherever they wanted to go. That was my job for weeks. Each morning I would fill up the car with petrol and be their tour guide for the day. I became quite good pals with them. On the last night they organised a party at the Pacific Hotel on the Strand. American warships were not a good location to hold parties as there was a standard instruction that liquor was not allowed on board these ships.

Another time, an Italian Navy training ship with a crew of about 1200-1500 berthed in Cairns for some time and the inspector gave me much the same job. I was instructed to look after the captain and several of the senior officers. I drove them on tours around Cairns and the Tablelands sightseeing and they were definitely impressed with the area. They held a party on board their ship prior to departing, which turned out to be a fairly grand affair.

Brian Gabriel was the one and only motorcycle policeman and he rode a BSA Golden Flash solo motorcycle. Unfortunately Brian was killed on duty when his motorcycle collided with a motor vehicle driven by a publican named Sonny Brifman, who was the licensee of a Cairns hotel. The full details of the accident escape me, but Brian was killed instantly. Brifman later became well known in police circles. Sonny married a barmaid named Shirley, who later became involved in some police matters and, I believe, committed suicide.

The death of Constable Brian Gabriel was a very sad affair and his body was transported by rail to Brisbane for burial. There was a police guard of honour at the railway station as the train carrying his body departed the railway station.

The police motorcycle was considered to be a bit of a jinx and it was difficult to find a police officer who was willing to ride it. One day the two inspectors, Tom Martin and James Hartley Cooke, called me into the inspector's office and Tom Martin said; "Kev, we just have to get that motorbike back on the road; there are quite a lot of traffic infringements. I know you have had some experience operating motorcycles, would you take it on for a time until we can get someone permanent?" I took on this role and became the sole traffic motorcyclist. Later on, the strength of the Traffic Branch was increased with the appointment of Sergeant Dennis Doherty and two additional constables, Bill Wilcocks and Keith Zupp. Later on, Desmond Vivian Fleming was also appointed.

I continued to ride this motorcycle for some time and in those days it took three police officers to detect the speed of a motor vehicle. A section of a particular roadway would be measured out and one man would be positioned with a white cloth, usually a white handkerchief. Some distance away would be a man with a stopwatch and a further distance along the road there would be a third officer. As the speeding vehicle passed, the man with the white cloth would drop it. That is, he would be holding his arm up high and as the vehicle passed he would quickly bring down his arm towards the ground. The officer with the stopwatch would then clock the speed of the vehicle as it passed him and the third man would intercept the vehicle. The driver would then be questioned and informed of the speed he was travelling and Court proceedings taken by way of complaint and summons.

There were not that many drink-driving offences detected. Society was more tolerant with regards drink driving than it is today. If you observed a vehicle being driven erratically you would definitely intercept it. You would make observations of the driver, checking for slurred speech, unsteadiness on his feet, bleary eyes. You would have him attempt to walk a straight line and have him attempt to pick up keys from the roadway. If you were satisfied he was under the influence, you would arrest the driver and convey him to the police station where he would be medically examined by the Government Medical Officer, who was Dr Donald Charles Cameron Sword. He would have the offender perform certain tests. There was a veranda situated between the main station and the watch-house and the doctor would have the offender attempt to walk a straight line, and another test was to have this person stand with his feet together, close his eyes and touch his nose with his finger. I remember one fellow who couldn't perform this second test saying to the doctor: "You try and do it, Don, you won't find it too bloody easy."

Dennis Doherty, the sergeant in charge of the Traffic Office, was a good-living, semi-religious man and we became good friends. He had three attempts to pass his sergeant first class examination and failed on each occasion: however, he studied law externally and passed his LLB with honours, was admitted to the Bar and eventually resigned from the Police Department, joined the Justice Department, was appointed a Crown Prosecutor and remained in that professional role until he retired.

Drink-driving legislation was starting to become more technical and in matters such as motor vehicle accidents or hit and run you had to undertake more in-depth investigation to secure a conviction. I remember one occasion when a vehicle had hit an electric light pole and failed to stop; however, you could see some green paint on the pole and Dennis said; "If we could get some of that paint it might be good evidence." We drove to my house where I secured an axe and, on returning to the accident scene, I put a couple of chops into the pole and it vibrated a little. Dennis said, "Go careful, we don't want the bally pole falling down". Dennis never swore. However, we did secure samples of paint, which did assist us with our investigation.

Regarding Dawn's position with the Queensland Tourist Bureau; at one time a boatload of Italian migrants arrived in Cairns and they were to be located on farms in the North Queensland sugar industry. Most of them could hardly speak English and Dawn had to interview them all and obtain their full names, date of birth and other particulars. She found this quite difficult and her boss said to her, "If you can carry out this task successfully it will result in you securing a much better position". Dawn recalls one incident where a busload of tourists were going to the Tablelands and some of them could not speak English very well: Somehow she didn't detail one man's movements and he was left behind, which resulted in him hiring a taxi to catch up with the bus. The fault was said to be Dawn's and it was the only time she was chastised while employed by the Tourist Bureau.

The Aerial Ambulance in Cairns provided an important service to North Queensland and one day when I was working in the inspector's office, Inspector Jim Cooke said to me: "Lad, the ambulance will be flying up to Arakoon to transport a mental patient to Cairns and we have to send a man with him. Would you like to go and have a look around?" I jumped at the chance. Tommie Biggs was the Ambulance Superintendent and Percy Trezise was the pilot of a volunteer group and flying a Rapide Rapid twin-engine plane. On the way up we were flying low and Percy pointed out to me hundreds of places in the ranges where wild pigs had been rooting around in the ground searching for food.

We arrived at the Arakoon settlement, which was run by the Presbyterian Church under the supervision of the Reverend McKenzie, a dour old Scotsman who had come out from Scotland some years previously. Percy Trezise was well known and he had with him a large sack filled with trinkets. As we were landing, you could see about 40-50 young maidens lined up in a "guard of honour" and these girls were topless and only wearing short green skirts. Percy received plenty of hugs and kisses as he handed out combs, mirrors and other trinkets to the young lasses.

The Reverend McKenzie did not drink, but kept a supply of very good Scotch whisky and during the evening provided us with a few rosiners of this good whisky. I was supplied with a bed and a mosquito net on the veranda and, after the Scotch, did not take long to fall into a deep sleep. The next thing I remember it was morning and there was a black face leaning over and shaking me from outside the mosquito net and a pair of rather large breasts very close to my eyes. One of the housemaids was trying to wake me up for breakfast.

We then picked up this patient from the mission hospital and she would have been the biggest Aboriginal woman I have ever seen. She was playing up a bit and we attempted to fit her with the straightjacket, which was probably manufactured about the time the Queensland Government was formed. She gave one shrug of her shoulders and all the stitching on the straightjacket broke and it was of no use at all. We didn't want to have to handcuff a woman and we were wondering what to do when Tommy Biggs said, "I'll fix her"; and with that he dived into his medical bag and produced the biggest needle I have ever seen and plunged it into her rump. She then slept all the way to Cairns.

During the month of September 1958 I was transferred to Roma Street Police Station, Brisbane and remained there for six years until October 1966. When proceeding on transfer it was necessary to have in your possession a "route" detailing all your government property on issue to you, such as – handcuffs, baton, official police notebook, firearm (if you had been issued with one), Policeman's Manual (two volumes) and other issue law books such as the Traffic Act and Liquor Act. I did own a motor vehicle at the time of my transfer, however, the Bruce Highway between Cairns and Brisbane was not suitable for long-distance motor-vehicle travel and by this time the Police Department had become more flexible and paid for the transportation of my vehicle to Brisbane by rail.

Within a short period of time after commencing duty at Roma Street I was seconded to the State Transport Section. Claude Wagner was the sergeant in charge with a staff of about eight. You travelled over most of Queensland intercepting trucks, checking their load and in particular the weight of their load. Road transport at that time was frowned upon by the Government as they wished most freight to be transported by rail. The transport companies had to have special permits to transport freight and that's what the State Transport police was all about, travelling the State, intercepting heavy vehicles, checking their loads and permits and instigating prosecutions where necessary. A rather humorous incident occurred early one morning at the Pine Rivers area on the old Bruce Highway. I had been up all night and was just about to cease duty when I intercepted this huge truck. I possibly could have commenced the questioning of the driver differently, but I said to him, "What's the size of your load?" He replied, "Twenty-seven hundredweight". I said, "Look, I have been up all night and I'm in no mood for games. What is the size of your load?" He again replied, "Twenty-seven hundredweight". I thought I had better try another approach so I said, "What type of load are you carrying?" He replied "Corn Flakes".

Dawn found it difficult to adjust to me being absent from home for so long so in January 1959 I returned to Roma Street and was seconded to counter duty at the Traffic Branch, which occupied an upstairs officer at the Roma Street building. A Sergeant Herbert was in charge and he was assisted by a police cadet who had a brother who was a well-known rugby league player. I was there for several months and my job there was mainly issuing drivers' licences and permits to women who wished to set up cake stalls at various locations throughout Brisbane. The Superintendent of Traffic at the time was Inspector Cec Risch.

There were two members of the Traffic Branch detailed to test applicants and one of them was a motorcycle officer. He tested applicants for motorbike licences who rode solo and this officer followed. The other was a senior constable who tested all applicants in four-wheel vehicles. If they passed, the applications were then handed to the counter staff and we issued the driver's licence and/or permits.

The inquiry staff numbered about 14-16 members and each evening two men worked 2pm to 10pm to serve summonses and execute warrants that would not be attended to during daylight hours. One particular night Trevor Blackwell and myself were working 2pm to 10pm when I received a telephone phone call from Inspector Cooke, who inquired from me who was speaking and the names of the men who were working. He then said, "How would you like to go to Mt Isa?" At that time there was a miners' strike in progress at Mt Isa and the previous night 20 police officers, mainly from Roma Street, had been flown to Mt Isa to assist the local police, who were having a fairly hard time on the picket lines.

I said to the inspector, "When are we going?", to which he replied, "Don't leave the station". I knew this could be a lengthy period of duty and at the time I was fortunate in that we had a telephone connected to our home, so I telephoned Dawn and asked her to pack a large suitcase for me and to include my khaki drill and khaki serge uniforms, which I had been issued with when serving at country stations. A car had been dispatched to Oxley to pick up a Sergeant Genricks and en route called at my residence to collect my suitcase.

Shortly after midnight 20 of us went by bus to Eagle Farm Aerodrome, where we boarded a DC3 aircraft for Mt Isa. After stopping twice for refuelling, we arrived in that town shortly after 6am. After a quick wash and some breakfast we went straight out on to the picket line. There was a line of distinction between the town area and the mine sites and striking miners were not allowed to cross from the town on to the mine site.

Finance was a problem encountered by most men as they never had time to make arrangements prior to departing Brisbane, and the absence of cash was an inconvenience to all; therefore the Police Department paid for our accommodation direct to the hotel management where we were billeted. There were about 60 extra police at Mt Isa who were billeted in the three hotels. Trevor Blackwell and myself were staying at the Argent Hotel and we were looked after extremely well. If you ordered a T-bone steak for breakfast it would cover the whole plate and the waitress would ask if two eggs were enough or if you would like three.

After we were there a few days Senior Sergeant King was becoming increasingly concerned with the flood of overtime claims as at that time the forms were very complicated documents, particularly at district office level. Des French was a plain-clothes officer at Mt Isa at that time and he informed the senior sergeant that I had previous experience working in the inspector's office at Cairns and would be competent with regards these particular forms. So the senior sergeant approached me and asked if I would do the job for him. I agreed on the condition that my workmate, Trevor Blackwell, could assist as I was only a two-finger typist and Trevor, a former cadet, was a proficient typist. As a result both Trevor and I finished up with a pretty good job for the rest of our stay at Mt Isa.

From memory there were about 65-70 extra police in that city during the strike. They were recruited from stations as far east as Townsville and south to Brisbane and from numerous country stations as well, and we were there for about eight to 10 weeks before we were gradually returned to our home stations. I always felt sorry for the permanent staff at Mt Isa as a good proportion of them were married and had to live there with their wives and children. During the strike they were reluctant at times to take action against local people who were endeavouring to break through the picket lines. After the strike was settled and the extra police had left the permanent members had to remain and carry on as normal, and no doubt it would be a difficult position for them.

While stationed at Roma Street I performed extensive duty at Parliament House, the Supreme Court and occasionally weekend duty at Government House. They were rather interesting jobs as you saw even in those days what a bit of a joke Parliament was. Duty at the Supreme Court was rather interesting in those days. If the jury was empanelled and held overnight, the jurors slept in beds on the veranda of the old courthouse building and their meals were brought over in big containers from the Daniel Hotel across the road. As well as the 12 jurors, there was always one of the sheriff's staff, the bailiff and two police officers.

At one time we had a new bailiff who didn't know the ropes, and when the meals arrived he fed the 12 jurors first. When we came to partake of our meal and looked in the pot there was bugger all left. It didn't take him long to work out that you fed the jurors last. Over time things changed with regards jury service and accommodation was secured for them down at the bottom end of George Street. We would walk them down after the evening meal and stay with them until 8pm when the police officers would cease duty. The bailiff would stay with them during the night and next morning the police officers would return, take up with the bailiff and walk the jurors back to the Supreme Court.

The Main Roads building was located just across the road from Roma Street Police Station, and if you had an inquiry from any police establishment in Queensland for the registered owner of a motor vehicle during office hours, you would walk across and see a particular person, who then detailed an employee to get the file. Once you manually obtained the information, you returned to Roma Street and telephoned the information to the relevant police station. If this required a trunk or long-distance telephone call you had to seek permission from your superior. Usually the information was transmitted by a series of local telephone calls to the inquiring station, which took a considerable period of time. Each police division had their own telephone allocation and you did not dare make long-distance telephone calls without permission. The particulars of each call were written in a special book with the nature and duration of the call. After termination of the call you contacted the telephone exchange, obtained the cost and also wrote that in the book.

After office hours you walked across to the Main Roads building gate and waited for the nightwatchman to appear. He usually arrived at the gate on the hour. He would give you entry and take you to the area where volumes of files were stored, light a hurricane light and search for the file. Once located you would obtain what information you required and then return to your station. This procedure was most frustrating if police were investigating serious crime ssuch as hit and run motor-vehicle accidents and stolen or wanted motor vehicles. It was not uncommon for police in the metropolitan area to wait for this information for up to one and a half hours. If you were from the country the mind boggles to think back on just how long it took for this information to be relayed.

There were no Police Department issue torches then. You had to supply your own. Apart from your issue handcuffs and baton the only other issued item was your notebook and an indelible pencil issued for the recording of particulars. Try using an indelible pencil to record particulars at the scene of a motor-vehicle accident in wet weather for an exciting exercise.

Roma Street police station in the 1950s, when I was stationed there, was used as a punishment station to some degree. There was a room off the senior sergeant's office with entry and exit through the same door, and there were two functions in this room, with one police officer manning the switchboard and another operating the radio. Later, when police patrol vehicles were fitted with radio equipment, this operator could communicate with operational staff in vehicles. These functions were usually reserved for police rank and file who had been transferred to Roma Street from various locations throughout the State and who were under some sort of cloud, usually alcohol-related problems. Some of these men, mainly unknown to the senior sergeants, made it their business to become quite friendly with the hotel staff across the road. They would have a piece of strong string or fishing line and when working late or night shift would arrange for staff members to bring over a bottle or two and attach it to their string or fishing line, which would then be hauled up through the open window where the staff would have a nightcap or two.

There was a canteen at Roma Street that never seemed to function at payable rates. It closed several times and reopened under new management with new people, but was never successful. At one stage the sister of Terry Flanagan, a serving police officer, tried to operate it for some time, but was unable to make it return a profit. There was also a liquor bar there that had been opened many years before. It was a liquor licence that could operate 24 hours a day. There was a clause in the licence that enabled this particular establishment to operate outside the bounds of the Liquor Act. It was a privilege given to the police by the then Premier of Queensland, Ned Hanlon. Premier Hanlon apparently looked upon police officers favourably and the purpose of this 24-hour-a-day liquor outlet was to enable police officers coming off duty at any hour of the day or night to have a few drinks before proceeding home.

There were always two serving police officers, attached to the Roma Street staff, who operated this liquor canteen and it was considered to be a prized job. At one stage I think it was just after I returned from the Traffic Office,

Inspector Woodbury called me in and said, "Young fellow, we need someone up in the bar at the Welfare Canteen. How would you like to work there?" I said, "Inspector, I can drink enough when I'm off duty without going up there to work". The inspector gave a bit of a grin and said, "Well we will have to send somebody else then".

Over the years there was "Diver" Mick Delves and Joe Peoples who worked at the canteen for some considerable time. One evening about 11pm, they decided to close and were cleaning up and partaking of an ale or two when there was a knock on the door. They replied with something like, "Go away, we're closed". The knock persisted and eventually this voice said, "Open up, I'm the Commissioner, Frank Bischof". One of the officers replied with a stupid remark, something like "I'm Bugs Bunny or Louie the fly". The knocking persisted and eventually the door was opened to reveal none other than the Commissioner himself, Frank Bischof. The Welfare Canteen never opened again.

During the late 1940s and '50s there was a rather large contingent of police at Roma Street with alcohol-related problems. If a police officer was stationed at a location anywhere outside of the metropolitan area and he misbehaved through overconsumption of alcohol and a transfer was warranted, he was usually transferred to Roma Street.

At Roma Street I had many years in the Inquiry Office and staff there had the job of doing up the fortnightly pay packets for the hundreds of men at both Roma Street and the Traffic Branch. All large police establishments like Roma Street, Fortitude Valley, Woolloongabba and the CI Branch were paid in cash, while suburban metropolitan stations and all other stations throughout the State were paid by cheque. The pay, with full details of who was to be paid and what amount, would arrive from headquarters in one big cheque and staff would proceed with an armed escort to the bank, after staff did the breakdown of denominations and coinage. You had to know exactly what notes and coins you needed prior to going to the bank so that the correct pay could be put into each envelope. There was no use going to the bank only to find when you returned to the station that you did not have the breakdown of notes correct. On paydays, wives of some of the police with alcohol-related problems would arrive to collect their husband's pay. It was an instruction issued by the inspector at Roma Street that the wives had to sign for and be given the pay and not the member. From memory, the pays at Roma Street and the Traffic Branch were processed by Tom Behm, Vince Crow and young Ron Youlles.

During the month of October 1966 I was transferred to Torwood Police Station, Brisbane. There was a staff of five, a sergeant first class in charge with four constables and I was a senior constable. In this division, there were two of the most traffic-congested roads at peak hour in Brisbane – Milton Road and Coronation Drive – and hardly a night would pass without a serious accident on either of these roads. If it was a wet Friday night, Dawn would remark, "A wet Friday night again. There will be another fatal road accident". And that was often the case.

We performed routine police work with normal day-to-day activities, which included the Lang Park football grounds, and we had football six months each year. We either performed rostered duty outside the grounds on traffic control or "special duty" on crowd control inside the football arena. After almost eight years at Torwood, I was completely sick of football matches.

I was promoted to sergeant second class and transferred to Gympie in March 1975 and back then it took about 22-24 years' service before you were promoted from senior constable to sergeant second class. Not that long before my transfer, Gympie had been proclaimed a police district with an inspector of police in charge. Jack Rawlings was the first inspector and he had retired and upon my arrival Phil Rheed was the inspector in charge. There was an overall police strength of about 28. We worked shifts on a 24-hour basis – 8am to 4pm – 4pm to 12midnight – 12midnight to 8am. My duty was mainly in charge of a shift, supervising activities from the office and monitoring prisoners in the watch-house. If there was a serious or fatal road accident you either took charge of the investigation yourself or supervised those who were.

During my time at Gympie I did not spend much time at the headquarters station, but was away performing relieving duty for some considerable time in charge of country stations. I relieved at Cherbourg, Murgon, Wondai and Kingaroy. I relieved in charge of Cherbourg for a period of nine months straight on one occasion and at another time I relieved at Maroochydore for a period of nine months. Even though I was out of my district I was still in the Sunshine Coast Police Region. Normally this duty would have been performed by a sergeant from the Nambour District, but because of circumstances unbeknown to me, no-one was available. Maroochydore was the busiest police division I worked in throughout my whole career.

On the many occasions I relieved at Wondai I grew to love the town and many happy memories from there remain with me. During the Whitrod years he had a standard instruction that country police had to conduct traffic patrols in their division each afternoon. This meant of course that during that time your station was usually unmanned. On these occasions at Wondai I was able to contact the girls working at the telephone exchange and they would take down any important messages and relay them to us upon our return.

At country police stations throughout the State, police wives were actually de facto police officers, receiving messages in the absence of their husbands and giving important matters immediate attention. If the matter was urgent there was an arrangement between husband and wife as to what action to take to contact an available officer. The country police wife, and women such as the women operating telephone exchanges, did a sterling job over the years and were never really recognised for their contribution to policing.

I did not realise it at the time, but while away from home on relieving duty, Dawn was at home managing the house and rearing three children, all reaching their teenage years without a father's influence.

I was promoted to sergeant first class about 1980 and remained at Gympie. I recall on one occasion I was detailed for relieving duty at Kingaroy when Senior Sergeant Dickson was transferred to Maryborough. Normally I would reside in an hotel when performing relieving duty, but at Kingaroy there was a problem with the telephone after midnight. The procedure was that when police ceased duty at midnight the telephone was switched through to the senior sergeant's residence and he took all calls until the station opened the next morning. So it was arranged for me to reside in the residence and do exactly that; attend to any telephone calls from the public after midnight. Suitable furniture and a refrigerator were obtained to make the home comfortable in the short term and I was completely satisfied with the arrangements. Charlie Dwyer was the regional superintendent and Pat Swan was the district inspector at the time and they both assisted and gave me their full support.

One Sunday morning I arose early, which was my normal practice, and the first thing was a visit to the toilet. I had rather regular bowel habits in those days and this was my location when the telephone rang. I crabbed it through the corridor in a hunched position to where the telephone was situated in the kitchen and on my right were a set of windows with no curtains, which opened out on to the street. I didn't realise it at the time, but as I was crabbing it through the corridor, all the early morning Catholics were leaving the church after Mass.

When I got to the telephone I was a bit anxious and as I picked up the receiver I simply said,"Hello". A voice replied, "Good morning, it's Joe here". I replied, "Joe bloody who?" He said, "Joh Bjelke-Petersen". I quickly stood erect and almost saluted. He then continued and said, "I only want to know what the weather is like. Is it clear, I'm thinking about flying up?" I said, "It's very clear, Sir, you can see for miles".

As I mentioned earlier, I relieved a number of times at both Murgon and Cherbourg. At Cherbourg you were usually in charge of a contingent of about

15-20 men, and I might add they were not very helpful. There were two small duplexes on the reserve and one of these was occupied by a male clerk who was a bachelor. The other was provided for the relieving police sergeant. This duplex had no floorcoverings and the floorboards were not tongue and grooved, but just hardwood timber with gaps between them, and the building was always bitterly cold in the depth of winter. It was quite an experience at Cherbourg to see the conditions those people lived under, which they alone were responsible for. During my time there, the Government built an elaborate watch-house that would do justice to any watch-house in Queensland and was provided with good-quality mattresses, mattress covers, sheets, pillows and pillowcases.

Normally the relieving periods there were from four to six weeks and on one occasion a work colleague of mine, Bob Claffey, was to relieve there for a lengthy period, however, he had domestic problems in Brisbane and didn't want to go so I went in his place. I was there for a continuous period of nine months.

On one occasion, after I was promoted to sergeant first class, I relieved in charge at Murgon and one day the recently arrived superintendent of the Cherbourg Mission, whom I had not met at that time, passed information on to me in person regarding a dispute between two families and the possibility of an impending riot that afternoon or night. I made inquiries and was satisfied there was some substance in the information. Later in the afternoon, I visited both hotels and appraised the publicans of the situation, informing them that police may have difficulty dealing with any problems they may encounter that night. They both volunteered to close their establishments immediately.

During the late afternoon you could see the number of Indigenous people in the town increasing and each of them were carrying what you would describe as a "waddy", a thin piece of sapling about three feet long. I could see that we might be in for real trouble so I commenced to telephone neighbouring police establishments for extra police and they came from as far away as Kingaroy, Goomeri, Maryborough, Gympie and Proston. During the afternoon, while discussing the situation with the recently arrived senior sergeant from Kingaroy, he remarked that the hotels were closed and I informed him of my discussions with the publicans and the action that they took. He said, "You have no authority to close them", to which I replied that they closed of their own accord to assist us in maintaining law and order in the town.

During the night it did get somewhat ugly. I had telephoned the Gympie district office and learnt that the district officer, Pat Swan, was absent in Brisbane, so the Gympie senior sergeant drove to Murgon. We had a conference and decided that we would not carry firearms as this may be more dangerous than beneficial. The rioting and fighting was mainly confined to the main street and we were concerned about the possibility of broken windows and damage to property, but that did not eventuate. We formed a line of police on the Wondai side of town and gradually moved them along Lamb Street (the main street), past the shire buildings and the picture theatre, out towards the Cherbourg road. This took a fair amount of effort and as they were moving along those who were not armed were pulling palings from wooden fences and we thought it would erupt at any moment, but fortunately for everyone concerned it did not. We eventually got them out and through the gate into the Cherbourg reserve and then formed a guard of police at the gate.

During this time there was a relief of female nurses waiting to go to the Murgon hospital and the nurses they were to replace were waiting to leave the reserve, however, we managed to successfully complete this exercise without incident.

Shortly afterwards, I saw the headlights of a motor vehicle approaching along the Wide Bay Road and it turned out to be Inspector Pat Swan, who had arrived back from Brisbane and drove straight up to assist us if necessary. I briefed him on the events as they had occurred, but was unable to inform him if any person had been injured. Once the inspector was satisfied, his instructions were to leave matters as they were until next morning, when we would get a better appreciation of events in daylight hours. Next morning there was not an Aboriginal person to be seen until we reached the township of Cherbourg, where it was found that most of them were still sleeping. Inquiries from the local hospital ascertained that no person had been admitted and over the next few days investigations showed no-one had sought medical attention.

I retired from the Queensland Police Department on 9 February, 1982 on my 56th birthday.

My first commissioner was C J Carroll and he was a highly respected man. In those early days I had met Commissioner Paddy Glynn when I was transferred to Camooweal and I recall the names of most of those who followed as Tom Harold, Frank Bischof, Norm Bauer, Ray Whitrod and Terry Lewis. I had great respect for Sub-Inspector Bill O'Connor who was stationed at Roma Street when I was stationed at Torwood. We often cashed our pay cheques at the same Commonwealth Bank and would compare the amount we received. This was just after a new superannuation scheme had been introduced when commissioned officers were paying very heavy superannuation and Bill would remark, "You're taking home more money than I am".

I had great respect for both Pat Swan and Charlie Dwyer. Pat was my district officer at Gympie and I had known Charlie Dwyer for most of my service. He was a plain-clothes officer when I was first transferred to Townsville and Charlie was instrumental in me remaining at Gympie when I was promoted to sergeant first class. In my retirement days I had great respect for Tom Pointing, who was the regional superintendent based at Gympie. Tom would always attend our retirement function and with a bit of prompting would occasionally recite "The Man From Snowy River".

In retrospect, I have not regretted my career as a police officer, but I certainly would not want to be a serving member of any police service today.

Over a three-month period in 1866, Sub-Inspector Uhr travelled some 3200 kilometres on horseback in pursuit of a horse thief.

*The Long Blue Line*, W Ross Johnston, 1992 (p 91)

# George Edwards

Throughout his career George Edwards was highly respected by members of the community and subordinates who served with him throughout the years. I would describe him as an ambassador for the Queensland Police Service and a role model for junior officers. He took his duties seriously and never expected a subordinate to perform a task that he was not prepared to undertake himself. He relished the life of a country policeman and enhanced the values of the Police Service in each community where he served. We must not forget the contribution made by his wife, who in many instances acted as a civilian police officer, answering the telephone receiving messages from members of the public, feeding prisoners and assisting in the general cleaning of the respective watch-houses. It is good to see son Philip carrying on the tradition, who at the time of writing holds the rank of senior sergeant.

Phil Edwards rose to the rank of Senior Sergeant and became the Officer in Charge of Gympie police division.

On 25 May, 2011 Phil passed to eternal life after a long illness. He is sadly missed by family and friends.

**Laurie Pointing**

# George Edwards

I was born on 19 October, 1923 at our family farm 12 miles from Stanthorpe. It was a broken-down returned soldiers settlement farm of 60 acres. My father was a returned soldier from World War I, 1914-1918. A bush nurse attended my birth. My family was in poor financial circumstances as was the case with numerous families in those days.

I attended school at a small settlement called Bapaume outside Stanthorpe. It was a one-teacher school and I attained a scholarship standard of education and left school at age 12½. There was no high school available, and even if there was our financial circumstances would have excluded me from higher education.

After leaving school I worked on farms in the Stanthorpe and Redland Bay districts for a few years. When I was about 14 I went seeking employment in the Redlands district on Moreton Bay. I remembered I arrived at Cleveland railway station with two bob in my pocket and the clothes on my back. It was late at night and I found shelter under a tree on the side of the road near a farmhouse. A Mr Burns, who was the owner of the farm, put me up and fed me for a few days, and in payment I worked on his farm. I ended up working a few farms in the area at the time and after a few months I returned to Stanthorpe. At 14 I saw an opportunity to get out of farm life and I joined the militia.

The militia was a voluntary army and I was attached to the 25$^{th}$ Battalion. I had to put my age up and no person in authority asked too many questions.

I undertook a three-months training course at Frazer's Paddock, Enoggera, followed by a three-months course at Redbank, near Ipswich, in the year 1939, and a further three-months course at Toowoomba. In between these camps we went into Stanthorpe one night every two to three weeks for training.

They asked for volunteers to go to Darwin and when I made my decision to join the permanent army and enlist in the Infantry Rifle Battalion they had intentions of rejecting me because of my age; however, after obtaining a letter of permission from my mother I was accepted. I turned 17 not long after I joined the permanent army and became a regular soldier in the 19th Infantry Battalion. Along with 140 other soldiers, I boarded a ship in January 1941 and sailed to Thursday Island**,** Bathurst Island, Melville Island and Port Moresby.

We were at sea for about a month and spent about eight weeks training on these islands, getting fit and in preparation for our duties at Darwin. I made some close friends in the battalion and I remembered not long after arriving in Darwin in 1941 we went out to one of the many naval ships that were anchored in Fanny Bay and we had a swallow tattoed on our forearms.

Most of my army service was spent in Darwin performing picket duties, rolling out barbed wire and putting in bomb shelters near the airports. Later in 1941, I remembered working near one of the airports and we could hear this loud noise coming from the air in the distance. The aircrafts were some distance away, but as they got closer the noise increased and you could see the larger formation.

I remember there was some conversation between us at the time. Comments were made like, "I didn't know we had so many planes" and "I wonder where they're heading". But as they got closer we soon realised that they were not our aircrafts, but were Japanese bombers. It was almost simultaneous as we hit the trenches and the bombs started whistling down and causing mayhem.

Every ship anchored in the harbour was sunk, all our aircrafts were flattened and had no chance to get into the air. There were hundreds killed that day. For a number of us our duties changed from rolling out wire and sentry duty to patrolling the foreshore and searching for bodies washed up for weeks after the first air raids.

I was in Darwin until the end of the war and there were 66 air raids by the Japanese in that time, with the last bombing raid at the end of 1943. It was a tough initiation for a 17-year-old, but I caught up with my older brother, who was also in Darwin at the time as an aircraft engineer in the air force. In 1944 I was transferred to the Atherton Tablelands until the end of the war. When I completed my service I achieved the rank of Warrant Officer and was discharged on 26 February, 1946.

After returning to civilian life I attended an army rehabilitation course at Toowoomba and eventually became a carpenter. I worked in the Cunnamulla district for some time and worked on a number of properties building shearers' quarters and shearing sheds. Most of my time there, however, was building on a property called Denevor Downs. It was 1.25 million acres and in 1951 they shore 150,000 sheep. The property was owned by the Toowoomba Foundry, which was owned by the Griffith Brothers, who still carry on business in Toowoomba today.

After finishing work in the Cunnamulla district I then travelled to Charleville, where I worked in the rebuilding of a hotel opposite the police station that had been destroyed by fire.

I remember that during this construction job a police officer would frequently walk past on his way to the post office. I think he was a clerk attached to the inspector's office at the Charleville police station. He would say to me, "Why don't you give that away and join the Police Force?" I would reply, "No, no, no, I don't want to be a policeman".

Petrie Terrace Depot, Brisbane. Tennis courts in the foreground, corner of garage and workshops on the right. *Queensland Police Museum.*

He continued with this line for some time and one day things were not proceeding as well as I would have liked on the job, so when this policeman approached the job site and again made this statement I said, "All right, I will be up at the police station in the morning". Well, that's what I did. I attended the Charleville police station the next morning, completed the necessary application forms and was duly accepted. I entered the Police Depot at Petrie Terrace, Brisbane on 13 December, 1948 as a probationary constable.

On the day I was called to the Police Depot at Petrie Terrace for my final assessment there were quite a number of young men gathered there who had all made application to join the Police Force. The first 16 applicants were rejected for a variety of reasons. I was starting to get the feeling that I would be returning to Charleville and carpentering, however, I was successful and subsequently accepted.

There were quite a few reasons why applicants were rejected. Some were over the recognised weight and some were underweight, not tall enough, colour blind or wearing glasses. You had to be at least five feet nine in height and under the age of 29½ as well. I was married when I commenced as a probationary constable, but if you were single when you joined you could not marry without first obtaining written permission and you had to have first completed 12 months' continuous service. When I first met my wife to be, Alma, she was serving with the Women's Australian Auxiliary Air Force (WAAAF), and we were married on 3 January 1948, just before I entered the Police Depot.

As an interesting note, my youngest daughter, Gwenith, got married in the same church at Kedron on 20 August 1977, some 29 years later.

When I entered the Depot I had a head start on the rest of the recruits when it came to the physical training because of my army service. The training instructor was Constable Tom Molloy, a former member of the British Navy who was born in Ireland. It is also noted that he was the training instructor and disciplinarian for my son, Philip, who joined the Police Force in January 1975.

Over the years many stories have circulated about the infamous Tom Molloy and his antics at the Police Depot, but I got on very well him. I was exempt from rifle drill and in its place I was given the strenuous duty of marking the tennis courts at the Depot and Fortitude Valley police station.

Even though I was married at the time, I lived in the old wooden barrack accommodation at the Depot and had no problem adjusting to that style of living because of my army discipline training. Alma lived at Woolwin in a flat waiting for me to finish my three-months training. We were allowed out on weekends and I would return to the flat at Woolwin.

Most of our training was lectures on law and police duties by a number of sworn police officers who were stationed at the Depot for that purpose. I cannot remember their names, with the exception of a rather polished, neat and tidy officer by the name of Alex Day.

On 1 February, 1949 our first child, Margaret, was born, and then a little over a month later I was sworn in on 4 March, 1949 by Commissioner Carroll at the Treasury building. I became Constable George Edwards, Registered No. 2402, when I was sworn in with 10 other officers in front of the Commissioner's desk.

My first posting after being sworn in was to Roma Street Police District. I was there for a few short months where I performed normal beat duty, walking the beat to the left at approximately two and a half miles per hour under the supervision of a senior officer, who gave you periodic bookings. I didn't like Brisbane and approached the inspector in charge to see if I could be transferred to the country. He said, "Young man, when I was first sworn in I did as I was told and went where I was sent and accepted my transfer, and you'll do the same".

However, he must have listened, because in a very short period of time I was transferred to Ingham in North Queensland. That was in June 1949, just three months after I was sworn in.

Prior to departing we had to buy some furniture, which was transported by rail, and my wife, daughter Margaret and I also travelled the long distance north by rail. Upon our arrival at the Ingham railway station we were met by local police. We arrived before our furniture and had to rent a furnished room in a boarding house until the arrival of our furniture some weeks later.

We then moved into accommodation in the form of an old private hospital building, which we rented for 30/-a week. We never had a car at this time because we couldn't afford one, and I used to ride a pushbike to work. I was earning about £22 a week and rent was about £1 a week.

I liked Ingham and I still have friends there today from those times.

Ingham was a 24-hour station, with about 15 or 16 staff under the leadership of Senior Sergeant J J Ryan. There was a sergeant first class of police who was second in charge and the rest of us were constables. Some may have had stripes, perhaps a senior constable or two, or several first class constables. The police station was an old wooden building and we were certainly cramped for room. There was a day room and the police office was small and cramped. The counter took up a fair amount of space and with no air-conditioning it became rather stuffy, particularly in the hot, humid months.

There was only one police vehicle attached to Ingham and that was a 1949 Ford utility. No air-conditioning of course. As a matter of fact I never enjoyed the comforts of air-conditioning in any police station during my whole police career. The main duties of police in Ingham were general duties, which included walking the beat, attending the counter, taking complaints and general arrests.

As well as routine police duties, residents obtained their driving licences and registered their motor vehicles at the police station and the police department was a vehicle for several other government departments. I played football at Ingham and generally became part of the community. While at Ingham, I utilised my carpentry skills that I obtained after the war and built some sheds, tank stands and living quarters on a friend's sugar cane farm. This friend was Roy Dowling, whose son was Greg Dowling, who played Rugby League for Queensland and Australia.

Our communication system was rather simple. There were no radios fitted to motor vehicles in those days and our communication system was the telephone. Telephone exchanges were operated by telephonists and if you were desirous of making a long-distance call, you telephoned the exchange and the girl would ask you what number you required and she would then connect your call.

You first obtained permission from your superior after explaining to him the nature of your inquiry and why you needed to communicate by telephone. On completion of your conversation you again contacted the exchange and obtained the duration of the call and the cost. All those particulars were then entered into your station telephone book. Each police station was allocated their yearly telephone allowance from the budget.

When relaying a message regarding wanted persons, stolen motor vehicles or other matters of importance you simply telephoned that information to your nearest police station and they passed that information to their nearest police establishment. You were encouraged to make local calls from police station to police station wherever possible because it did not affect your local telephone budget.

I spent five years at Ingham and during this time Alma and I had another daughter, Lois, on 1 November, 1951. While at Ingham we saved hard and managed to buy our first family car, an Austin A40. However, after five years we felt that it was time to have a change. I then successfully applied for a transfer to Ipswich. Alma, Margaret, Lois and I then drove to Ipswich. It was 1760 kilometres and took us three days travelling on dirt roads and sleeping in the car on the way. One night was a blessing when we stayed with my brother-in-law, Norm Rudd, who was then a policeman in Mackay.

We arrived in Ipswich and lived with my retired mother, who lived in Whitehall Road. We only stayed there a short time before we found accommodation in Clay Road for 30/- a week. I took up duty at Ipswich station in January 1954.

Ipswich was strange after Ingham. It was a headquarter station and controlled policing activities and the administration functions for all police stations in the district. The inspector and the sub-inspector were in the same building, as were the inspector's clerks, who were responsible for the flow of administration duties. There was a Criminal Investigation Branch and a Traffic Branch, a number of police motor vehicles and a much larger contingent of staff than Ingham, and it was in close proximity to the capital city of Brisbane.

Staff worked around the clock in three shifts and a senior sergeant was in charge of each shift. From memory we worked 6am to 2 pm, 2pm to 10pm and 10pm to 6am. I recall there was quite a lot of night work. Communication had improved by 1954 and there were radios fitted to the police vehicles, which enabled the officer in charge of the shift to communicate with patrolling officers.

I was stationed at Ipswich for 18 months and spent 12 months of that time performing relieving duty at Forest Hill, Boonah, Redbank and Goodna police stations. There were varied vehicles used at the different stations. There were no vehicles at Forest Hill, a Land Rover at Boonah, motorbike at Redbank and a motorbike with sidecar at Goodna. While at these stations I improved and developed my administrative skills required for running a station.

During this time I had applied for a transfer to Kalbar, a one-man station within the Ipswich police district and I took up duty there in July 1955. During my time at Kalbar we had two more children. Our youngest daughter, Gwenith, was born on 3 December, 1955 and our son, Philip, was born on 28 July, 1959. Phillip is also now a police officer. During our time at Kalbar, our oldest daughter moved to Brisbane for employment and lived with her aunty.

I spent a few months over 10 years at Kalbar, which was a typical one-man station. The police office was attached to the police house and you carried out normal police duties as well as being an agent for several government departments. You issued driving licences, transport permits; you also registered motor vehicles and a variety of other duties for departments not associated with your police duties.

The police residence was not cemented underneath the house. There was no air-conditioning, no screens, floorcoverings or curtains. Matters such as floorcoverings and curtains were the responsibility of the incoming police officer. You were paid a small amount of money on transfer, which was supposed to compensate you for incidentals.

Once again we communicated by telephone as this was the only means of communication available. Upon my arrival in that town the police vehicle was a pushbike and the officer in charge was not paid an allowance to use his private motor vehicle to carry out police duties. However, you were able to fill out a voucher for a taxi to go to traffic accidents, although this was impractical a lot of the time due to time and often unavailability of the taxi.

There were 24 miles of the Cunningham Highway in the Kalbar police division, which included Cunningham's Gap. The highway was only two lanes and in my time I attended to and investigated, without any assistance from other sections of the force, 30 fatal road accidents. The pushbike was eventually replaced with a Harley-Davidson motorbike and sidecar and, while this was a huge step forward, it was most difficult carrying out police duties such as fatal and serious road accidents in the wet weather.

You used your private motor vehicle to investigate serious incidents. I completed numerous reports over the years in an effort to obtain a police vehicle, but on each occasion received the advice that there were insufficent funds. The closest I went to receiving a police car was when I was advised by the Police Depot that I was receiving a Mini Minor. However, after waiting several weeks for its arrival, I was advised that it was reallocated to the wharf squad (so close!).

It was Commissioner Whitrod who introduced the policy that you transferred from small police stations after you had been stationed there 10 years or more. My brother, Arthur, was also a policeman, stationed at Ipswich. He was performing relieving duty at Marburg when I received a telephone call from him, and he asked "When are you going?" I replied, "I'm not going anywhere". Arthur replied, "Have a look at the Police Gazette". I had not received the Police Gazette at the time, but it did arrive shortly after that conversation and sure enough there it was: I had been transferred to Gatton. I had not been officially notified of that transfer by my superiors at Ipswich, which I considered unprofessional. I moved to Gatton with Alma and our three children who were still at home and thankfully the Police Force provided a police residence.

However, the timing of my transfer was not thought through too well by the transfer board. I was a senior constable getting close to promotion. Once I settled into life at Gatton I commenced applying for positions and after a relatively short period of time was promoted to sergeant second class and transferred in charge of the Mundubbera police division, a two-man station.

With more planning and some consideration, my transfer to Gatton could have been avoided and less expense incurred by the Department. That happened a lot under Commissioner Whitrod. He seemed to have this fixation of transferring police officers who had been stationed in small communities for over 10 years at any cost. I wasn't entirely against the policy, but there were quite a number of police who were in a similar situation to myself who were due for promotion and were transferred, then shortly afterwards promoted and again transferred, at unnecessary cost.

I took charge of Mundubbera in December 1966 and spent seven years and eight months there., A new police residence was erected while I was there which was greatly appreciated. During my time at Mundubbera I was fortunate to have good, competent constables with me. Lou Olsen was the first and over the years I had Brian Pitman and Glen Durrie. Brian Pitman was one of the most meticulous officers I ever encountered. He was extremely thorough and advanced confidently through the ranks. During the Fitzgerald inquiry he spent quite a period of time as Acting Deputy Police Commissioner. His children followed in his footsteps. They were a real police family. I am not sure how many are there today, but I believe his four sons are current senior serving police officers with the Queensland Police Service. On another point of interest, Allan Davey served under me while I was the officer in charge at Murgon years later and he is currently a serving Assistant Commissioner.

There were a couple of incidents of note while I was at Mundubbera. One involved two single brothers, Gilbert and Robert Netz, who owned a dairy farm called "Nantylyn" at Mundurran, near Mundubbera. Gilbert, aged about 37, married a young woman who was aged about 20. They had an argument with the result that she left him and came into Mundubbera to catch the train to leave the district. Anyway Gilbert followed her and walked on to the railway platform carrying a .303 rifle and he shot her while she was standing on the platform. She was holding her purse in her hand and the bullet went through her arm, through her purse and through a $1 note in her purse. She collapsed on to the platform and he again fired another shot at her while she was on the ground and this bullet entered her right shoulder and exited through her chest.

Gilbert Netz then left the scene. I was immediately notified and quickly summoned the local doctor. It was amazing that this young woman was still living and she survived. Shot twice with a .303 rifle and survived, amazing. I think Tom Pointing may have arrived from the Bundaberg CI Branch to take charge of the investigation. Netz was committed to stand trial at the Supreme Court, Brisbane on a charge of attempted murder, but when the trial commenced, the complainant flatly refused to give evidence, so the presiding trial judge dismissed the case and discharged Netz. Naturally, the Crown appealed the decision.

I attended the appeal at the Supreme Court, Brisbane and was sitting at the back of the Court when Judge Mansfield asked if the sergeant from Mundubbera was present. When it was confirmed that I was, I was called to the witness box to give evidence, and during my evidence Judge Mansfield said to me, “Is it true that the accused once said to you during a conversation ‘One of these days I am going to go off pop?” I replied, “Yes, I did have an occasion to speak with him concerning a domestic matter and he said, ‘One of these days I’m going to go off pop’ I asked what he meant by that statement and he replied, ‘You’ll know one day’. Anyway, the appeal was successful and Netz was convicted and sentenced to a term of imprisonment.

Policing at Mundubbera was the normal routine country policing. This meant being part of the community wherever possible and ensuring the public that your duty was to uphold the law and, at the same time, involving yourself in day-to-day community affairs and carrying out your duties in a professional manner. Traffic offences notices had been introduced and traffic patrols were part of your daily routine along with the issuing of tickets to offenders. There was not a great deal of serious crime committed, but we had our fair share of sudden deaths, fires and domestic disturbances.

I always prided myself in maintaining strong community ties and while at Munduberra it was no different. I was a member of several clubs and groups, holding executive positions such as president of the Rotary Club and golf club.

Five people drowned in one accident at Munduberra when a car went over the side of the low-level bridge that spanned the Burnett River and plunged into the river. It was after dark and the driver and his four passengers were all intoxicated. The water in the river was low at the time and the vehicle travelled about 30 feet to the river bed. The five occupants of the vehicle were from Allies Creek sawmill. Brian Pitman was working with me and he said, “I can’t swim, George”. I positioned the police vehicle by driving it as far as I could on the sandy dry section of the river bed before becoming bogged.

This allowed the vehicle to shine enough light on the spot where the vehicle had landed. It was practically submerged in the water. I think I pulled three bodies, maybe four, from the vehicle. I first tied a rope around the bodies and guided them to the bank so they could be removed. We located one body next morning. It had been dislodged from the vehicle and was positioned about one and a half miles downstream from the bridge. A crew from Channel 7 television station arrived next morning and filmed me in the water. I was wearing shorts so they took a few shots of me in the water from my waist up.

No counselling those days, not like it is today. I saw on the Channel 7 news recently where police went to a fatal road accident at which one person had been killed and the officers all had to have counselling after the investigation was finalised. Makes you wonder what the job is coming to.

I thoroughly enjoyed my eight and a half years at Mundubbera until in t August 1974 I was promoted to sergeant first class and transferred in charge of Cunnamulla. I moved to Cunnamulla with Alma and my son. By this time, my youngest two daughters had obtained employment in Brisbane in administrative jobs.

There were quite a number of Aboriginal people living in camps near Cunnamulla-one on the north side and one on the south side of the township. They caused quite an amount of trouble, with arrests every day, mainly for alcohol-related matters. I was the watch-house keeper and Alma prepared prisoners' meals and washed the watch-house towels and blankets, for which we were compensated. It was acknowledged at the time that Cunnamulla had the highest arrest rate per capita in the State.

There were a number of large towers situated in the town, at the rear of the police residence and in the police quadrant. I remember looking out the kitchen window early one morning and observed this Aboriginal man starting to climb one of the towers so I quickly followed after him. By this time he had secured the wire on a part of the tower and was determined to commit suicide. I was up the tower ladder about 25 feet, holding on with one hand with the fellow on my shoulder. Other officers arrived after my wife raised the alarm and with their help we were able to save him. The wire had cut into his neck, however, he survived. I was about 50 at the time so it was a bit of a struggle, but it came to a successful end.

I enjoyed Cunnamulla and knew what it was like before I applied for the position as I had worked in that country as a carpenter before I joined the police. The majority of the residents were good people and I was fortunate in that I had good staff. Greg Tutt, Ted Swift and John Fox were the three CI Branch men I had over the time and they were all active and competent detectives.

During my time at Cunnamulla, my son joined the Police Force and went to the Police Academy at Oxley in January 1975. I qualified for the rank of senior sergeant and eventually submitted an application and was promoted to the rank of senior sergeant at Rockhampton, which is a headquarters police station providing a 24 hour service with plenty of night work.

Alma and I moved to Rockhampton by ourselves, as all our children had left home by the time. I commenced duty at Rockhampton in July 1978 and was one of a number of senior sergeants working around the clock in charge of shifts. While my stay at Rockhampton was only short it was enjoyable, as I was friendly with a bank manager there who was at Kalbar in the early days of my career. We played golf two or three days a week, which was a good release from shiftwork.

Verne McDonald, the Deputy Commissioner at the time, came and saw me and asked if I would be prepared to transfer in charge of the Murgon Police Division, a post that was being upgraded to senior sergeant at the time. After discussing it with Alma, I accepted the position and took up duty at Murgon in March 1979.

On my first day of arriving at Murgon, I attended the front counter and spoke with the administrative officer, John Wex. I have had reason to return to Murgon in recent years after my retirement and have had the pleasure of seeing John at the Murgon station.

Murgon was a 24-hour station with a staff of about 17, including one detective. The police station and my residence were reasonably new at the time, so both the living conditions and working conditions were rather comfortable. In my time there, Dennis Arndt was the detective and in one year we had 4600 arrests, the second highest in the State. Two murders and a couple of riots were among some of the serious matters that occurred in my time there.

As was the case at Cunnamulla, I was the appointed watch-house keeper and, with the assistance of Alma, provided meals and washed the towels and blankets, for which we were reimbursed. Assistant Commissioner Greg Early made comment once that I was the highest-paid watch-house keeper in the State at that time – I would believe him because the amount of work needed to look after the watch-house was enormous.

I attended the commissioned officers' course at Chelmer College while at Murgon and obtained very good marks, but was not accepted at the time. I was not given the reasons why, but on reflection it may have been my age. I was about 56 and they may have thought there was no value in promoting an officer of that age to commissioned rank. I might add though that I was a dedicated officer who loved the Police Force to the day I retired and would have had no issue with continuing my service through until age 60.

After I returned from the course I was contacted personally by the Deputy Commissioner, who offered his support and encouraged me to attend the next available commissioned officers' course.

I discussed my future with my family and retired from Murgon at the age 57 on 17 January, 1981. I had had enough by this time and realised it was time to move on to the next phase in my life. Alma and I purchased a block of land at

Victoria Point near where I had worked all those years before as a young boy. We built our home there in the semi-rural environment that we loved and lived an active life in retirement. There was only one other house built in the street when we constructed our house. It is amazing how the area has developed over time.

I saw a lot of changes in technology during my service. I never enjoyed the comfort of air-conditioning in any police vehicle or police residence, however, the police house at Murgon was of brick construction and reasonably new. During my service I saw the introduction of traffic offence notices, two-way radios in motor vehicles and breathalysers. Prior to improved technology to obtain evidence for a drink-driving offence you had to observe the condition of the offender, whether they had glassy eyes, flushed face, slurred speech or were unsteady on their feet. You would have them attempt to walk a straight line and attempt to pick up car keys from the roadway. The offender would be examined by the Government Medical Officer who would obtain blood from the offender, which would be forwarded under escort to Brisbane for examination, and more often than not it would be several weeks before you received the blood-reading results.

I recall in my Ingham days the Government Medical Officer would come to the police station and first inquire the name of the arrested person prior to him conducting the medical examination. We must always bear in mind that in some of the country districts in days gone by, the Government Medical Officer may have held that position for 20-30 years and had brought into the world some of the local drink-driving offenders.

To obtain evidence for a simple breach of the Traffic Act or Regulations you would interview the motorist and record the conversation in your official police notebook and furnish a breach report, which was then forwarded to your district headquarters. Eventually the file would be returned, instructing you to prosecute the offender by way of Complaint and Summons.

I worked under several Police Commissioners. Carroll was the Commissioner when I first joined and he was followed by Paddy Glen, who was succeeded by Tom Harold. Then we had Frank Bischof. When Bischof retired Norm Bauer took over for a short period of time and then Max Hodges, the Police Minister in the Bjelke-Petersen Government, was given authority to select his own Commissioner and he recruited Ray Whitrod, from New Guinea. I think Hodges and Whitrod both served together in the Air Force during World War II. While he was a reformist he was not my type of person. He wasn't a man's man. Terry Lewis was Commissioner when I retired.

I had tremendous respect for Norm Bauer and Terry Lewis. You could talk to them anywhere, at any time, on any subject. They would listen to your complaints and assist you wherever possible.

I experienced a fulfilling life and have no regrets. I enjoyed my police career and if I was starting out now would do it all over again.

In the 1880s Birdsville police rode camels. Sub-Inspector Little considered "two good camels will do more than six horses".

*The Long Blue Line,* W Ross Johnston, 1992 (p 37)

# Don Braithwaite

I asked Don Braithwaite to write a chapter for this book for several reasons, including the fact that he chaired the committee that was responsible for the publication of The Long Blue Line, the first official history of the Queensland Police Service.

Like me, Don was a country boy who came off a farm and knew how to work draught horses. He carried through life fond memories of a country environment centred around Finch Hatton in the Pioneer Valley.

We follow that career from cadet through to Assistant Commissioner (Personnel). He set his sights on personnel management and welfare in mid-career and tailored all his studies accordingly. The choice was fortunate for Don - and the Service because, having had frequent dealings with him on matters of police administration, including particular aspects of welfare, I can say he is a straight shooter and a man of compassion.

This chapter also touches upon the yesteryears of Queensland policing in such areas as policewomen, pay and conditions, transport, accommodation, communication, Petrie Terrace Depot days, the Oxley Police Academy and its ethnic dinners, and the foundation of the Juvenile Aid Bureau by Detective Sergeant Terry Lewis.

Don has good memories of the Service. Two years ago (2008), with Terry McMahon and Allan Hilker, he organised a reunion of those retired members who passed through the Depot 1948-1952. A coat and tie affair, it was held at the Police Academy with Commissioner Bob Atkinson as guest of honour. It was a memorable last hurrah for a lot of old blokes.

**Laurie Pointing**

# Don Braithwaite

My good fortune was to be raised in Finch Hatton in the picturesque Pioneer Valley to the west of Mackay. Born in 1931, I was the fourth of eight children. Dad was a cane grower on a modestly sized farm, which grew no more than 1200 tonnes in the best of seasons. Mum was a full-time mum.

Dad worked the farm with eight draught horses. Seven cows kept us in milk and butter, the separated milk going to the pigs. Chooks provided eggs and on Christmas Day a couple would give up their lives for a good cause. A cranky old Smithfield cattle dog kept the stock under control and the farm relatively free of snakes. We had a number of fruit trees.

During the decade into which I was born, Charles Kingsford Smith, Don Bradman and Phar Lap were the recognised heroes. This was the first great age of radio. Historians tell us the Great Depression struck hardest in 1931, the year I was born. Sure, we were born into a frugal environment, but you don't miss something you never had. If we had no spare cash, neither did other families in the valley. But the eight children enjoyed a wonderful sense of security as our hard-working, no-nonsense parents stood between us and the ills of the world.

Some 800 people lived in and around Finch Hatton, which was a typical representation of small-town Australia. Besides Cattle Creek sugarmill, it boasted three churches, three pubs, two picture theatres, four general stores, a sawmill and the usual butcher, baker, barber and blacksmith. Railway and loco lines ran through the valley and the village, servicing the people and the mill. A sergeant and constable staffed the local police station. I grew up in the best of childhood environments.

As did some 20 other farm boys, I rode a pony to Finch Hatton State School with its enrolment of 110 pupils and three teachers. Six one-teacher schools were located within a radius of 15 miles. But the halcyon days of my youth saw me in an encounter with the law. After school came out the farm kids would race their horses up the main street, pedestrian kids scrambling to safety. One afternoon as we rested our puffing ponies in the shade of a tree, Constable Ron Horsford, himself mounted on a magnificent bay gelding, rode up and quietly told us that if we did not walk our ponies through the hamlet we, ourselves, would be walking. I was boyishly impressed by the horse, accoutrements, uniform and particularly the manner in which the constable cautioned us. All this was in accord with the respect in which the citizenry held the local constabulary. My thoughts turned to being a policeman.

World War II started in 1939 and affected everyone. Because many of our young men enlisted, the resultant labour shortage on the farms demanded that farm kids take up the shortfall. Gathering horse feed for the chaffcutter, feeding the stock, milking the cows, planting cane and cultivating it with teams of heavy horses: These were some of our tasks over the school holidays, before and after school and on a Saturday. Sunday was for church-going and swimming in the deep holes in Cattle and Finch Hatton creeks.

I thought I was well paid for my work by being allowed to go to the pictures every second Saturday night. The picture theatres of those days were the palaces of the poor.

My parents were determined that all their children receive a secondary school education and skimped and saved to that end. In turn the six sons and two daughters went to boarding schools in Warwick (The Scots College and Presbyterian Girls College) for two years each to gain their Junior Certificates. All the siblings have been enduringly grateful for the hard work, sacrifices and foresight of our parents.

In 1947, my second year at Scots, I made application to the Police Commissioner for admission to the Force as a cadet the following year. The headmaster provided a helpful reference. In an acknowledgment I was advised I would be contacted in 1948. I heard nothing more until October that year when I wrote a reminder letter.

Two police cars and four motor bikes outside Roma Street Station. Ford Coupe. Note: Traffic car loud speaker system and motor cycles with sidecars. *Queensland Police Museum*

Meanwhile, Dad employed me on the farm. He gave me and another man a contract to harvest the 1948 crop. This consisted of cutting the cane by hand, shouldering it up on to trucks and conveying the trucks to the loco siding by way of a three-horse wagon. This proved a useful experience because after cutting and loading burnt sugar cane in the dew of a chilly morning and in the noonday heat, all work thereafter was relatively easy.

The police recruiting centre responded to my reminder letter with telegrammed advice that I go to Brisbane at my own expense for medical examination which, if I passed, would permit me to be admitted immediately.

I became a cadet on 24 October, 1948 and was assigned to the Inspector's Office at the Police Depot. In early history this site was a prison that in 1883 became the Police Depot, imposing brick barracks being built in 1939 at a cost of £41,000. Fate did not permit me to enjoy a room in those barracks. Instead, for the whole two years and seven months I spent at the Depot my accommodation was in the old wooden barracks, which possibly were there when Captain Cook discovered Australia.

(Sixty years passed before I returned to the cradle of my police career. In May 1987 the Department moved the remaining Depot functions to Alderly and the following month the old site was publicly auctioned with a reserve price of $3m. The investors were required to retain and restore the brick barracks as a condition of development. They did a grand job of it. You can enjoy free parking for two hours to take in a movie, shop or dine at a restaurant, one of which is located in what was formerly the classrooms. Treat yourself to a nostalgic walk through the entrance of the barracks and read its history and see a photograph of Tom Molloy leading a squad of marching probationaries. Another photograph, taken in the 1930s, shows a lineup of 40 lance-carrying mounted policemen in full dress uniform. Best of all, the complex is named and known as The Barracks. This name is important to all those older officers who passed through its gates in that it helps us to reach back through the mists of time and place a hand on the shoulder of our youth.)

Looking back, those Depot days were the springtime of my life. Young, healthy and full of life, why would I want to think ahead to when I would be in my 70s? If only we had been paid a fairer wage for routine duties that consisted of processing correspondence, filing and conducting tests for recruitment. Two nights a week we attended the technical college at the end of George Street for typing lessons, from which we were exempted only when we reached a speed of 35 words per minute. I became a competent touch-typist.

When I joined as a cadet, Tom Molloy was a probationary and even in that capacity he was then bellowing drill instructions to fellow recruits under the watchful eye of Sergeant Day. He shouted the same instructions at me when I became a probationary for three months.

Finally, on Monday, 4 June, 1951, Probationary Donald John Braithwaite was sworn in as a Constable, Registered No. 5176.

A group of us was inducted by Commissioner Smith in his office in what is now the Treasury Casino. Policing had to be important, I thought, because we had to take an oath to carry out our duties properly. Journalists, company directors and public servants are not oath-bound.

The following Monday saw me starting work as a clerk in the inspector's office in Townsville. The police station was a rambling old wooden structure with first-storey barracks housing some 30 men. We had our own mess. Country officers found a bed there when they came in on escort duties. Once again I was in accommodation that was not too flash. Using lockers, I boxed off a room for myself at the end of a veranda enclosed on two sides with glass louvres. In heavy rain a mist of moisture settled on my bedclothes. The absence of fans (forget about air-conditioning) left us to face the brunt of stifling days and nights in summer. But the short winters were delightfully benign.

We were always on call. One late afternoon a shark found a hole in the netting of a swimming enclosure on The Strand and dragged a struggling man out to sea. We were called to walk the shore until we found the body washed up with a leg missing.

When the inspector's office ran out of filing space, my task was to make room by destroying old records dated back to the 1880s. How interesting to read some of those old reports with their handsome copperplate writing, but how sad that part of our recorded history was burnt.

While in Townsville I married a Mackay girl, Pam, and 57 years later we are still together. We had three sons and have been grandparents 10 times over and now we are great-grandparents.

By 1955 I recognised the need to enlarge my police experience beyond office work. Also, we wanted to set up a home in Brisbane. My application to perform general duties at Roma Street Police Station was approved and I began duty there in April. But after only six weeks I found myself in the Communications Section of the Criminal Investigation Branch – an old converted church at the corner of George and Elizabeth streets. This section was the 24-hour nerve centre of police operations in Brisbane, with a very busy switchboard receiving all manner of complaints and information.

The Communications Section was built around the radio system that controlled all those cars connected to it. The section was always overhung with an atmosphere of urgency, with its constant chatter of typewriters, endless flow of reports and the ongoing static-ridden radio exchanges. I enjoyed my time there.

In March 1956 I was appointed a plain-clothes constable in the Brisbane Criminal Investigation Branch and posted to the Company Squad (now Fraud Squad). Fortunately, I was paired with the officer in charge, Detective Sergeant Allan Duncan. There were no training courses, as such, in those days and you had to learn on the job. You adopted those police practices that you thought worthwhile and discarded those with no merit. In these circumstances, the quality of the senior partner was very important for a young officer learning the ropes. My good fortune was to be paired with some outstanding police officers – Don Becker, Jim Voigt, Terry Lewis, Gerry Cremin and Ivan Clark.

Let me outline the working conditions and salaries of those times. The CI Branch accommodation and conditions in the 1950s and '60s were absolutely abysmal. Over many years a little old stone church in Queens Park had been resurrected, refurbished, restored, renovated and revamped for the purpose of providing working accommodations for more people than would have made up its original congregation. A modest wooden extension at the back housed the company and the car squads as well as providing a dining room and toilet block. The other squads and field staff members were crammed into little rooms carved out of the old church. One of those field staff detectives was Bill Hayden, the future Governor-General. The three inspectors and detective senior sergeant, plus the prosecutor, had to have their own offices. Clerks in the inspector's office found refuge in one corner. The Communications Section occupied another corner. Room had to be found for our old wooden lockers and space for a day room for assembly to hear the daily readout. Squeezed along one side was the very important Modus Operandi Section, with the Gazette Section beside it.

Another occupant was the occasional rat, which when baited died under the floorboards. It was an embarrassment to have a witness call to give a statement and have to explain to them the source of the dreadful smell.

We used trams and did a lot of walking because of the scarcity of transport. Besides one car used exclusively for night work, we had three cars, a utility and a motorcycle. Usually you booked a day ahead for the use of a vehicle.

Our pay was miserly. Married with three children and paying off a home, we lived from pay to pay, and even though in those days I was a non-drinker. Looking back I have to say that the Government and the public received a much higher level of good police service than they were prepared to pay for. Put it down to the dedication and sense of responsibility on the part of most officers. Almost all households were single income because wives were considered homemakers who should not work outside in the wider world.

During the 1950s the department employed a handful of policewomen – say five or six. Unsworn and in civilian dress, they were stenographers, assisted with shoplifters and gave care and comfort to female victims and children. Any thought of broadening their duties and responsibilities ran into a brick wall of tradition and male chauvinism that echoed those times, not just in the Queensland Police Force, but within the community as a whole. For example, if a government-employed female married, she was required to resign. The Whitrod administration later began to enlarge not just the role of policewomen, but also their expectations and promotional prospects.

After five years in the City CI Branch, I was assigned to the Fortitude Valley office so as to be afforded the opportunity to investigate a wider range of offences. This office was run by a cantankerous Irishman, Detective Inspector Ben McNicol, and staff numbers were 30. By this time my classification was detective senior constable.

In those times Queensland police officers were required to give all their evidence – no matter the length – from memory. Although one's notebook contained details of conversations and observations, an officer was not permitted to refer to them. I remember a flamboyant homicide detective sergeant, big Don (Buck) Buchanan, giving 95 pages of evidence from memory in a murder trial, but he took all the preceding week to learn it word perfectly.

If an officer got stuck for words in a witness box the magistrate or judge might permit a quick reference to his notebook to "refresh his memory", but there was to be no reading. The notebook had to be closed and put away. The requirement to memorise evidence gave rise to a stupid impasse: If an officer gave lengthy evidence, defence counsel would argue that at least part of it must be inaccurate or deliberately false because it was unnaturally word perfect and no-one could recall such a volume of detail with certainty. On the other hand, if the witness had to refer briefly to his notes, again false testimony would be suggested because a police officer was a professional witness trained to remember every little detail. Lawyers enjoyed an advantage with these specious arguments and had no wish to see the system changed.

In 1962 I caught up with a dodgy character who was wanted in Victoria for defrauding an old lady. Arrangements were made to extradite him and a Box Hill detective, Eddie Snell, came up to interview the offender and take him back. Eddie asked me to participate in the interrogation by contemporaneously typing a record of the interview while he asked the questions. A few weeks later I stood in a witness box in Melbourne and gave evidence about the interview procedure, identified the record of that interview and the signatures of those involved. It was all so easy. I dearly wished that the same processes were in place in Queensland.

When starting a shift on the Valley night wireless patrol with plain-clothes constable Warren Dinte one night in November 1962, little did I anticipate that 36 hours would pass before I went home. We were directed to take up with the Chermside police at Cash's Crossing regarding the rape of a 16-year-old girl by five men. One offender – Clarke – was detained at the scene. From Clarke we obtained the names of his four companions and with the help of other staff eventually we rounded them all up.

With Eddie Snell's record of interview still fresh in my mind, I decided to give it a go. After all, there were five separate interrogations to be undertaken as well as the five conversations involved in confronting the offenders with the victim. I knew Dinte to be a fast and accurate typist and he typed the 10 separate conversations contemporaneously while I conducted the interviews.

The five offenders appeared for committal hearings before the Chief Stipendiary Magistrate, Mr McKenna, who permitted me to read from the typewritten records, which were then admitted as exhibits. This was no real test for the new system, however, because none of the defendants was legally represented.

The Chief Crown Prosecutor, Mr Lloyd Martin QC, called me in for discussions about the oncoming trials in the Supreme Court. He proposed to present indictments on charges of rape. Mr Martin raised the matter of the method of my recording the interviews and I advised him of the Victorian experience. He suggested that I still memorise the evidence because defence counsel would certainly object to my reading the record, and most likely the presiding judge would sustain that objection. I respectfully and sincerely informed Mr Martin that I wished to make a determined attempt to read the records. He made it clear that it would be on my head, and although he would argue the issue for me, I should be mindful of the penalty for contempt of court. I must say that this advice worried me, so I contacted the Police Union, which said it would back me up if things went wrong.

The trials were held separately, the first being an indictment of rape against Clarke. Mr Justice Stanley presided over the hearing, which lasted four days. Mr Martin prosecuted and Mr Eddie Broad QC acted for the defence.

I was the first witness and although I strode purposefully forward to take the oath, I was quite apprehensive. Looking up at the gallery, I saw several detectives who were interested in my bid to read the record of interview. I gave introductory evidence and a few sentences leading into the facts. Then, turning to the judge, I explained the manner in which Dinte and I had recorded the evidence and asked permission to read from the typewritten record. Mr Broad was instantly on his feet and loudly objected, correctly pointing out there was no precedent. For some 10 minutes, argument was joined between His Honour and the two barristers. I felt trickles of sweat running down my spine. Justice Stanley then ordered, "Witness, carry on".

I gave a couple more memorised sentences and again halted. In an incredulous tone of voice, His Honour demanded, "Witness, is that all you can remember?". "Yes, Your Honour," I replied. "Should I give further evidence without reading from the record, I cannot swear as to the veracity of that evidence."

A deafening silence. The trickle of perspiration became a stream. Throwing up his hands in exasperation, His Honour scolded, "Then the witness will just have to read from the record".

During the following months all five offenders were found guilty and sentenced to imprisonment and the contemporaneous typewritten record of interview was quickly adopted throughout the State. No more would police officers have to walk the floor and memorise evidence until 2 o'clock in the morning.

In 1963 Commissioner Bischof, upon his return from an overseas trip, decided to start a section that dealt exclusively with problem children and the problems of children. He named it the Juvenile Aid Bureau and appointed Detective Sergeant Terry Lewis and policewoman Yvonne Weir to run it. The Bureau proved to be a big success because at that time police officers generally did not like handling cases involving juvenile offenders because they little understood the special procedures involved, or the workings of the Children's Court. They were only too glad to hand such cases over to the Bureau and soon there was a call for additional staff.

At that time I was still working at the Valley CI Branch, but again I was looking to widen my field of experience. Also I admired the work ethic and style of Terry Lewis. I applied for a vacancy and became the third member of the bureau, which was accommodated on the top floor of the old police headquarters.

I enjoyed the new position and after many years of night work I also appreciated a more regular home life. The bureau expanded rapidly and within a couple of years I became a detective sergeant second class and took charge of staff members handling cases on Brisbane's north side. An old friend, Boyd Barrett, ran the south side. All the staff were dedicated and hard working and this was a cheerful and contented bureau under the leadership of Detective Sergeant Lewis.

Although I held the Junior Certificate standard of education and performed well in internal police examinations, I felt the need to further my education. I was permitted to enrol as a miscellaneous student at the University of Queensland and attended night lectures to study Criminal Law. Then I became interested in speechcraft and for over two years attended weekly meetings of the Brisbane Toastmasters Club at the Canberra Hotel. Arising from this experience I gave several public lectures on the conversion of the pound sterling into decimal currency. The Commissioner heard about this and farmed out a number of speeches to me.

My supervisory role in the bureau called for ongoing involvement in personnel matters and it appealed to me to the extent that I decided to base my career in this field. In 1969 I enrolled at the Kangaroo Point Technical College to undertake a four-year course in personnel management, my Junior Certificate gaining me entry. The course comprised 17 subjects that demanded a weekly attendance of two nights – three nights in the final year.

Not long after I had enrolled, two staff members inquired what areas of study might be available to them with their scholarship (Grade 7) standard of education. I discussed their situation with the college principal, Mr Vowles. He was most cooperative and said that if a course catering specifically for police needs was drawn up, his college would make it available. Who could have anticipated that in implementing Mr Vowles' advice, I would eventually find myself holding a tiger by the tail.

Let me explain this by observing upon the standard of – and attitude towards – education in the Force in the 1950s through to the late '70s and its effect upon promotion. In the '50s, with a total strength of some 2500, only five or six men enjoyed a senior (Grade 12) education. Only one serving member (Bob Matheson) held a degree. But such a standard was in keeping, roughly, with the standard of education of the general population.

Promotion was based almost solely on seniority. Do your work (and some didn't always do much work) and pass the internal examinations on Law and Police Duties and with the attrition of time you were slowly – but surely – promoted. This system gave the average officer some sense of direction and a feeling of security in knowing that eventually he would become at least a sergeant. No demand was placed on an individual to face the challenge of external studies, to keep pace with what was happening in the field of education in the outside world.

Things began to change in the 1960s. First, the Department introduced various internal training courses that were held at Chelmer Police College under the direction of Inspector Barlow. Mockingly, the college became known as "The Charm School". Perhaps this training stoked a desire for further study in a few officers because some went about gaining their adult matriculation (and the right to university enrolment) by passing two senior subjects, one being English. A couple used adult matriculation to study for the Bar Board examinations to become barristers.

In another way I became part of this modest groundswell by developing a framework for a technical college course for all police officers, no matter their standard of education. I was an alien in such an endeavour, but brought together those who knew what they were about. Besides Mr. Vowles and his staff, Paul Wilson, a criminology professor, made a valuable contribution, as did Col Bevan, Chief Probation and Parole Officer. As things were coming together I enlisted the help of John Dautel, who worked in the Commissioner's Office, and Inspector Clifford, who was in charge of Probationary Training. Finally I approached Inspector Barlow, who suggested the title "Police Arts and Science Course".

I did not collaborate with the union, and looking back that might have been a mistake. Perhaps I sensed (correctly as it turned out) what would have been their displeasure for such a project.

At about this time a new Commissioner took over the Force. University educated, Ray Whitrod was experienced in policing and enjoyed an impeccable war record. I must say I welcomed the appointment.

By this time the proposed new police course was being given its finishing touches and I set about compiling a covering report. I wrote that the course represented a well from which any police officer could quench a thirst for further education if he/she were so disposed. In emphasising that the course should not be a prerequisite for promotion, the point was made that its merit could speak for itself in a Promotions Appeal Court. I was very mindful that there would be a widespread mind set against the course if it was made compulsory. The covering report was also signed by Dautel, Clifford and Barlow.

With Commissioner Whitrod's approval, the course was implemented. There was a rumble of discontent across the Force and immediately the shining star of new police thinking was named "The Art and Farts Course". The union called meetings of protest. I attended as many as I could to support the case, and although occasionally catcalled, mostly my views were received civilly because I argued that the course was not a prerequisite of promotion.

A pleasing number of officers took up the course, which was made available by classes in larger cities and also by way of correspondence. For the very keen student, an incentive was that upon completion the member became eligible for university enrolment.

With the course bedded down reasonably well, the Commissioner made one of his many bad decisions. He decreed that the course would be a prerequisite for promotion. His timing was terrible. Not only did Whitrod bring down ire on his own head, but as I was the author of the course, also on mine. The union believed itself and its members to be betrayed. The rancour that this decision engendered lingered for years. I felt the bitterness as old hard-headed policemen tried to come to terms with the awful fact that there would be no more promotion unless they bowed to the will of "the academics". One night, as I was leaving a class at Kangaroo Point Technical College, I encountered a detective I had known for a long time. Looking me in the eye he said, "Except for you, Braithwaite, I would now be at home with my family". These were distressing times that were brought about because two of my staff asked me to find an avenue of study for them.

In 1971 Commissioner Whitrod saw the need to establish a Planning and Research Section and selected Doctor Mal Colston to head it. He then seconded me from the Juvenile Aid Bureau to work with Colston and some months later we were joined by Senior Constable John Dautel. I gained useful knowledge in areas previously beyond my ken.

At that time Mr Harry Allsop, a Senior Lecturer at Brisbane Grammar School, had been appointed as the first Director of the Queensland Police Academy, which was to be opened at Oxley the following year (1972). Mr Allsop was ensconced in an office at Police Headquarters on the same floor as Planning and Research. In his preparation for the opening of the new academy, he had frequent recourse to our section's resources and we became friends. He asked if I would consider going to the academy with him when it opened. My answer was "yes", so he spoke to the Commissioner who arranged the transfer.

Upon the opening of the academy I took up duty with Sergeants Noel Dwyer and Yvonne Weir to lecture cadets on police subjects. Using eight civilians teachers, cadets were taken through to the end of Grade 12 when, if 19 years of age, they were sworn in.

The academy was opened too early, with frenetic construction still going on. We had to constantly improvise. While the police officers were used to performing in a circus, the civilians were restless. These hectic and trying times were made no better by the frequent appearances of Commissioner Whitrod, who was determined to micromanage his pet project. My disenchantment with the man and his inability to give the Force a unifying sense of purpose and direction deepened, until in mid 1973 I resigned to go to the Justice Department. Because it was well known that in earlier times I had been a strong Whitrod supporter, he took my resignation as a personal affront and demanded three months' notice. Of course he could do this legally, but the provision was never exercised in any other instance before or after my resignation.

Mr Whitrod's final act of spite was the action of a little man. How sad for the Force that someone who entered our service with such acclaim and promise delivered so little. Sure, he took on a difficult task to improve a fossilised organisation, but he lacked the patience, insight and finesse of a leader. At times his scorn for his Force was thinly veiled and he quickly lost its goodwill. He soured relationships with key personnel and too often his ham-fisted approach to relatively minor issues turned them into problems. But due credit to him for turning a modest groundswell in police education into a healthy wave for the future.

Becoming a probation and parole officer with the Department of Justice in 1973 saw my work purpose change from catching crooks to rehabilitating them. Col Bevan was my boss and I was impressed with the professionalism of my fellow workers as we operated out of the old Mansions building in George

Street. My police experience was a big help in handling cases, but the duties were not as challenging.

Twelve months later saw the opening of a State Ombudsman's office headed by Sir David Longland. Vacancies existed for two investigators and I was very pleased to be selected for one position. I found myself surrounded by lawyers. The work was rewarding and enjoyable and involved a deal of travel throughout the State. How I appreciated the luxury accommodation, the good pay and working conditions. I worked there for seven years and was promoted to executive officer.

In 1981 Commissioner Terry Lewis asked me to consider returning to the Force and offered me the position of senior police officer at the Queensland Police Academy on the rank of inspector. I ran the figures on pay and superannuation and found that the proposition would involve considerable financial disadvantage. I declined the offer.

Some three months later the Commissioner renewed the offer, saying he wanted a person with police experience, but with a balancing perspective of community needs and expectations that could be instilled in the academy students. This time I accepted the offer.

My return to the Force on commissioned rank raised some talk because it was such a rare event. The academy director was a retired army man, Colonel Jock Jenvey. Wayne Bennett was in charge of the physical training program and one of his constables was Mal Meninga. The original cadet system that was in play when I left the Force in 1973 had been replaced with probationary training.

I found that in my absence the organisation had changed for the better. Certainly it was a happier place and ongoing training and study was an accepted part of life.

Mindful of the Commissioner's interest in the needs and expectations of the community and their application to police training, I thought about conducting a public survey in these areas. I floated the idea with Mr Lewis and he approved.

Not having any expertise in this area myself I enlisted the aid of the academy's senior educationalists, Manuel Anthony and Frank Putland, and they worked tirelessly on the project. They made sure that the sample would be truly representative of all public voices. The survey enjoyed a public launch and some 3000 forms were sent out to the citizenry across the State. They were asked for their views on various aspects of policing, including police attitudes and behavior, and were invited to suggest the degree of emphasis to be given in a training program to their areas of concern and approbation.

The response was gratifying and the many answers and suggestions were collated and introduced into police training. We were able to identify the standing of the police in the community and work towards improving it.

I shared a long standing friendship with an Italian house painter named Lou Colavitti. He had spoken about some of his unpleasant experiences as a new migrant. Although some of these hurtful situations arose from racial intolerance, most were misunderstandings born of differences in language, culture and customs.

I discussed the situation with the director and suggested that a good purpose would be served by setting up a program that permitted a healthy understanding between police recruits and the various ethnic groups through personal contact and thoughtful communication. In 1982 a dinner was arranged at the Italian Club with the attendance of its members and our probationaries. Commissioner Lewis was there and gave enthusiastic support for the initiative.

Such was the success of that dinner that over the following 18 months we reached out to some 12 more ethnic groups in a similar manner. We would collect the stipulated cost of the meal from the recruits and staff members and pay up front. The Vietnamese community had no suitable venue of their own so we lent them the academy kitchens and dining room. What an occasion!! Over 400 people attended and as we ate the various courses of exotic food we were entertained by Vietnamese dancers.

The Department continues to hold an annual dinner to which is invited a wide range of ethnic groups. This interaction of police and community must add to an atmosphere of public tranquillity that is the hallmark of good policing.

In 1984 I was posted in charge of the Juvenile Aid Bureau as a detective inspector. Although staff numbers had risen to over 100, I felt that I had returned home. My nine months there was the happiest time of my working life. For me, new features of the bureau were the several suburban offices and a dedicated child abuse section.

I set time aside to personally interview every staff member. Treat people with respect and they will reward you with a store of goodwill and a happy working force.

Office statistics showed that a disproportionate number of Indigenous children were coming to notice. Hearing that a Sandgate detective, Bill Schofield, had done some work in this area, I asked him to become the Aboriginal Liaison Officer for the whole of Brisbane. Bill agreed and the community elders welcomed his appointment.

In November 1984 I was sent to the Australian Police College in Manly to undertake a Senior Police Officers Executive Course over four weeks. On the shores of Sydney Harbour I mixed with some 30 other police officers from all Australian States and New Zealand. The Governor-General was the guest of honour at the graduation dinner. For the purpose of rating students, class results were divided into thirds.

In January 1985 I was promoted to Assistant Commissioner (Personnel). Apparently all the study I had done in this area and the fact that I was graded in the top third of my class in Sydney carried the day for me.

Brian Stevenson became my personal assistant. The sergeant had been long involved in the field of police administration and I became his willing student. He knew every procedural requirement and steered me away from what was policy quicksand for the unwary.

Also available to me was a first-class Welfare Section headed by Inspector Bob Kirkpatrick. Just one case study tells of its worth: We flew a Cairns officer in the final stages of terminal cancer to the Royal Brisbane Hospital accompanied by his wife. Bob telephoned me at 5 o'clock on a Sunday morning to say the man was fading fast. Entering the hospital room I saw Bob holding a blood-stained bowl into which the patient strained to vomit. On the other side of the bed sat his wife, her face suffused with care and tenderness. As I stood at the foot of his bed, the poignant tableau before me graphically bespoke the extraordinary bounds of human experience in suffering, love and compassion. Bob had held the bowl all night. The poor man died within an hour of my arrival and Bob took the widow in hand to find accommodation and make funeral arrangements. Police welfare does not come better than this.

But there was one gap in our welfare service – the absence of chaplaincy. Following discussions with Father Wally Ogle, an Anglican priest, he agreed to become our first police chaplain, albeit an honorary one, because of the perennial budget restrictions that always plagued our badly underfunded department. Father Wally was a real self-starter and proved to be a huge success. He was very fond of police officers and their environment and spent more time with them than with members of his flock. Within six months we had chaplains representing the Anglican, Catholic and Uniting churches as well as the Salvation Army. These were quickly followed by appointments across the State. Father Wally had a lot to do with the setting up of the first Police Remembrance Day.

Alcoholism had always been a problem in policing. In earlier times the problem was swept under the carpet and remained hidden and untreated. Thanks to such people as Greg Hogan and Laurie Pointing, and the formation of a police group of Alcoholics Anonymous, the problem began to feel the benefit of the warming rays of honest disclosure.

I gave the AA movement my strongest support and attended a number of meetings and celebrations. Members saw that their department would no longer be coldly judgemental, rather understanding and helpful. In retirement Greg became an employee who travelled the State selling our message of trust and good intentions.

Maintaining a healthy level of morale is a major challenge for the Personnel portfolio so I travelled extensively. A 1985 trip took me to Croydon, where the hospital matron showed me an enlarged photograph of a policeman and his wife standing beside a newly turned grave. The scene poignantly depicted Constable and Mrs Hasenkamp at the burial of their 11-year-old son near Croydon in October 1893. The two sad faces remained with me and led me to ponder the injustice that the exploits of police pioneers had never been recognised because no-one had taken an interest in recording the 120 years of Queensland Police history. Upon my return to Brisbane I made a formal application to Commissioner Lewis to explore ways and means of writing the first comprehensive history of the Queensland Police Force. He approved the project.

Again I had bitten off more than I could chew. I knew nothing about the writing of history. Again I turned to other people for help. Les Padman, the owner of Boolarong Publications, provided me with the names of appropriate persons to help set up a committee, of which I became the chairman. I remain humbled by the wealth of assistance that was offered. The outcome of so much work was the writing of The Long Blue Line by Professor W Ross Johnston. My honour was to write the foreword. The turbulent whirlpool of the Fitzgerald Inquiry delayed publication until 17 July, 1992 when the Governor-General, Bill Hayden, publicly launched the book.

The Fitzgerald Inquiry into Queensland police corruption extended from May 1987 to June 1989. Over 238 days of public hearing, 339 witnesses were called to give evidence. I was the third witness and gave evidence regarding the processes of promotion. I had nothing to fear; my integrity was never questioned.

The frenetic first week of the Inquiry was an accurate harbinger of things to come. The Inquiry's blowtorch to the police belly was unrelenting. Newspapers had never reaped such dramatic headlines so easily; the public thirst for more revelations could not be slaked.

In the face of such an onslaught, police morale went pear-shaped and the standard of that morale was my personal responsibility. I travelled widely to give regular updates on what was happening. My constant refrain to all officers was "Sure, things are tough, but hang in there and do your job. We will come through all this OK. Things will get better".

But it took a long time to get better. For me, the nadir of all the ongoing misery was the standing down of Commissioner Lewis. I was awfully saddened. He had been a popular Commissioner, approachable, progressive and hardworking, with an achievement-studded career behind him. I very much valued his friendship and support for such worthwhile initiatives as the police history project and ethnic dinners. I am mindful of Shakespeare's melancholy observation that man's imperfections are engraved in brass; his virtues written on water. Thus it has been for Terry Lewis.

Mr Ron Redmond became Acting Commissioner and I was upgraded to Acting Deputy Commissioner. For some six weeks when the Minister and Mr Redmond were overseas I was Acting Commissioner. You could say, then, that I got to the top of the police tree, but in the taxing environment of the times it was a hollow honour, undeserving of exultation.

The workload of the four remaining senior officers (Ron Redmond, Terry McMahon, Allan Hilker and myself) was formidable. Four vacancies in the upper echelon were not filled during the Inquiry. I was responsible for three portfolios.

As the Inquiry ground to a close, the opportunity arose for me to draw some good from the ashes. I spoke to an old friend, Ron Richards, the managing director of the Queensland Courier Mail. I first knew him as a police roundsman. I pointed out that his paper had feasted for two years on the carcass of the Department. What about returning something positive by sponsoring a scholarship to send an officer overseas to study some particular aspect of policing? He agreed and the annual Courier-Mail Police Scholarship has been ongoing, with Sergeant Mark Lyell winning the $15,000 award in 2010 to study how police forces in the United States, Canada and the United Kingdom are using body-worn video.

At last the Inquiry closed down, its findings and recommendations made public. A police era had passed. Time for new blood. I was exhausted. I retired on my 58th birthday in 1989.

If asked if a particular personal experience left me with a lingering regret, it would be this. Like many police officers who have had a long affiliation with a typewriter as a tool of trade, I enjoy using words. Every year the London Home Office holds the Queen's Police Gold Medal Essay Competition. Any officer in the British Empire is eligible to compete and annually it attracts some 400-500 entrants. Having won second prize in 1969, I tried again in 1985. This time I slipped to third. So much for the adage "try, try, and try again".

Permit me a brief observation to bring this chapter to a merciful close. Policing is a most honourable profession in that it is the grassroots guardian of the public good. Today's fresh-faced young constables look back on my era as quaintly old-fashioned, little realising that one day they too will be viewed in the same light. Let them remember that the future is based on the past as each generation tries to build a better platform for the next. In this sense, today's police officers stand on old shoulders such as mine, peering into the future to identify the new challenges and opportunities that lie ahead. I wish them well.

How is this for disciplinary punishment - in 1872 at the hands of Sub-Inspector Clohesy:

Constable Egan fined £1 ($2) for allowing a prisoner to escape from the watch-house.

Constable Meade fined £2 ($4) for refusing to work in the stables.

Three constables fined £9 ($18) for disobeying his order not to be found "out of uniform at any time about the streets day or night".

Constable Fitzgerald fined £1 ($2) for neglect of duty in not bringing back his horse, which died out on patrol.

*The Long Blue Line,* W Ross Johnston, 1991 (p 30)

# Neville Bruce Travers-Jones

I was stationed at Biloela in Central Queensland, which was then situated within the large and sprawling Rockhampton Police District. Traffic Branch officers from that city carried out both motor vehicle and motorcycle patrols along the many hundreds of coastal and country roads and clocked up thousands of kilometres during the course of their duties. One such motorcyclist officer was Neville Travers-Jones. A feature of those days was the inappropriate technology available to all general duty police officers performing patrol duty in both remote areas and lonely and isolated country roads, particularly officers performing motorcycle patrols. When we look back on history and now realise the importance of "Work Place & Safety" legislation the mind boggles when we stop for a moment and reflect on officers such as Neville Travers-Jones and his numerous colleagues patrolling lonely stretches of highways such as the infamous "Marlborough stretch from Rockhampton to Marlborough and then on to the city of Mackay during the hours of darkness". Neville was a successful country and coastal police officer and when officer in charge managed his police stations with a high degree of efficiency. He was highly regarded by all members of the community and his fellow police officers, particularly his peers and subordinates. As a young woman, Pam Travers-Jones was employed as a non-sworn member in the Police Department and her experience in that field was an added bonus to Neville, particularly in Normanton where he was frequently absent from home in the course of his duties for lengthy periods. Since leaving the Queensland Police both Neville and Pam have become successful business people, still residing in the township of Bowen.

**Laurie Pointing**

# Neville Bruce Travers-Jones

I was born in Murwillumbah, New South Wales on 21 October, 1951. I was first out of a family of six. I was raised on my parents' small beef and dairy property in the McPherson Ranges of Northern New South Wales.

My father supplemented our income with timber cutting. It was a tough, primitive existence with no machinery, all done by hand, which was hard on my mother. By my eighth birthday I knew about handling stock in the mountains and how to swing an axe. I learnt how to drive wedges and break down a log for fence posts.

I attended small primary schools at Pumpenbil and Tyalgum, NSW. I attended Murwillumbah High School, graduating at the end of my fourth year with a NSW school certificate. I was 16 when I left school. I had performed strongly enough in science and agricultural science to receive an invitation to study at the Hawkesbury Agricultural College. All my mates had left school earlier, had jobs and money in their pockets. I decided I was finished for good with schooling and that it was time I made my way in the big world and earn some money for a change. It was a poor decision.

My world was restricted to the Northern Ranges of NSW. I knew nothing else. I gained employment as a stockman for a large cattle company in our area. I lasted about six months before injuring myself in a horse accident while showing off. I quickly discovered two things – stockmen don't receive sick pay and the money doesn't go far when young and unable to work. My mother suggested I look into a career with one of the military or police forces.

According to Mum you received your pay there even if you were sick or hurt and couldn't work. All your basic living costs were looked after and they fed you. I couldn't believe my ears, so with plenty of enthusiasm I applied to join the Air Force, Army and Queensland Police. The Police Force responded first and in no time I was called up for medicals, etc. in Brisbane. Before my 17th birthday I was accepted and commenced training as a Police Cadet at Petrie Terrace under the watchful eye of Sgt Tom Molloy.

I spent three years in the barracks. I was homesick for the bush and at times wondered what the hell I had got into. Our day would start at six in the morning with Tom bellowing over the public address system, "All cadets and all probationaries out of bed". This wake-up call was varied occasionally, generally after Tom was tired from a big night on rum at the Depot and had camped the night.

Urged on by the uniform staff at the front office, the wake-up call would be, "All cadets and all probationaries hand off – and on with socks". Once out of bed the panic was on to be shaved and dressed, with beds and room immaculately prepared for Tom's inspection at 7am Parade and inspection over, it was downstairs to the mess for breakfast. A contractor named Bushby ran the mess, with three or four ladies who worked for him preparing the meals. The tucker was filling, but dull and repetitive.

After breakfast we would change into our gym gear and run down to the gymnasium in Petrie Terrace. There would be a session of calisthenics, life-saving resuscitation drill and judo followed by a rough and tumble all-in version of basketball. A couple of mornings a week there would be swimming and life-saving training in the pool. We all had to reach bronze medallion standard. We were a fit-rough mob and injuries were frequent during our morning training sessions. After physical training there would be an hour in the classroom learning to type and fatigues around the barracks. Fatigues were general cleaning details, polishing brass door knobs around the barracks.

We would then have lunch at the mess or, if earlier, collect sandwiches and walk to our designated stations where we would perform clerical duties. My station was Traffic Headquarters in Herschell Street, Brisbane. I met Pam, my wife to be, at Traffic Headquarters where she was working as a typist. We worked to 5pm each day before walking back to barracks. The evening meal was served between 6pm and 7pm in the mess. There was limited choice and often the remains of lunch and breakfast were mixed together with gravy poured over the top to disguise the concoction. After our meal we had a few hours to ourselves for showering, washing, ironing, cleaning shoes and preparing our room for morning inspection.

Cadets could go on leave for a few hours at night. The procedure was to present yourself to the front desk neatly attired where a uniformed officer would book you out. You had to book back in by midnight and any late returns incurred a penalty detail arranged by Tom. Hazing among cadets was constant ,with a group of senior cadets making it their business to give new cadets a hard time. First-year cadets received constant attention, only easing when they moved into their second year.

Many left, unable to cope with barracks life, and I'm sure the hazing played a significant part in their decision to leave. The military had exactly the same problem in Duntroon and occasionally scored a bit of adverse publicity over the practice.

I was sworn in on 19 February, 1971 on the parade ground at the Police Depot, Petrie Terrace, and our brand-new Commissioner, Raymond W. Whitrod, officiated.

I became Constable Neville Travers-Jones, Registered No. 8177.

I was transferred to Woolloongabba Police Station and it soon became apparent I would have to buy a typewriter. I bought an old Royal for about $20. I was assigned to mobile patrols and quickly realised I would have to purchase my own revolver. I was struggling financially so the gun dealer had to search the bottom drawer for a weapon that was in my $30 price range. I ended up with an old .38 Webley revolver. It was so worn in the break-open pivot axle I had to aim off to the left to compensate for the trigger pressure pulling the barrel around to the right. The barrel was easy to clean because there was hardly any rifling left to collect any residue.

Features of my Brisbane service included the Springboks riots and the baton charge at the tower mill to clear rioters and protesters, three weeks' full-time duty at the morgue and qualifying for departmental motorcycles.

I was then transferred to Longreach where I performed general duties as a single constable. The barracks were new and first rate. Features of my Longreach service included attending some big blues with shearers and yard builders who were working in the area at the time. On my days off I jumped on a livestock truck when I could and travelled further out into the desert country.

I married Pam in 1972 and was transferred to Rockhampton. Like most newly- weds of the time we had no money and we were a long way from our families. No-one seemed to have any idea at Rockhampton station of my posting there so naturally no inquiries had been made for rental accommodation. Normally this was attended to properly, but somehow our case fell through the cracks in the system. We managed to find a little one-bedroom beach house with a back room, which we converted into our entertainment area. It had a dirt floor, which was handy on dart nights. If the dart fell out of the board it would fall to the ground tip first and dig in without any damage to floor or dart. Our little home was in a village called Zilzie.

Despite our poor accommodation and the 40-minute drive to and from the station we were happy. I served in general duties for a while before being appointed to a traffic position on motorcycles. In those days when you were assigned to the bikes you had your own machine and you rode it on duty, all weather, day and night. As it turned out, my patrol logs were checked for other reasons after I had left, and they showed I had logged just over a million patrol miles. I managed to survive without any sort of a prang, which was a bit of a record. We provided traffic enforcement to outlying stations and it was during this time I first met Laurie Pointing.

I had been directed by radio to intercept a suspected drug courier travelling from Biloela to Rockhampton. I made the intercept and shortly after the Biloela car with Laurie and another officer arrived and we carried out a search of the villain's van, recovering a small quantity of hashish.

Housing for constables in Rockhampton back then was a problem. Young married constables resorted to renting a house, then divided it in half and shared with another couple. With the strain of shiftwork, babies and babies on the way the stress was too great for many marriages.

Among the memorable features of my Rockhampton service was my time on the bikes. You worked alone, often a long way from any support and often out of radio range. What you started you had to finish. There were many occasions I was sent north late at night to investigate road accidents on the infamous Marlborough stretch. Generally these accidents were fatigue related and were either numberplate to numberplate head-ons or single-vehicle diversions into the scrub. Both types of accidents inevitably resulted in deaths or serious injury due to the high-impact forces of such accidents. We were generally first emergency unit on the scene.

We had no medical kit on the cycles and usually were out of radio range. When the ambulance arrived it was generally crewed by only one officer and we just muddled through the best we could. We had no training in serious road -accident investigations, nor did we have any equipment. I had my own small 10-foot tape and clipboard I kept in the panniers on the motorcycle. Any long distances were measured by pacing out and recording the steps as yards. This was the evidence we gave in court. Serious road-accident investigations during the '70s in major towns and cities were initially investigated by an experienced traffic officer.

He would concentrate on recording the visual evidence, the physics of pre-impact, impact and post-impact. His intimate knowledge of motor vehicles, motorcycles and equipment helped him greatly in determining whether or not any mechanical issue may have contributed to the accident. If he felt there was a mechanical issue that needed more attention it would be reported to the nearest police mechanic, who would carry out a full mechanical inspection of the vehicle. At this stage a member from the Criminal Investigation Branch would be assigned to the job and would liaise with the traffic officer and go over all information gathered so far. The CI Branch member would then move towards examining the level of criminality and negligence of people involved.

I was involved in a few jobs where firearms were being used by offenders. A District Court judge formally commended my actions on one job and made a recommendation to the Commissioner through my district inspector. Trouble was, at the same time Rockhampton-based barrister Robert Hall, who was representing the baddy, lodged a complaint about injuries I had inflicted on his client.

This job started off when a number of triple O calls reported shots being fired from a heavy-calibre weapon within a residence in the Lakes Creek area. I was on city motorcycle patrol at the time and was directed to attend. I was armed with my service revolver, a .38 Smith and Wesson Special. The difficulty facing all officers attending such calls is the lack of information. Have people been shot? Where is the gunman directing his fire? Where is the gunman firing from? How many gunmen are there? What weapon does he or they have and how skilled is he with it? Are hostages involved? How should I approach the address without becoming a victim myself? No tactical response groups back then. All these thoughts are rushing through your head while travelling at high speed to the job.

I parked my cycle a couple of addresses away from my objective then began the longest and loneliest journey that many police officers make. Leaving your vehicle and getting to the front door of the baddy's house over open ground is where you are most vulnerable. If bravery is to be spoken of, this is the point where the pucker factor is up in the 10's. I slipped in through the open front door and started moving quietly from room to room in the house. All was quiet. The Lakes Creek car had responded to this call as well and I knew I would have another officer on the scene soon. I found a woman and young girl hiding under a bed, the baddy's wife and daughter as it turned out.

They were terrified and unable to speak. I kept moving through the house towards the back room. The house was a high-set, three-bedroom weather-board with the kitchen and dining room at the back of the house. I was a few metres from the dining area moving down the hallway when I saw the gunman. He was sitting in a chair at the dining-room table with a .303 jungle carbine levelled at a young man seated across from him facing my direction of approach.

As I moved closer the gunman started to rise slowly out of his chair. He was still unaware of my presence and started to aim his rifle at something outside. I could see the weapon was cocked and his finger was taking pressure on the trigger. At that moment I saw the subject of his attention was the constable from Lakes Creek coming through the back yard. I put my finger to my lips signalling to the hostage to be quiet as I came into his view. Well, that didn't work. His head shot up and his eyes opened as wide as saucers, giving the gunman all the warning in the world that someone was behind him. In a flash he was on his feet and spinning around to meet me, trying to bring his weapon to bear.

No bravery here, just bucketloads of fear and the animal instinct of survival. I moved fast into him and smashed the weapon into his face, stunning him and causing him to lose his grip on the rifle. I managed to wrestle the rifle from him, then I handcuffed him. At no time did I draw my weapon and to this day I think how stupid that was. What was the point in the Department ever issuing me with one if I didn't use it on this occasion? Good question. I think the answer lies in the fact that all police instinctively try to preserve and protect life, not take it. They may not want to go on about it too much, but their whole being is to help others, and in some instances it is tested to the extreme.

Big dilemma for the Police Force was do we decorate the constable or charge him. I had my problems as well. I had very little service and no money. I had a barrister talking about a civil action he was going to take against me to cover his client's medical and dental expenses. My employer seemed to be ready to carry out their investigation when I felt they should have been backing me to the fullest. Both sides went back to their corners and took no further action. I served in Rockhampton from 1972 to 1979. Our first child was born and Pam had stopped working. I had to get a second job, but permission was still required upon application and usually was denied. My only option was to join the Army reserve. I served two years in the 42nd Royal Queensland Regiment as a mortar gunner.

My next station was Tully, a six-man station as I recall, with one Criminal Investigation Branch officer. Sometime around this period my registered number changed to 2133. The station was the poorest building I had ever seen the police use for that purpose. From memory it seemed to have been an old dwelling cut in half. Somehow we squeezed in there, with exhibits and lost property stuffed into cupboards and corners. Tully is one of the wettest centres in Queensland, which didn't help the old building. Structurally it was unsound, the roof leaked in a number of places and in heavy rain water used to pour down through some of the lights mounted in the ceiling. The building was eventually condemned by the council.

Russ Hinze, who had relatives in the area, called in one day unofficially to look at our working conditions. Well, the rockets went up then – he abused the local member in front of three of us on duty at the time and said our conditions would be changing immediately and they did. An old council building was renovated nearby and we moved into much better circumstances. Career-wise Tully was an important stepping stone for me. The one and only detective was limited in what he could achieve on his own without a collaborator. I was fortunate to work with Peter Pascoe, one of the best detectives around.

He was patient enough to pass on his knowledge and investigative skills to me, which served me well for the remainder of my career.

We had two young children to support now and it was necessary to get a second job. I had no problem getting work on my days off on banana plantations in the area. I didn't worry about approval from the police this time round. My Tully service broadened my knowledge and skills in criminal investigation work. I passed promotional exams for the rank of sergeant and started thinking about applying for officer in charge positions.

While stationed at Tully I was involved in another incident with an offender playing with guns. Late one afternoon I was on general patrol with a junior constable when we were directed by radio to intercept a vehicle containing a male offender who had fired a number of shots at a residence in the Tully rural area. This was a domestic that had escalated to a point where a young man had completely lost control, armed himself, then set about terrorising his in-laws and other relatives. Once again the information was sketchy. We knew shots had been fired from a heavy-calibre weapon by one gunman and that he was travelling in a Ford Falcon sedan.

At that stage we did not know who he was and whether anyone had been killed or injured. More information over the radio advised us the offender was likely to drive to a location west of Euramo. Night had fallen as we drove steadily up a dead-end road leading up to Tully River Station. The gunman took us by surprise about 20 kilometres up this road. He must have been watching our approach and accelerated his car out of a side track in front of us, blocking the track. He jumped out of his vehicle with a 30.06 rifle and a 12-gauge shotgun. He took aim at us with the rifle using his vehicle for cover.

We braked and scrambled out of our patrol car the best we could, taking cover behind it. The range was probably about 25 metres and we were only armed with our personal issue weapon, the .38 Smith and Wesson Special. The .223 Ruger rifle issue was still some time off. The baddy called out for us to back off or he would kill us. He then said he was going to sool his pig dog on to us. By this time my pucker factor was about seven and rising. We were hopelessly outgunned and the future looked bleak.

He opened the car door to release the dog. My partner, Gerry Hibbard, and I had a quick conference and decided I would try and shoot the dog if it advanced and he would engage the gunman while I moved to a better position for a shot at our man. To our relief the dog raced out of the car, down the little gully nearby and had a huge pee. Poor bugger had probably been holding it for hours. At this point I thought I would try a bit of bluff. In a loud authoritative voice I called on our man to drop his weapons, step away from his vehicle and he would not be harmed.

I was in for another surprise when he replied: "Is that you, Neville? I've had a beer with you with my Uncle John at the Lower Tully pub. I know you are a battler and do extra work to look after your family. You back off, I don't want to kill you." A glimmer of hope. I still didn't have a clue who he was, but I felt there was a chance we might get out of here without loss of life or injury. We slowly got back into our police vehicle, keeping our weapons trained on our man and reversed out of there in retreat.

But the problem hadn't gone away. We met Detective Pascoe and Mick Smith, our officer in charge, further down the road and set up a roadblock. I think Peter and Mick might have brought their own long arms with them. A short time later our baddy approached in his vehicle and was stopped by our block. I remember well even now how annoyed I was with myself for not having resolved this problem earlier further up the track. Now more people were involved, with the potential for death or injury rising. No bravery here, just absolute anger and frustration.

I was going to finish this one way or another right now. As our man stopped, my mates aimed their weapons. I left my pistol holstered and approached the gunman. I remember saying: "This has to finish now, either way we are going to leave here together." He said: "I've got a rifle pointed at your guts, I'll shoot you through the door." He certainly had the weapon pointed at me, with both hands holding the rifle. I simply reached in the window, turned the ignition off and pocketed his keys.

I told him it was over and slowly reached in and took the rifle from him. He offered no resistance. I think he was glad it was over as well as we were.

The weapon was cocked and loaded. We found a considerable supply of ammunition and some food in his car. I think things went very close to going bad. I was commended again and this time the recommendations passed through the system. The Commissioner responded with a commendation. A few months later I was decorated by the Queen during her visit to Australia for the Commonwealth Games.

In 1983 I moved on promotion to Normanton as officer in charge. Normanton was in the Mount Isa District. I was 31 years old, which wasn't bad progress for an operational officer back then. I had 30 days to move after official notification of my transfer. In that time I had to clear any bills I had around town, buy a reasonable four-wheel-drive vehicle that would get me there and buy additional refrigerators and freezers necessary to handle bulk buying. We had to carry sufficient food to carry us through difficult wet seasons. We had prisoners to feed as well as ourselves.

Our children had to be kitted out with new school uniforms and books. I took three weeks leave before I moved and worked full-time on a cane farm in the area. This brought in enough money to cover all the above. A dislocation allowance was paid, but could only be described as a small supplement for anyone transferring over long distances. The wear and tear on furniture from constant moving was severe and it paid to own strong, durable furniture.

Serving as officer in charge in the remote regions of Queensland has its own unique challenges. I think it would be fair to say, "You will finish your tour of duty a changed man". I found I became independent and confident in my ability to command my patch. I was intolerant of nonsense policies and tomfoolery that flowed out the backroom of some district offices. My views on policing and commitment narrowed down to looking after the community I served. Somewhere along the line while serving in O/C positions I found I was moving in a different direction in policing to that of the service. This little section on my career and that of other officers who served in places such as Burketown, Arakun and Kowanyama could be worthy of a book, and some day someone will write one.

The accommodation in Normanton was disappointing in every respect. The residence for the officer in charge was an old Queenslander with a fully screened veranda. It would have been a good home in its day. However, time and a harsh climate had taken their toll. The cracks in the walls were so wide I could look through them from the comfort of my lounge room and watch fights developing outside the Central Hotel.

Normanton Police Station, September 1973. *Queensland Police Museum.*

When the hot westerlies were blowing, the salt and sand off the salt pans would blow straight through the walls and into our house. We had to battle for almost a year to get ceiling fans. Bureaucracy had decreed we lived on the coastal strip and did not rate fans. It was understood by Q-Build, or whatever they were called then, that Normanton's average summer temperature was just behind Marble Bar. This made no difference at all to the score.

Our district officer wasn't particularly interested in pursuing the nonsense. Pam won the day, however, when she invited the housing chief over for lunch when he was doing his six-month visit. Pam cooked up a big baked dinner and sat the chief down in the kitchen while she cooked. When I arrived home for lunch I saw an overweight public servant red in the face and fairly dripping with sweat. Q- Build couldn't change the coastal policy; it was just too hard. Our lunch guest jockeyed with funding for electrical repairs, which just happened to cover the cost of installing ceiling fans the following month.

The police station was in a light pre-fab modular complex we shared with the courthouse, the Aboriginal and Island Affairs Office and the Department of Primary Industries. The police office had no secure interview room and every interview that was conducted during office hours was shared with the Aboriginal and Islander Affairs Office. Fortunately for the police, the manager and his staff were on side and understood the difficulties we faced policing Normanton.

The watch-house and gaol section was probably a hundred years old and I'm sure was on the Historical Register. What a hopeless show if there was a death in custody within these walls: An inquiry would have knuckled a few heads, including mine. There were always plenty of guests in the watch-house and gaol section. I had to take some unusual measures to reduce the chance of a prisoner becoming depressed and hanging himself. I won't go into detail here, but it worked for the three years I was there.

Our patrol vehicle was a short-wheel-base Toyota four-wheel-drive. It was well equipped with a winch, high-frequency radio and security cage. They were as rough as guts and a trip to Mount Isa or Kowanyama would leave you with sore kidneys and back for days. These vehicles were air-conditioned and when the service re-equipped with the long-wheel-base models we had a very good patrol vehicle indeed. Normanton had only one police vehicle and it became necessary to use my own vehicle on many occasions for police work. The division was about half the size of Victoria, which caused us to be away for days on a specific job or on patrol. This left the other officers in town without a vehicle, which of course was not acceptable.

A feature of my Normanton service was the isolation from any back-up. What you started you had to finish and win every time. We managed our own criminal and stock investigations; we also covered our prosecution and training needs for the young constables.

I worked with Nardoo Burns, the last of the old Aboriginal police trackers. The courage and loyalty this old fellow displayed to Normanton officers was commendable. Recognition of his outstanding service to the Queensland Police Force was acknowledged by the Commissioner of Police. I worked with Nardoo in stock investigations and on searches for people lost or injured in the bush. We also hunted criminals who were on the run and on foot in the bush doing their best to evade police. Some were armed and I had complete confidence in my tracker to cover me if we came under fire. Nardoo was armed on these occasions with a heavy-calibre rifle and was a crack shot. He was a competent horseman and we spent days in the saddle on searches and stock investigations.

There is not enough room here to cover Nardoo's gift in tracking. The best I can do is sum up his ability in this way. Nardoo was born and raised at a time when his tribe would still go on walkabout and live off the land. When they were working on cattle stations such as Inkerman, Dorunda and Dunbar the job of moving the station's horses back to higher ground during the wet was left to them. Naturally Nardoo had an intimate knowledge of the country. He knew where to get tucker and which country was to be avoided during the wet when moving stock.

Nardoo Burns

He knew all the trees, where they grew and their uses in the bush. What singled Nardoo out from other Aborigines who could track were his spiritual powers to foresee where the person we were looking for would go. If the person being pursued was an Aborigine who knew Nardoo and in turn was known to him then things would get easier. Nardoo seemed to be able to get into their heads and after a couple of days they would just give up. The first thing the offender would say would be something like, "I knew Nardoo was after me, I felt it yesterday, so I reckon I better just sit down and wait for you".

I will describe one particular stock job we carried out on Miranda Downs where Nardoo's abilities were used and how it all can be tied into a good brief of evidence. The manager of Miranda rang me one morning and said a large mob of cattle he had been holding in reserve had been stolen. He reported he had last seen the cattle a fortnight earlier. The mob was 2000 in number, made up of breeders with calves at foot, herd bulls and steers ranging from two to five years of age. All the calves were unbranded and there were a number of cleanskins with this group. All breeders, herd bulls and steers were branded and had been mustered at the close of mustering the year before.

I knew the manager and I accepted his complaint as genuine. An immediate response by police on this complaint was necessary because there was a fair chance the offenders were still working in the area midway through the commission of the offence of stealing these cattle. Mareeba stock squad was still looking after our area at this time and I contacted them immediately. After a lot of messing around and phone calls, it became clear the stock squad wouldn't be looking into this job for some time.

I gathered a small team together for this job – Dick Arnold, a young DPI stock inspector, Nardoo and myself. We packed some gear and kicked off our investigation the following day. The missing cattle had been gradually moving out of the scrub as water dried up. The country was strong and had a good water point, which eventually became the last decent water for cattle on this run.

The station manager had been watching this mob come together over the preceding months and monitoring the condition of the fats. He decided on a date to muster and had booked trucks for the stores. On muster day he sent his stock team, horses and supply truck out in advance and a couple of hours later he followed in the muster chopper. He flew over his team en route to the southern waterhole. Five minutes later he was looking out over the plains where this mob had been grazing and to his amazement there was not a beast in sight. He made a brief search of the area in the helicopter and later found a bullock stressed and pretty knocked about. Horse and motorbike tracks were visible and he became convinced a crew had come into his country and cleaned him out completely. He rang the police for assistance and offered any resource we might need.

It didn't take us long to determine the complaint was genuine and that a large mob had indeed been mustered and driven off their run. For three days we followed the path of this mob through poor tea-tree country, heading in the direction of a cattle station called Clotilda. We struck a section of boundary fence that marked the boundary of Strathmoor and Miranda Downs. The gang we were tracking used this section of fence to lean on with the cattle.

It became evident they were having trouble pushing cattle out of good country into bad with no water. There was evidence everywhere of bulls being thrown, tied, then winched up on to vehicles. Poddy night yards in the form of wire netting strung between trees were scattered along the herd's passage throught the tea-tree. We recorded and photographed all this as we went. Finally the trail ended at a newly built set of timber yards and nearby holding paddocks. The yards were well built and had been extensively used, with bulldust about a foot deep throughout. Nardoo was particularly useful at this point of the investigation.

As we examined the yards and surrounding area for evidence, we were able to learn much about what had occurred at these yards. We learnt the timber for these yards was not from the Clotilda area. We found where someone had dropped a killer and blooded him in the yards. The butchering occurred a short distance away under a tree. We were able to draw a clear picture on how the mob was broken down into smaller mobs for drafting and finally for trucking out. Our knowledge was so complete that when we eventually started interviewing some of the ringers involved in this job, they became convinced we somehow had them under observation the whole time. This would not have been possible without Nardoo's involvement. This investigation carried on for a long time with some arrests being made.

Ron Odgers wrote a song titled "Nardoo Burns", a song about this wonderful old man, which is sung by the late and great country music singer Slim Dusty. It is recorded on Slim's CD Coming Home.

Time for a little war story from the Gulf. For some reason a big mob of Aborigines from Doomadgee moved into Burketown for the weekend. The officer in charge of Burketown told me he expected plenty of trouble and asked if my crew would be in a position to provide back-up if needed. We were having our own problems at the time. The stock camps had just shut down for the wet and everyone was back in town with heaps of money and a big thirst.

I was monitoring the high-frequency radio as best I could, in case Burketown called for help. The district officer had been alerted and apparently was keeping watch as well. Later during the evening I heard the Burketown O/C broadcast over the air that he and his constable had withdrawn from the street and taken refuge in the station. He said they were under pressure from a large mob of Aborigines armed with spears and fighting sticks and they required assistance. Mount Isa replied, "You are not alone, Sergeant, we are supporting you and monitoring the radio". Then an unidentified voice replied over the radio, "Well I hope you blokes are armed, that should help a bit".

I suspect it was Borooloola police who made this call. Six months later at a barbecue I tried to get some admissions from them, but they wouldn't wear the allegation at all.

During my tour of duty in Normanton I had a particularly interesting job helping the director of the International Crane Foundation, Professor George Archibald, find some missing cranes. This job came to me in the form of a Ministerial file directing me to assist George, a United States citizen, in his mission to locate these birds. Probably the main thing I had to do was to see that nothing unpleasant happened to the professor while he wandered around the wetlands of the Gulf on his quest.

Briefly the background to this story is the Thai Royal Family asked the International Crane Foundation for assistance in finding out why the Eastern Sarus Crane had pretty well disappeared from South-East Asia. They wanted to know where they had gone and, if possible, wished to re-establish them back home. They had disappeared from Thailand, the Philippines, Vietnam and Cambodia sometime during the late '50s, early '60s.

George established that high human populations, along with social disruptions and war, had been responsible for their demise. What George didn't know was where they had all gone. He followed up a hunch he had developed when reading a article written by some chap studying the brolgas on the Gulf wetlands of Northern Australia. This particular article was describing the visual difference between a male and female brolga and how they mate for life. George felt this fellow could be mistaken and what he was actually describing as the coloured features of the female brolga belonged in fact to an Eastern Sarus Crane.

A few days after I received this file I saw this man striding down towards the police station with cameras and bags hanging off him everywhere. His dress was different to anything I had ever seen before and I had a feeling I was about to meet the professor I was supposed to take care of. It didn't take long for us to get acquainted and George got down to business straight away. He asked Pam if she would mind looking after all his money, travel arrangements back to the US and any correspondence that came to hand while he was out bush.

Pam agreed and George promptly handed over his moneybelt full of travellers' cheques, US and Australian dollars as well as his passport. When George described the birds he was looking for and showed me a photograph of one of them, I told him I thought there were plenty of them hanging around the flood plains between Normanton and Karumba. I told him that I always believed this pink-legged, red-necked bird was a female brolga. I had to drive up to the Karumba station and asked George along. I took Nardoo along as well, just in case our professor suddenly had the urge to go for a walk in the bush.

On the way up to Karumba we saw brolgas on the plains doing their meeting dances in the rain that was now falling quite heavily. Suddenly, I had three big red-necked brolgas walk out of the long grass and across the road in front of me. The professor corrected my observation by exclaiming, "Goddam, I have found my Sarus Cranes". With that sighting George was out of the vehicle in a flash. I left him and Nardoo wandering around the wetlands in the rain while I continued on to Karumba.

I later made arrangements to settle George on Delta Downs cattle station, a property owned by the local Aborigines, so he could carry out his studies and search for nests and eggs. I arranged for an Aboriginal local, Roy Beasley, to be George's minder, with instructions never to leave his side. George Archibald's mission was successful and he subsequently moved eggs from Australia to his headquarters in the US. The chicks hatched successfully and the Eastern Sarus Crane was slowly re-established back into Thailand under the protection of the Royal Family.

Two years was the normal tour of duty in places such as Normanton. It took me three years to get out and by that time I had had enough. The Department, to their credit, allowed isolation leave with free air travel for police and their families serving in remote areas. This concession was both generous and important for the welfare of these people. The Department also had a policy of offering O/Cs a choice of the cream stations in nice, quiet areas. I was offered a choice of three two-man stations at the time and I chose Giru. The transition from Gulf service to the quiet lifestyle of Giru was good therapy for all of us. It was good to see our kids going off to a normal school. They made plenty of friends and became involved in team sports. The police house and station were excellent quarters. The watch-house was perfect for storing horse feed, which is what I used it for. I figured my horses had served the Police Force well for two and a half years at my expense so it was time the Department responded by supplying storage for their lucerne hay.

I have been regularly asked over the years why I had to use my own horses in the Gulf when the Police Force owned horses and what did I use them for. I had not been in Normanton long before it became obvious we were going to have to manage stock investigations in our division ourselves. If you can't ride a horse and you don't have access to one then you don't have that option. I could ride and I did have marginal access to horses if I borrowed them off properties. We did borrow some for a while, but most stations took advantage of the situation and lent us horses that hadn't been handled or ridden for years.

I suppose they figured it was a reasonable trade. We break and handle their horses for them as payment for the use thereof. We had horses standing on their heads trying to tear the girth off with their teeth, throwing themselves upside down when one tried to tighten their girth. This sort of thing can be a lot of fun for a bunch of young blokes messing around in a good set of yards. We didn't have the yards, and while we were young enough we didn't have the time for messing around breaking horses in the scrub. We were working trying to get a job done quickly and quietly so we didn't fizz up the cattle we were checking. Try checking brands of cattle and recording same in your official police notebook while your mount is doing his best to get rid of you. The other problem is the gulf run is big country and the heat excessive. You need fit, strong horses with good endurance, regularly fed on good feed and in work.

The stock squad horses I saw certainly didn't fit the bill and cattle properties were never going to lend us such animals. There were a number of occasions where horses and good horsemen were needed in searching for people lost in the bush. Some of these people were young Aboriginal stockmen who had gone into the horrors. This was caused from prolonged excessive drinking then going out to the properties to work after going cold turkey off the grog. From a medical point of view I have no idea why all the demons would visit these unfortunates and send them clean off their heads. There were three such cases while I was in Normanton and all occurred out on stations.

One was found dead on the third day, having run off from a stock camp late one afternoon. He died of thirst basically 10 metres from a waterhole that would have been clearly in his view if he was of sound mind. The second was found the day after he had run off. He was near death, wearing no clothes and suffering from a multitude of cuts and abrasions from running into barbed-wire fences and other obstacles. I interviewed three other ringers who were with this fellow during the day he ran off. They stated he came out from town on the mail truck two days before and seemed all right. The day he went off his head they had pushed some strangers (cattle belonging to another property and caught up in the muster, cut out during drafting for collection by the owner) out into a cooler paddock and had then done a couple of hours' light yard work.

Just before lunch, after they had cleaned up, they noticed their mate was sitting on a log about 30 metres away from the camp. He had removed his shirt and boots and seemed to be twitching about, shaking his head and talking to himself. They had lunch, but he didn't join them and ignored calls to come and eat. Suddenly, without warning, he let out a loud howl and ran flat out towards the scrub. On his way he ran headlong into a four-strand barbed-wire fence. The impact threw him back over on to his back. He got up and just dived through the fence and ran off into the scrub faster than they thought it possible for anyone to run. When this sort of thing happened out in the Gulf, the stations had to stop work and put in a big effort to search for the missing man. Woe betide any police or cattle station that didn't put in a maximum effort to find an Aboriginal stockman gone missing; you could guarantee making page one.

The third fellow was luckier in that when he ran off he had been acting a bit strangely for some hours and his mates were keeping a bit of an eye on him. When he bolted the head stockman and his offsider were nearby on horseback. They rode the man down, tackled him and tied him up. The flying doctor took him out later that evening. This seemed to work well and it became standard practice to have mounted men in the search for such men.

A person in the horrors is difficult to track and find even if you have a tracker like Nardoo with you. There is not much time in which to find these fellows alive. The clock is literally ticking the instant your man runs off. Generally he will be running flat out, changing directions at random and diving behind logs and bushes, hiding from the demons, which could in fact be some of the people in the search party. They don't follow tracks, roads or watercourses, but just run completely out of control. Trouble is, they are burning up large amounts of energy and perspiring heavily.

Dehydration rapidly moves in and it is no consolation that the man is in well-watered country. His brain won't tell him he needs to drink or rest. He will continue on his mad journey until complete physical exhaustion and dehydration brings him down. It gets harder then, because the search party is looking for a person down and not moving. Mounted men are essential at this stage. Motorbikes are often used, but are a poor substitute. A mounted man naturally has a better view from his higher position and is free to use his hearing and eyes to search for his quarry. His horse will take care of looking for the best course to travel. A motorcyclist does not have a commanding view, he can't hear anything and most of his eye scan is used to watch where he is going. The motorbike is quite happy to continue straight on into a stump or ant hill, where a horse will make every effort to step around such obstacles. Thus the need for a couple of good horses.

Our house at Giru was an old weatherboard high-block home, well built and maintained. The house was battened in down below, all cement floor and lock-up carport. There were no ceiling fans again because we were in the coastal strip, just like Normanton. The police station was air-conditioned and well appointed.

Giru community was a very pro-police town, with Townsville close by if support was needed. We were happy there, but eventually I had to consider moving on to higher rank. Our children were in their final years of education. Our daughter, Sonia, was at James Cook University and our son, Kevin, in his last years of high school.

Among the features of my Giru service were handling major flooding of the township and surrounding areas, with a category two cyclone thrown in for good measure. The town was inundated on eight occasions during a six-week period. It is during these sorts of prolonged major incidents where officers in charge work around the clock until the emergency has passed. Their wives man the phones and radio, providing a communication base for their husbands as well as running the home.

It was soon after this spate of bad weather in the Townsville district that a conference was convened to look at the high cost in manpower to manage these prolonged weather events. A portion of the conference was devoted to looking at the age-old problem of O/Cs and their wives giving 150% in working hours.

It was noted they had worked hours well above any remuneration or benefit from the Force. There has never been any disagreement on the commitment to service given by these people. There has never been any doubt on the degree to which communities rely on these officers and their wives. It was around this time that the time and motion experts had examined the service and among many other revelations concluded that the level of responsibility of O/Cs often equalled, or exceeded, that of many inspector positions. Corporate management of any large organisation faced with such information would have to take positive steps to address such imbalance to gain legitimacy in the area of Human Resource Management.

The conference turned out to be a round-table event where the issues just went round and round. I would not be surprised to learn that after all these years this anomaly still exists. The second feature of my service in Giru was the downfall of Commissioner Lewis and associates. Morale among country police dropped to rock bottom and was probably no better in Brisbane. Some of the brightest constables I had trained and worked with left the Force in disgust. I was stunned by the revelations pouring out from the media and the loss of good men leaving the service. I began to realise how naïve I really was when it became obvious that there was a well-aged level of corruption and greed embedded in the service. I still must have held that little boy notion of "I will strike down the wicked and protect the weak with my last breath for mankind".

As I reflect now on my service while writing, I think the shining light of honor and integrity important to me as a police officer to keep serving began fading out. I served five years in Giru and in my last year attended a five-week development course at Chelmer.

The law content and general structure of this course was first rate. The instructors were experienced investigators and prosecutors who had earnt their spurs with many years in the field. All operational police on this course knew these fellows and respected their proven abilities in the real world. We also respected their ability to change from police operations to lecturing in a classroom environment. The knowledge I gained at Chelmer would have been a big help to me for my Normanton tour.

I qualified for the rank of sergeant first class and moved on promotion to Bowen as office in charge. Pam and I are keen sailors and have always had some sort of sailing boat. I must admit 90% of my motivation centred on the Bowen move was about lifestyle and 10% on career advancement.

I think the uniform strength for Bowen was eight, with two detective positions. The station was a modern brick-veneer building, air-conditioned and well furnished. The watch-house, like most throughout Queensland, was unsuitable for holding prisoners. This facility was eventually upgraded at considerable cost to meet the stringent requirements now in place for watch-houses. The police houses were all good, solid, high-set, three-bedroom homes with secure carports.

Bowen division had a few problems and there were some serious discipline issues left outstanding for the incumbent O/C to deal with. The friction that had developed between the serving officers from this untidy situation had knocked morale for a six. The promotional and transfer procedure of that time was slow to the extreme. Stations and men were left in limbo for long periods of time under the command of acting O/Cs operating in a caretaker role. I wouldn't be surprised if this problem still exists in the service today. Discipline issues don't just go away with time: They usually manifest themselves into something pretty ugly if left unchecked. The damage was done by the time I arrived and it became necessary to transfer two of the married constables out of the station.

The next problem to look at was the limited hours of police coverage for Bowen. Bowen's commerce group felt they were hard done by with the limited police resources allocated for Bowen and that was having a detrimental effect on all commercial fronts in the town. It was perceived by this group that the police shut down and went to bed when the drunken villains of the village came out to play. The clergy, Social Welfare Services and Licensed Victuallers Hotel Association were united with the commerce group on this point. The station was hopelessly undermanned and my predecessor, Ron Clark, had put a lot of time and effort in trying to raise the station's strength.

Ron had prepared a solid brief for upgrading the station to 24-hour operations. He warned me about hostility I could expect from district office if I followed up on his efforts to improve police resources in Bowen. The third problem I had was Bowen division sitting on the boundary between Northern and Central Police Regions. For at least two years, despite efforts on secrecy, Bowen hung in a vacuum while it was debated whether the station would remain in the Northern Region or move to Central Region. Resources and budgets were closely guarded by both regions. Naturally neither region wanted to commit assets to Bowen.

Bowen eventually moved from Northern Region to Central Region then later on back to Northern Region. After many years of constant pressure from the Bowen community, Sergeant Clark and myself, the station was upgraded. Bowen moved to 24-hour policing with 22 uniform positions. The community was most grateful, especially the commerce and welfare groups. As expected, I paid a heavy price for my efforts, but that's another story.

The position of Senior Sergeant – Officer in Charge Bowen was gazetted and I was unsuccessful in my application for the job. There was a large public outcry from the community and much in the press about injustice on the O/C appointment. A number of community leaders met with senior officers and aired their displeasure over the way Sergeant Travers-Jones had been overlooked. An application for a street march was lodged by a community group through my office.

I was able to persuade them to withdraw their application. I pointed out their march would have a detrimental effect on future relations with the Police Service and certainly would not do me any good. I had been in the Police Force long enough to know I would somehow be seen as provoking such sentiment within the community. I decided to take recreation and long service leave and move interstate for a good break. I believed the dust would settle and the incumbent officer in charge, Mick Isles, would be able to establish himself quicker within the civil and police community.

I returned off leave and resumed duty back at Bowen. I was tipped off by two Bowen community leaders that senior officers in Townsville were convinced I had caused all their headaches in Bowen, despite assurances from these leaders that this was not the case at all. I asked to be excused from second in charge duties. This request was granted and I moved into the field on general duties. My old second in charge, Sergeant Cameron, continued to perform duties as second in charge and relieving duties when the O/C was absent.

I had very little to do with Mick Isles; we were courteous to each other, but that was it. I had no contact with senior management in Townsville and felt they had got over their problems with me and were just going to leave me alone. After two months back on the line and still trying to adjust to rotational shift work I was told a comprehensive report on policing problems in Bowen had been furnished by Mick Isles. I was told I featured in that report and the service had endorsed Mick's assertion I was the reason he was having difficulties policing Bowen.

I was advised senior Townsville officers made no investigation into Mick's claims before sending the subject report down to Brisbane. My informant advised the service had already passed judgement against me. I would not be made aware of the existence of this report and I would have no opportunity to apply for redress. I spoke with Superintendent John Howell about the existence of this report. He eventually came to Bowen and handed me the report. Mick had stated in this report that I was directly hindering policing in the Bowen Division. I was disappointed to see senior officers up to the Deputy Commissioner had concurred with the report and the accompanying submission that I should move on to Townsville.

These officers placed their signatures on this report without one querying the veracity of the allegations. It would seem my past service and track record meant nothing to these men. I complained to John Howell and asked for the matter to be investigated thoroughly. If it was found that the allegations were false then nothing less than a full retraction under his hand would be required to address the wrong. To John's credit, the investigation was carried out and he furnished a comprehensive report finding the allegations made against me by Isles were false and without substance.

John handed me his report for noting and I asked him to assist me in leaving the service with my voluntary retirement entitlements as soon as possible. I officially left the service in July 1996 with my entitlements after years of continuous service in the line. Mick Isles continued to have difficulties in Bowen and eventually transferred to Ayr. He had further difficulties there and eventually went absent without leave. He is still missing.

I am happily retired from the Police Service enjoying quality time with my wife and family. Pam and I are both in business and in good health. I served the Bowen community for five years giving all I had to improve policing in the area. I have been warmly welcomed into the community as a long-term resident. We have no plans of moving.

In 1893 Constable Duffy of Winton, with a tracker, set out on horseback in pursuit of Henry Ward, who had murdered an Aboriginal with a stirrup iron. Duffy eventually arrested Ward and for the next five days they were handcuffed together until their return to Winton after travelling 709 kilometres over 11 days.

*The Long Blue Line,* W Ross Johnston, 1992 (p 58)

# Osmund Ertman (Ossie) Cislowski

The Courier-Mail, Monday, August 16, 1954.

**Constable is saved**

Townsville---- Doctors at Townsville Hospital are confident that they have won a six-day battle for the life of a 27-year-old police constable. He is Osmund Cislowski, married, who was critically wounded in a shooting at Townsville on Tuesday night. Cislowski received wounds in the thigh and stomach when he grappled with a man while investigating a noise inside a building.

Cislowski was on the dangerously ill list and developed pneumonia. A 24-year-old labourer has been charged with unlawfully attempting to kill Cislowski.

**Gunshot wounds failed to stop policeman**

**The Sunday Mail** – 11 November, 1996.

**Queensland's heroes.**

There was no doubting the courage of Constable Osmund Ertman Cislowski when he tackled a criminal one August night in Townsville in 1954.

It was to earn him the first George Medal won by a Queensland policeman.

Constable Cislowski, then 27, was patrolling the Townsville shopping centre with another policeman, Earl Needham, when their attention was drawn by a late-working office employee to the sound of footsteps on the roof of a building, Constable Cislowski saw a man acting suspiciously and called on him to stop; but the suspect responded by firing from the hip with a pistol.

The bullet struck Constable Cislowski in the chest, but he continued.

What followed was described in court later by Crown Prosecutor Ralph Cormack as "an epic of courage, tenacity and devotion".

The gunman fired a second time – the bullet punctured Constable Cislowski's lung and passed out through his back.

The policeman caught the man by his trouser leg, but he broke free. As Constable Cislowski grabbed him again, the gunman fired a third shot. This time the bullet entered the Constable's thigh, but he continued the struggle.

Constable Needham had heard the shots and by this time had come to Constable Cislowski's assistance. He grappled with the gunman, risking being shot himself.

The gunman was to fire two more shots before he was finally subdued. One of the rounds passed through Constable Cislowski's hip.

Mr Justice O'Hagan described Constable Cislowski's performance as "courage and devotion to duty" deserving of the highest praise when he later sent the police officer's assailant to jail for 14 years.

Constable Cislowski recovered from his multiple wounds and continued his career in the Queensland Police Force.

**Paula Doneman – Crime Editor**

## Ceremonial Police Parade

On Friday, 11 May, 1956, a most impressive ceremonial parade of members of the Queensland Police Force took place at the Petrie Terrace Police Depot, Brisbane. The parade included representatives of the uniform sections of the General Police, Traffic Police, Traffic Motorcycle Squads, Water Police and Mounted Police and the various squads of the Criminal Investigation Branch.

The Ceremonial Parade was called to mark the occasion of the award of the George Medal to Constable First-Class Osmund Ertman Cislowski, the award of the British Empire Medal to Sergeant Morgan Francis Clark, Senior Constable Wesley John Cooke and Constable First-Class Earle Leonard Needham and the Queen's Citation for Bravery to Constable First-Class Clifford Henry Lebsanft. The circumstances leading up to these awards were published in the March, 1956, issue of The Police News.

The strength of the parade consisted of 16 commissioned officers and 200 non-commissioned officers and other ranks. The Queensland Police Force on parade made a colourful and most impressive spectacle and created a deep feeling of pride in our Police Force. The setting and staging of the parade was superb and reflects great credit on the Deputy Commissioner, Mr T Harold, Officer in charge of the parade, The Master of Ceremonies, Senior Sergeant A Day, and each and every member of the Police Force who participated in the parade.

In addressing the parade the Commissioner of Police, Mr P Glynn, welcomed the guests of honour, their relatives and friends, representatives of Government Departments, members of the Executive of the Police Union, and other invitees.

He said the parade had been called to mark the occasion of the bestowing of Imperial Awards by Her Majesty, The Queen, on five members of the Queensland Police Force. He quoted the words of the gazette notice referring to the circumstances leading up to the conferring of the awards and stated that the award of the George Medal was the first occasion that this distinction was earnt by a member of the Queensland Police Force.

He said that the conduct and bravery of each of the recipients showed action of the highest order and that no award previously earnt was more richly merited or so arduously earnt.

Police News – **June, 1956, Page Nine**

Ossie was to become the first Queensland police officer to receive the George Medal – Civil Division.

**Police Bulletin – Police Museum – Page 4**

On 16 November, 1954 in the Supreme Court, Townsville before Mr Justice T C O'Hagen, Kevin Morris was sentenced to a term of 14 years' imprisonment with hard labour for attempting unlawfully to kill Osmund Ertman Cislowski. On a second charge of breaking and entering he was sentenced to a term of three years' imprisonment with hard labour, and on a third charge "of having been found at night – having in your possession without lawful excuse implements of housebreaking" he was sentenced to a term of imprisonment with hard labour for five years. The sentences were ordered to be served concurrently.

Photograph of Ossie Cislowski receiving his medal from the then Queensland Governor, Sir John Lavarack. It was the first George Medal awarded to a Queensland Policeman

The weapon used by Kevin Morris was a .22 calibre Woodsman Colt Automatic pistol, which he had stolen after breaking into the shop of Kenneth Vincent James at Townsville on or about 6 August, 1954.

Ossie Cislowski was sworn in as a member of the Queensland Police Force on 4 October, 1948. He was shot and wounded while on duty on 10 August, 1954. I was sworn in as a constable of police on 3 December 1958. I knew Ossie during the time I was stationed at Biloela in the early 1970s; Ossie was then a sergeant first class and officer in charge of the Emerald Police Division. I was not aware of the shooting incident until the article 'Queensland Heroes' appeared in the Sunday Mail on 11 November, 1996, some three years after my retirement.

After returning to duty from his injuries, Ossie continued his career and retired with the rank of Senior Sergeant at age 56. During his career he was awarded 'Commendations' in the years 1954 and 1958 and a 'Favourable Record' in the year 1956 for good police work.

**Laurie Pointing**

# Osmund Ertman (Ossie) Cislowski

## Part One

I was born at Bundaberg, Queensland on 2nd February, 1927. I attended the Pheebee State School at Bundaberg where I attained a scholarship standard of education and left school at 14. During my school days my parents operated a pine and hardwood timber sawmill at Bundaberg where I carried out my fair share of work after school and of a weekend when time permitted. About the time I left school my parents moved to Gympie where they operated a similar type of sawmill at the One Mile. I continued working with my father until I reached the age of 21. I thought to myself, "There has to be an easier way to make a living than working in sawmills among the sawdust, heat, flies and dust". My older brother, Chris, had joined the Queensland Police Force about 1944 and he inspired me to join, so I decided to give it a go myself.

I entered the police depot at Petrie Terrace, Brisbane in June 1948 and lived in the old police department wooden barracks at that location. I found barracks life quite comfortable as I was used to living in rough conditions working in the timber industry. Barracks life never worried me at all. At the time of entering the Police Depot my hands were stained black from timber sap and I was physically fit. The physical fitness instructor would call me out to the front of the group of recruits to have me demonstrate particular activities we were about to undertake and my fellow probationary constables would follow on from there.

Sergeant Alex Day was the senior instructor and his junior was an Irishman, Tom Molloy. At the time of my entry into the Police Service Paddy Glynn was the Commissioner of Police. I was sworn in on 4 October ,1948 by Commissioner Glynn after we marched down to the Commissioner's Office situated in the Treasury Building. There I became Constable Osmund (Ossie) Cislowski, Registered No. 4598.

I was transferred to Roma Street Headquarters where I performed beat duty for the next two months. There was nothing very exiting about performing beat duty in the city; however, during my time at Roma Street there was a hit and run motor vehicle accident, which was very rare in those days, and I was instrumental in identifying the vehicle responsible for the accident. After all these years the circumstances of the accident escape me, but I do know that I was not the arresting officer.

I received notice of transfer to Townsville on or about 1 December, 1948 and travelled there by train, which took two days. I was a single man then and, upon my arrival, was allotted accommodation in the police station barracks at the Townsville police headquarters in Stuart Street. There would have been about 20-30 young police officers in barracks, which was fairly cramped. There were no females.

The barracks accommodation was situated on the top floor and was dormitory-type accommodation. You did not have a room to yourself, but shared with a fellow officer. Downstairs there was a mess, where a cook prepared our meals. There was also a shower recess and toilet block in the same vicinity and conditions were reasonable. The Townsville police district in those days extended as far west as Cloncurry, Mt Isa and Camooweal. There was a huge amount of relieving duty when officers from their respective stations were absent for a variety of reasons and relief officers were always selected and detailed for relieving duty from the single staff at Townsville.

Motor-vehicle transport was very limited and the duty senior sergeant was in charge of all motor-vehicle keys. He was also the officer who delegated the use of vehicles to personnel in the course of their duties. Some of these old gentlemen treated the police motor-vehicle fleet like their own property and you had to convince them that you needed a vehicle to carry out a particular duty that you couldn't complete while performing foot patrol. Attached to the Townsville headquarter police district during my early days of service was a BSA motorbike and side car, which, was used mainly by the inquiry staff for general inquiry work. The district police inspector in charge had a motor vehicle allocated to him for personal use. On some occasions when staff members were extremely busy and motor vehicles were in short supply he would occasionally lend his vehicle to some member of the Criminal Investigation Branch during the day to carry out an investigation, provided it was returned to him by late afternoon. Apart from this vehicle there was probably another four or five vehicles for use by members from the Criminal Investigation Branch, Traffic Branch and general duty police. The fleet of motor vehicles were mainly Holden utilities.

There was a communication room upstairs on the same floor as the barracks, but at the opposite end of the building there was a large community room with a billiard table, which provided some entertainment to off-duty police. The communication system was rather primitive; however, officers at the station could communicate with officers on patrol performing duty in police vehicles. That's how Constable Earl Needham and I received the broadcast of a possible "burglar on premises" the night of my shooting. We were on traffic patrol at the time and we were not armed.

There was no official issue of firearms to individual police in that period. The ones provided were those taken from criminals or handed in at police stations by individuals who had no further use for them. They were kept under lock and key by the station senior sergeant and issued out usually only in cases of emergencies. These firearms were mainly .38 revolvers and .303 rifles. Nor was there any departmental issue of torches. We had to purchase our own.

Initially when I first commenced duty at Townsville I worked in the office of the superintendent of traffic behind the counter, where the majority of my duties pertained to the registration of motor vehicles, issuing driver's licences, firearm registration, measuring commercial vehicles for registration and numerous other functions, which today are attended to by other departments such as the Transport Department.

In 1951 I was transferred to a permanent position in the Townsville Traffic Branch where the bulk of our duties were traffic patrol and performing point duty. We performed point duty, as it was known, at almost every intersection in Flinders Street. There was no system of controlled traffic lights installed. They had not been either invented or manufactured for use in Queensland. You really had to concentrate when performing point duty as you directed the traffic by arm movements, and one error on your behalf could result in traffic congestion or possibly a motor-vehicle accident.

That same year, the Townsville Traffic Branch vehicle was a white-coloured Dodge utility and the larrikins around town called it the "white ghost". When you were patrolling the inner-city area people would congregate in groups and the young larrikins would call out loudly, "Here comes the white ghost. Here comes the white ghost". It was very hard to detect breaches of the Traffic Act and Regulations in the inner city as every person knew where the "white ghost" was.

I recall very few arrests for drink driving in those days. When an arrest was made you had to observe the behavior of the vehicle first. If you observed the vehicle travelling in a manner that alerted your attention, that is, swerving from side-to-side, crossing over white lines, travelling too fast, you intercepted the vehicle and then observed the behavior of the driver. You obtained evidence to support a charge of drink driving by observing if the driver's speech was slurred, eyes bloodshot, breath smelt strongly of liquor and unsteady on his feet.

You would then have the driver alight from the vehicle and attempt to walk in a straight line. If he was unable to do so this was further evidence of his behaviour while under the effects of alcohol. The charge of drink driving was supported by your evidence. There was no technical evidence or blood reading.

Once you detected a breach of the Traffic Act or Regulations you took down all particulars of the driver and the motor vehicle and the elements of the alleged offence, recording them in your official police notebook. You then typed up your breach report, which was submitted to your superior and, should he recommend a prosecution, you typed out the summons, which was duly signed by the Superintendent of Traffic. Following this you served the summons on the offender personally, for identification purposes, and that summons then proceeded through normal channels to the Magistrate's Court. Your court brief of evidence was then typed and handed to the Police Prosecutor.

At about nine o'clock on the night of 10 August, 1954, Constable First Class Earl Leonard Needham and I were on traffic patrol and were working the Townsville traffic car - the white ghost - when a call came over the two-way radio regarding a possible breaking and entering and burglar on premises occupied by New Zealand Loan and Mercantile Agency in Denham Street. As we were in that vicinity we immediately responded to the call.

On arrival we spoke with a youth by the name of Frank Morris (no relation to the offender, Kevin Morris) at the front door of that building and he told us that there was a person on the roof of the building. Needham walked around to the Cleveland Street side of the building and I walked further along the street and turned into Hamilton Street, which then ran at the rear of those premises. I commenced to walk backwards and forwards along that street looking up on to the roof and over a nearby fence in search of a possible prowler. There was a street light on a pole at the rear of those premises on the opposite side of Hamilton Street. I was in that street for approximately two or three minutes when I saw a male person jump from the top of a galvanised iron fence surrounding these premises. He landed in the street and commenced to run in my direction. I commenced to move towards him calling out, "Hey there, stay where you are, police here".

This man was about nine yards distance from me and, when I called out, he changed direction and commenced to run up a track that led on to Melton Hill. I closely followed and was only a few yards behind him when he arrived at a galvanised open shed about 30 yards up the track. He ran into the darkened shed and wheeled about and called out, "Don't come near me". I did not heed his words, but continued to follow and then grappled with him. As I did so I saw a flash of fire come from about his left hip and I heard the sound of a shot and something strike me in the chest. I was unable to get a good grip of him and he pulled away from me and ran back down the track towards Hamilton Street.

I gave chase and succeeded in catching him by the back of his trousers, which resulted in the outer half of his left trouser leg coming apart in my hand and he kept running down the track. I continued the chase and caught him around the hips and upper part of his legs just prior to him reaching Hamilton Street. As I caught hold of him I stumbled on the rough ground and my grip on his body slid down to the lower part of his legs, but I still held him as he struggled to get free.

While I was on the ground he twisted his body back in my direction and fired several shots at me, but I did not feel anything strike me. I was being dragged over the rough ground and the stones into Hamilton Street. I could not regain my feet and he broke free and commenced to run along Hamilton Street towards Cleveland Street. I regained my feet, continued the chase and overpowered him, throwing him face down - with his arms out in front of him - to the ground. I was more or less in front of him holding his arms to the roadway. It was at this stage that Earl Needham arrived at the scene and he dropped down across the man's shoulders where he was sprawled on the roadway and Needham took hold of his wrists and I stood up in front of them. I saw this man struggling with Needham and noticed that Needham was endeavoring to turn the firearm that the man held in his hand skywards. During the struggle with Earl Needham this man fired another shot, which struck me in the left thigh. A further shot was fired, which narrowly missed hitting Needham's head.

I think he had the firearm in his left hand at this stage. After this shot was fired I saw Needham force his arm holding the firearm down on to the roadway and I was able to wrench the firearm from him. I noticed Constable Pitt assisting Constable Needham and I walked away to a parked police utility. I dropped the revolver into the back of that utility and I said to the police officer in charge of that vehicle, Constable Bohl, "Drive me to the hospital, I have been shot". On examination at the Townsville Base Hospital it was revealed that I had been shot three times: once in the chest, once in the left thigh and once in the upper right leg. I am not aware when I received the wound to the right upper leg. It may have been when I stumbled and he was trying to get away from me while I was holding on to his legs.

Retired Superintendent Gordon Scott Duncan was a uniform constable stationed at Townsville at the time of this shooting incident and was greatly affected by the shooting of Ossie Cislowski, as were many other police officers and members of the community. A strong friendship developed between Duncan and Cislowski and that friendship still exists today.

## Recollections of Ossie Cislowski

## Gordon Duncan

During the May 2010 I had the opportunity to interview Gordon Duncan and he said that at the time of this shooting incident, Dr Scott Young was the Chief Surgeon at the Townsville Base Hospital. "He was that competent," said Gordon, "that he could cut your head off and then replace it and you wouldn't die. Dr Scott Young was a good friend of mine and told me that he was of the firm belief that Ossie would die and would not be alive the following day. Ossie was in Intensive Care and naturally we couldn't see him, but I kept in close touch with the hospital and his wife, Gwen. They had two small children at the time and Gwen was marvellous. She kept it together and approached the situation in a cool and calm manner. Earl and Maureen Needham went out of their way to assist Gwen and gave much needed support to the family."

Townsville police received regular updates from Dr Scott Young regarding Ossie's health and gave strict instructions that no other doctor or member of the medical staff were to treat him without first consulting him. The district police inspector detailed two police officers to look after Gwen and the children every day and provide transport whenever she required it, especially to and from the hospital to visit her injured and sick husband.

Ossie's injuries were enough for any person to afterwards suffer trauma and mental stress. We were all of the view that once he sufficiently recovered he would be retired medically unfit. No-one believed that he would even contemplate returning to duty. How wrong we were. The fact that he eventually returned to duty and retired at age 56 with the rank of senior sergeant speaks volumes about the calibre of the man. I do not recall the period of time he was absent from duty on sick leave, but he got himself motivated, came back to work and just got on with his life.

> Gwen Cislowski said that after the shooting incident Earl and Maureen Needham were very good to her and the children. Both kept in touch and provided assistance to her whenever she needed it. Gwen speaks warmly of police personnel who were stationed at Townsville at the relevant time and expressed her sorrow for the parents and other members of the family of Kevin Morris, the offender responsible for Ossie's injuries. In Gwen's view the part played by Earl Needham in the capture of Kevin Morris did not receive the recognition it should have, even though he was awarded the British Empire Medal for bravery.

Gordon Duncan recalls that the Police Department decided they would look after Ossie when they realised his determination to return to duty. The Department transferred him in charge of Stuart Creek police division, a one-officer establishment and a small township situated some eight to 10 kilometres south of Townsville City. His superiors in their wisdom considered Stuart Creek to be a nice, quiet location capable of providing him with a quiet lifestyle and a reasonable amount of police duties to keep him occupied. This division, at that time, among other things, supported Alligator Creek livestock abattoir, a cement works, one hotel and the Stuart Creek Prison.

At the time of his transfer to Stuart, Ossie held the rank of constable first Class. Duncan had been the relieving officer in charge of Stuart Creek police station for a period of four months when Ossie, Gwen and the children arrived on transfer on the afternoon of 11 September, 1955. Gordon had reasonable accommodation at the police residence and partook of his meals at the hotel. According to Duncan he was extremely pleased when Ossie secured the position at Stuart Creek and, at the time of Ossie's arrival at Stuart Creek, he (Cislowski) had not performed duty since the shooting on 10 August, 1954 and his first day back at work was to be at Stuart Creek.

In August 1955 there was no allocated police vehicle attached to Stuart Creek. Their means of transport was a beautiful big gelding (horse), about 15½ hands, which came from Dotswood cattle station. "Dotswood" was the name given to the horse. "I could ride a horse," said Gordon, "but I wasn't sure if Ossie could. Anyway, he was a tall animal and I was not prepared to take the chance and have Ossie suffer an injury from a fall from a horse. So I arranged to have the old patrol horse returned to Dotswood so he could see out his remaining days in retirement."

At this particular time Duncan was the owner of an Austin A40 sedan motor vehicle with a rag hood and frequently utilised this private vehicle to carry out general inquiries in the division. Prior to his relieving duties at Stuart Creek Gordon had performed a period of security duties at Collinswood and had been issued with a .38 automatic revolver and ammunition.

The main telephone was situated in the Stuart Creek police station office, which was attached to the residence, and there was an extension to the residence for convenience when the station office was closed. The Cislowski family bedded down for the night in the residence that was to be their home for the next 10 years. Just on daylight the telephone rang, which caused both Ossie and Gordon to leave their beds with the intention of answering the call. The message that was received alerted them to a shooting at the Stuart Creek Prison. Duncan said there was terrific noise issuing from the direction of the prison, which indicated to him that shots were being fired and it sounded as though prisoners were banging their cell buckets against the steel cell doors. According to both Ossie and Gordon the noise was unbelievable.

It transpired that a criminal named William Henry La-Vere had been released from that prison on 8 September, 1955, after serving a lengthy prison sentence for a crime of "Robbery with Violence" and, during the early hours of 9 September, 1955, armed himself with a concealable firearm and broke into the prison with the intention of releasing some of his prisoner friends. According to Gordon this criminal was somewhat of a "heavyweight" in jail and commanded some respect among his fellow prisoners.

After Kevin Morris was arrested for the serious crime committed on Ossie Cislowski his home was searched and several firearms located, however, one concealable firearm was not. Morris had given this to his grandmother for safekeeping. The scheme to escape from prison was hatched by Morris, La-Vere and possibly five or six other long-term criminals, which included Platz, who was serving a life sentence for a murder committed at Mt Morgan, and a man named Taylor, serving a sentence for armed robbery.

Kevin Morris (24) leaving the Supreme Court yesterday with a police escort, after he had been sentenced to 14 years' imprisonment on a charge arising out of the wounding of Constable O. E. Cislowski. *The North Queensland Newspaper.*

Once the scheme was put into place Morris instructed his grandmother to bring the concealable firearm to the prison for his inspection to satisfy himself that she was still in possession of it and was available to La-Vere upon his release. These criminals knew that La-Vere could gain entry through the dwelling house of the chief prison officer, but that would only allow him entry between gates and not into the prison proper where the prisoners were housed. This is why La-Vere needed the handgun to hold up or shoot, I believe, the only night officer on duty, who happened to be Chris McCann.

"As you entered the big main steel flat gates at Stuart Prison," said Duncan, "there was a bar gate some 20 metres inside the grounds and erected nearby was the prison armoury La-Vere had broken into the armoury and had removed a quantity of the prison firearms to assist in the planned escape."

The interior gate in those days was made of metal bars with a small gate built into it so that warders could enter or exit into the prison without opening the extra-large gates. This small gate is kept locked for security purposes and the night officer carried the key on his person. McCann heard noises coming from between gates and went to investigate, which was part of La-Vere's plan. McCann opened the small gate, stepped inside and saw La-Vere armed with guns and immediately jumped back through the open gate. He later remarked, "Thank the good Lord I didn't lock the gate behind me".

McCann then quickly positioned himself behind a 44-gallon drum located in a circular garden and commenced firing in the direction of La-Vere, while La-Vere was spraying bullets in every direction. A later inspection showed bullet marks on both sides of the 44-gallon drum.

In his only day of freedom La-Vere, as well as securing the handgun, made a rope ladder with a hook affixed to one end. The plan was that once he either shot or overpowered McCann he would secure the master key to the cells of Morris and the other prisoners earmarked for release. Aware that the alarm in all probability would have been raised, the plan was to quickly release his criminal friends, arm them with rifles from the armoury and use the rope ladder if necessary to effect their escape.

Ossie and Gordon moved as quickly as possible and travelled to the prison in Gordon's private motor vehicle. As they commenced the journey Duncan threw Cislowski the .38 revolver and a handful of bullets and said, "Load her up, mate". Ossie replied, "I better be careful, Gordon; the last job I went to I got shot. I don't want to get shot again".

At this period of time Stuart Creek Prison only rostered one prison officer on night duty and La-Vere was aware of this fact. Arming himself with several firearms he removed from the armoury he began just firing indiscriminately, hoping that one or several bullets would find their mark. Eventually prison officers gained control of the situation and La-Vere knew he had lost the battle, put his gun down and surrendered to prison officials, who by this time had arrived at the prison, opened a steel trapdoor and let Ossie, Gordon and other back-up police, who had arrived from Townsville, into the prison.

Gordon Duncan said that during his time at Stuart he was deeply involved with inquiries at the jail, which was a dimly lit establishment housing a couple of hundred male prisoners. With only one prison officer on the midnight shift until six in the morning, both prison officers and Stuart Creek police were always anticipating that attempted escapes were possible.

At the Supreme Court, Townsville on 16 December, 1955 La-Vere was convicted on two counts of "Attempting Unlawfully to Kill" and one count of "Breaking and Entering with Intent". He was sentenced to a total of 14 years' imprisonment with hard labour, the principal arresting officer being Detective Constable First Class C D (Charlie) Dwyer assisted by Plain Clothes Constable First Class J M West. Dwyer had a distinguished career with the Queensland

Police Service and at the time of his retirement held the rank of Assistant Commissioner.

Duncan recalls that Ossie had not yet returned to duty on the morning of the shooting at Stuart Creek Prison, and Duncan was of the view that the incident would trigger a relapse of Ossie's health and would surely be the determining factor in him retiring medically unfit. This was not to be and became just another chapter in Ossie's life

During Duncan's relieving period at Stuart Creek, prisoners Platz and Taylor did escape from the prison. They closely examined the key used by the prison officers by looking at it whenever possible. After leaving their cells they removed bricks from a wall and executed their escape. Assisted by Constable Ron Youells, who at the time was performing relieving duty at Mingela police station, Duncan borrowed horses from Dotswood cattle station and spent seven or eight days searching on horseback in and around a location called Sellum before the two prisoners were recaptured.

Roy Hielscher, a senior police officer now living in retirement at Townsville, said that in the year 1954 he was stationed at Kuranda. Shortly after Ossie was seriously wounded he had occasion to visit his police headquarters, Cairns, where he found anger among rank-and-file police there to be intense. Bob Maynard, also a retired police officer residing at Townsville, told me that he was transferred to Townsville some six or seven years after Ossie's unfortunate incident and the shooting was still the talk of the town.

In 1954 the general public knew that police officers were not armed while performing their duties. The public were angered by the fact that an armed criminal carrying out a breaking and entering offence callously opened fire on a police officer with a revolver and shot him. "It was assassination in my opinion," said Duncan, "and the anger within police circles and the community remained for years."

# Osmund Ertman (Ossie) Cislowski

## Part Two

Continuing his story, Ossie said, "I spent 10 years of my service at Stuart Creek and shortly after I settled in I applied for a police motor vehicle and was eventually allotted a 1956 Holden utility with a lot of mileage on the speedometer. My duties there were consistent with duties at most one-officer establishments, such as general inquiries, dead bodies, fires, motor-vehicle accidents, issuing of drivers' licences, registration of motor-vehicles and a multitude of duties now carried out by other government departments. General inquiries at the prison and officework took up quite a bit of my time".

It was a large police division extending north to the Ross River, south to the township of Giru where the police strength was a sergeant second class and a constable, then to where my division joined the Mingela division at the Charters Towers Range road. There were numerous cattle properties in the division and huge mobs of cattle were driven on foot and by road transport to the Alligator Creek Abattoir, which employed a large number of fairly rough seasonal workers. The issuing of stock permits to those people engaged in the cattle and livestock industry was also an important part of my duties.

About 40,000 head of cattle walked from Western Queensland and other far out places to the meatworks yearly, where about 600 head were killed daily. That

40,000 head did not include the number of cattle regularly transported there by rail.

There was a lovely old Record book at Stuart Creek Station that recorded the history and reports from previous officers stationed at Stuart over many years, and it was common to read of packhorse patrols of some 1300 miles lasting for months For many years the old patrol horse "Dotswood" was the main patrol horse. Before I was allocated the Holden police utility, it was common for property owners to lend me a motor vehicle to carry out some inquiries such as checking and updating the Electoral Roll. This generous offer had also been extended to previous police at Stuart before my time.

A large part of my duties at Stuart Creek were general inquiries at the prison, and this is where Kevin Morris was detained after being sentenced at the Supreme Court, Townsville during November 1954. It was not uncommon for me to encounter Morris during the course of these inquiries and we frequently engaged in general conversation over the years. I bore no ill will towards this man. What happened had happened and I was determined to get on with my life and remain positive.

During February 1966 I was promoted to sergeant second class and transferred back to the Townsville Traffic Branch where Roy Hielscher was the officer in charge and superintendent of Traffic. The duties of a sergeant second class of police at the Townsville Traffic Branch in the mid-1960s was mainly supervision of staff, preparing the roster, officework and correspondence, delegation of staff, some patrol duty and occasionally relieving the officer in charge during his absence.

Townsville was rocked by a serious of explosions on five consecutive nights commencing on 9 May, 1969 and the residents of that city were in fear. Explosives were used to destroy clubhouses, railway bridges, churches and a toilet block. Gordon Duncan by this stage of his career was a detective sergeant attached to the Townsville Criminal Investigation Branch and I was still attached to the Townsville Traffic Branch. Tension and fear throughout the community was such that Townsville people were demanding action from their police, and our superiors were putting pressure on rank-and-file police to extend their efforts in apprehending the person responsible.

I was fortunate to have the confidence of a local resident who passed information to me that indicated the identity of the person possibly responsible for this massive destruction. I passed that confidential information to Gordon Duncan and we worked together on the investigation. As a result Gordon interviewed a male person - a local resident – and, after lengthy questioning, did not secure evidence to charge him with an offence so further inquiries had to be carried out. On the night of 11 May, 1969 a set of brick toilets on the Hugh Street side of Gill Park were destroyed by explosives that sent bricks and sheets of iron hurling across Hugh Street. A motor vehicle was seen near the toilets at the park and information was supplied to the investigating police by a taxi driver and an electrician. This information was then thoroughly examined by Gordon Duncan and his team of investigators.

We had not ruled out the suspect that Gordon originally questioned and, at one of the earlier explosive blasts, Gordon found pieces of brass that became vital evidence. Our suspect was an 18-year-old man named David John Moore and he worked for Bill the Wrecker, who operated a demolition business. Bill was an old showman who had spent many years on the show circuit and was demolishing the old red-brick powerhouse out at Ross River, but he wouldn't let Moore do any explosives work, as he considered him to be careless and dangerous in that field of work.

Gordon telephoned me at home on the Monday morning and informed me that, as a result of further investigations, he was now positive that Moore was responsible for the explosions and asked me to accompany him to further question this young man. As we walked towards the workshop where Moore was cleaning up rubbish for scrap metal, Gordon picked up two pieces of pipe, which proved to be further evidence of vital importance. As we approached Moore, Duncan showed him the pipe and said, "Where did this come from?" Moore replied, "From the signal box we demolished".

Confronted with the evidence we had compiled, Moore subsequently confessed that he was the sole person responsible for the extensive damage recently caused by explosives. As it transpired he was resentful that his boss, Bill the Wrecker, would not allow him to perform any blasting in his demolishing work so decided to experiment on buildings throughout the city.

The Police Department in those years was very frugal and you were expected to perform your duties on a "shoe-string budget". Being paid for overtime worked was frowned upon unless you had a very good reason such as arresting an offender on a serious charge. As we were driving from Moore's place of employment to the Townsville Police Station with the offender in the police vehicle Gordon contacted our district inspector, Ted Osborne, by radio and informed him that we were working on the Mad Bomber case and enquired as to the possibility of overtime. The reply we received was, "No arrest; no overtime".

That's how it was in the old days if you were following up positive leads in an investigation and your shift was close to being completed. Your superiors in most cases would not approve overtime unless you could almost guarantee them that you would make an arrest.

We drove into the back yard of the police station and parked and I remained in the vehicle with Moore while Gordon went to speak with the inspector. Gordon said to Ted Osborne, "Ossie and I have got the bomber in the vehicle out in the yard". Inspector Osborne replied, "Don't bullshit to me, Duncan," to which Gordon said, "I am not going to; don't worry about that". Moore had already admitted to us that he was the person responsible for the bombings prior to Gordon approaching Inspector Ted Osborne.

At this juncture our superiors were in the process of arranging additional police officers to proceed to Townsville from centres like Charters Towers and Ayr to assist in the protection of buildings such as churches and other important landmarks. The arrest of Moore at this stage of the investigation avoided a very expensive exercise.

Ted Osborne was so elated that he decided to interview Moore and allowed himself to become involved in the investigation. He accompanied us when Moore directed us to the buildings he had damaged and destroyed. At the trial Moore's defense alleged that, during the interrogation, Gordon Duncan had assaulted Mooce, or to use a phrase barristers loved to use against police in those days, "flogged a confession out of him". Inspector Ted Osborne was called to give evidence and, following the completion of the trial, said to Gordon Duncan, "Duncan, I will never stand within a hundred yards of you when you are talking to anyone again".

Next morning Osborne informed us that Moore had spent some time at Mt Isa and, during his time there, the single-men's police barracks had been destroyed by fire and Moore was a possible suspect. So we interviewed him again and he said, "It's bigger than you think. Yes, I burnt the barracks down and five more houses here in Townsville as well".

Moore pleaded not guilty to every charge and later, in 1969, David John Moore was sentenced to a total of 10 years' imprisonment on numerous charges of arson and attempting to damage property by explosive substance.

In the month of November 1973 I applied for and was promoted to sergeant first class as officer in charge of the Emerald Police Division. Emerald, at the time, had a staff of about 10-12, which included a detective and one female non-sworn member - a female who performed clerical duties. I loved the life and work at Emerald, however, Gwen could not settle into the country way of life. So, in about April 1975 I was transferred as the officer in charge of Clayfield Police Division. Clayfield, at that time, was a Brisbane suburban police station. At both Emerald and Clayfield my main duties were the efficient functioning of the police station and division and supervision of my staff.

Photograph of Detective Sergeant Gordon Duncan and Sergeant Ossie Cislowski – escorting David John Moore – to the Magistrates Court, Townsville when Moore was first arrested.

During December 1977 I was promoted to senior sergeant and returned to Townsville performing general duties, mainly as the senior sergeant performing shiftwork in charge of shifts, supervision of staff and the allocation of duties and administrative duties. On my return to Townsville police personnel were housed in a new police station and working conditions had improved considerably. There were more modern motor vehicles and technology had taken a giant step forward.

I retired on 2 July, 1983 at 56, having thoroughly enjoyed my 35 years as a member of the Queensland Police Service. Certainly, there were one or two incidents along the way that made life difficult at times, however, this was balanced by the fact that Gwen was a loving and supportive wife and we have two loving daughters. A policeman's life is not always pleasant, although over the years I have met and made friends with some remarkable and wonderful people, and worked beside some outstanding police officers. I have developed a lifelong friendship with some of these officers, men like Gordon Duncan, a most experienced and capable investigator whose friendship I value dearly.

# Recollections of Ossie Cislowski

## Jack Farrell

John Douglas (Jack) Farrell is a retired Queensland police officer who rose to the rank of inspector of police. During his police career he undertook the study of law, and after completing all stages of the examinations conducted by the Barristers Board of Queensland, was admitted as a barrister of the Supreme Court of Queensland on 30 September, 1996. On being admitted to the bar he eventually resigned from the Queensland Police Service and experienced a successful professional career in private practice. He is now retired from the bar.

Jack has some interesting recollections concerning Ossie Cislowski. His father, the late John Arnold Farrell, retired Chief Superintendent of Prisons, joined the Prison Service of Queensland in 1947. In those days Queensland had two prisons, Brisbane (Boggo Road) and Townsville (Stuart Creek), and some prison farms as well. In order to gain experience and seek promotion, Jack Farrell (Senior) moved to Stuart Creek, Townsville in 1950. When John Farrell (Senior) took up duties at Stuart Creek, young Jack, who was born on 20 December, 1944, was aged five years and a few months.

In those days Stuart, a suburb of Townsville, was much the same as it is today. There was Stuart Creek police station, which had one police officer. The police station in those days was situated close to the cement factory and the sole officer was Constable Bill Brackin. At some stage the police station was rebuilt where the police house now stands. The officer who replaced Mr Brackin was Constable Ossie Cislowski.

For most of my primary schooling I attended the Railway Estate State School. It was there one day that I learnt that a police officer (Mr Ossie Cislowski) had been shot while attending to a break-in alarm in the premises of New Zealand Loan and Mercantile Agency in Denham Street. His partner at the time was the late Sergeant Earl Needham. As children, we knew nothing else about the matter except that the prevailing wisdom was that Constable Cislowski, the shot officer, was going to die.

Nobody at that stage knew the toughness and resolution of the man. He did not die, but went on to have a distinguished and lifelong career as a police officer. At the time of the shooting I was aged nine and a few months away from reaching my 10th birthday. A proportion of my story surrounding the following incident was related to me by my late father.

The man who shot Mr Cislowski was named Kevin Morris. Morris was, as my father described him, "wild and woolly and full of fleas". He was a known criminal who had no hesitation in shooting at police who were attempting to carry out their duties. It was later shown that Morris had obtained a firearm that he used on Cislowski, together with other firearms, from breaking and entering the premises of a gunsmith named Rex Penny. These premises were in Flinders Street, Townsville, across from the large, round garden bed outside the Townsville railway station.

When Morris was apprehended some stolen firearms were taken from him by the police. However, not all firearms were recovered. Morris was sentenced to 14 years in prison for the crime committed upon Mr Cislowski and it seems from early stages of incarceration he had no intention of staying in prison and doing his sentence quietly.

His visitors included his grandmother, an elderly lady who would draw no special attention to herself. However, Morris had given her one of the stolen firearms, a concealable firearm, and had instructed her to carry the weapon with her on all occasions when she came to visit him in prison. It seems that this is precisely what she did. On each visit, she brought the firearm with her in her purse or bag and was required to produce it to Morris on each visit so that he could be satisfied that she still had it and it was still available to him when he wanted it. This is my recollection of this event as related to me by my late father. Apparently security in those days was not as fine tuned as it is today.

The scheme devised by Morris went even further. One of his fellow prisoners was a man named William (Bill) Henry La-Vere. He and Morris devised a scheme that they hoped would get Morris out of prison and into freedom. In September 1955, La-Vere was released from custody and then headed off to see Morris's elderly relative who, of course, Morris knew had a concealable firearm waiting for La-Vere. So from shortly after his release from prison, La-Vere had custody of a loaded concealable firearm. His intention was to use that to get back into the prison and forcibly cause the release of Morris.

To do that today by breaking into the prison may seem a rather daunting task. However, life was different in the 1950s. On either side of the large gate at Stuart Prison was a residence. The residence to the right of the gate was occupied by Chief Prison Officer Les Beatty and his wife. The residence to the left of the large gate was occupied by Chief Prison Officer Tom Nolan and his family.

One member of that family became well known in police circles. Tom's son, Brian, became an inspector of police and was known as co-ordinator of the Regional Duties Officer Scheme in Metropolitan North for many years.

These residences ran along the side of the in-between gate area. In order that the Chief Prison Officer could check on the staff without having to announce his presence, there was a doorway between his quarters and the prison itself. All that the Chief had to do to gain entry to the prison was open the door and walk in. This was, no doubt, convenient and effective for supervisory purposes. However, it also provided a very easy access to the inside of the prison. For if the prison officer could easily enter the prison, then so could anyone else who knew of the scheme gain easy access to the prison by simply walking in through the Chief's residence and opening the door, as the Chief would do.

It should also be remembered that from 5pm until 10pm and from 10pm until 6am the prison, in those days, was staffed by one officer. At 5pm quite a number of prisoners were still out working and had to be locked up later. If a prisoner already locked up had to be removed from his cell, then the prison officer on duty had to gain the assistance of one of the Chief Prison Officers residing on site. So gaining entry to and from the Chief Prison Officer's residence was not particularly difficult. Both Morris and La-Vere knew of this arrangement and used the security weakness to their advantage.

After his release from prison, La-Vere immediately went to Morris's grandmother and got the loaded concealable firearm. Early the next morning he travelled to the prison and made his entry through the doorway of the residence of the Chief Prison Officer. Without any resistance or problem, La-Vere was able to gain entry to any part of the prison that he wanted and that is precisely what he did. The officer in charge of the night shift was Mr Chris McCann; Chris is long dead and gone, but would be remembered by police, having retired as Deputy Superintendent at Stuart Prison. At the time of McCann's retirement, his position may have been classified as Manager as the rank of Superintendent was being phased out during the late 1980s and early 1990s. McCann found La-Vere in the prison, armed, and a gunfight ensured, with La-Vere on the veranda of a building firing down towards McCann. McCann had taken cover behind some rose bushes planted in a half 44-gallon drum. A number of shots were traded between the two.

I am not sure how Prison Officer Walter Frank Hoger came to be on the scene; however, records show that he was unarmed and led two other staff members into the gate area and overpowered L-Vere. For his courageous effort he was awarded the British Empire Medal. Hoger at the time of his retirement held the rank of Superintendent. Other prison staff members involved in this event received letters of appreciation from the relevant Government Minister.

In those days, a large number of prison officers lived on-site in the houses, some of which are still at the prison today. I can recall with my brother, Barry, hearing the shots coming from the direction of the prison. In those days, very few if any of the staff owned a motor vehicle and very few had a telephone. I recall men coming out of their houses, speaking briefly together about what the shots meant. It was quickly decided that whoever was manning the prison must have been in trouble and the men headed off hurriedly across the paddock towards the prison to assist their fellow officer. They left very quickly. Some wore pyjamas, or underpants, or whatever they happened to be wearing at the time. The important thing was to get there quickly to assist.

This, however, did not apply to our next-door neighbour, Mr Frost, who had come from England and had served in the English prison system. Mr Frost arrived at the prison with all the other men, except that he was in full uniform, including a tie. My father, in later years, always marvelled at how Mr Frost could get dressed as quickly as he did. Dad used to remark that only a Pommie could have done it. Mr Frost later returned to England and is now deceased. He did, however, have a further distinguished career in the British prison system before his retirement.

It was quickly ascertained by the first prison officers arriving at the prison that Prison Officer McCann was being pinned down by La-Vere. They were able to get behind La-Vere through a doorway between them and him. They decided that the only way to finalise the situation was to push the door open very quickly and hopefully subdue La-Vere before he had a chance to use the firearm he was carrying and using. Their problem was further compounded by the fact that although they had a sufficient number of men to do the job, there was a limit as to how many could get through the door to La-Vere at one time.

In any event, they carried out their plan, quickly pushed the door open and before La-Vere could see what was happening he was subdued and overpowered.

La-Vere received the same sentence as his friend Morris – 14 years' imprisonment. I understand that both Morris and La-Vere served out their sentences without any further drama and were released after having done so. I understand that neither of these men were ever charged and convicted of any further crimes.

Having known Constable Ossie Cislowski early in my life, I formed an extreme admiration for the man. His bravery along with Constable Earl Needham on the night Ossie was shot is something that legends are made of. Ossie Cislowski was a police officer universally admired and respected. In 1974 I joined the Queensland Police Force and on occasions saw Ossie in the various jobs we undertook. To me he was the type of police officer every young recruit officer could aspire to be.

Before I resigned from the Police Service I gained commissioned rank. Ossie did not do so, and no doubt had no desire to do so. But technically I finished my career in a more senior capacity than he did. However, the greatest thrill that I got as a senior police officer was to be in the same room as Cislowski and wearing the same uniform as he was. The badges of rank meant not a thing. That is how much I have always admired this courageous police officer.

I would have expected that the problems at Stuart Creek Prison during August 1955 involving the criminal La-Vere would be etched in the folklore of the prison. A few years ago, however, I had a beer one night with some long-serving prison officers and had a lengthy discussion took place concerning Morris and La-Vere. None of these men had heard of the incident.

I was not aware until recently that at the time of the La-Vere incident retired Police Superintendent Gordon Duncan, then a constable of police, was relieving in charge of Stuart Creek Police Division and had spent a considerable period of time performing that relieving duty, between the departure of Bill Bracken and the arrival of Ossie Cislowski. I was also not aware that on the date of La-Vere's release, Ossie Cislowski and his family had arrived at the Stuart Creek police residence where Ossie was to take charge the following day.

Nor was I aware that both Gordon and Ossie were two of the many police officers who took part in the initial investigation at the prison on the morning of the La-Vere break-in. This happened to be the first police investigation Ossie attended since being shot by Kevin Morris some 12 months before and once again involved firearms.

However, it is great to hear that Ossie Cislowski, now in his 80s, is still alive and enjoying reasonably good health and is actively involved in retired police matters. To my mind, if any young police officer wanted to know how high he should aim to be in the Police Service, he should be told to be half as good as Ossie Cislowski. He is the stuff that real police officers are made of.

(1) The policeman's lot became a lot happier when - in 1957-58 - a sick-leave bank was created to which all sworn-in personnel contributed one day of their recreation leave.

(2) The Queensland Police Credit Union was formed on 2 July, 1964 to provide financial assistance to its members

(3) The Queensland Police Club was revived and renamed and moved to new premises in 1979.

*The Long Blue Line, W Ross Johnston, 1992 (p 302)*

## Mervyn John Bainbridge

Barbara Bainbridge summed up her late husband Merv correctly when she referred to him as a "unique man". Because that is exactly what he was – a unique individual - and there will never be another Mervyn John Bainbridge. He was a competent uniform police officer, experienced in all facets of policing. Merv gave loyalty and demanded loyalty. He was particularly interested in the welfare and careers of younger officers and gave freely of his time to assist them, not only while on duty, but in their private lives if and when they needed a helping hand. Some not so pleasant experiences with some hard-nosed senior officers when he was a junior officer himself influenced him to pursue police union activities and this he did with relentless vigour. Merv possessed a sense of humour that drew people to him. He was a great storyteller who loved nothing more than to reminisce about the past. A character who is greatly missed by his friends and, in particular, those people who have been associated with the Police Service.

Rest in Peace, Merv, your memory lives on.

**Laurie Pointing**

# Mervyn John Bainbridge

As I head towards old age and reflect upon my life so far, I am reminded that in considering times gone by it is quite easy to slip into the mindset of wearing one's "rose-coloured glasses", or selectively only remembering the hard times. I shall in recounting my life and times from 1966-2002 attempt to be objective, but be warned, this account is seen from my own cynical perspective.

I was sworn in as a constable of police at the Police Depot, Petrie Terrace on 30th March, 1966 and transferred to Moorooka Police Station after surviving three months' intensive training at that establishment. Memories of those three months are twofold. First for the good times, friendships made with the people there, and the feeling that you were about to be admitted to a special group of people, a sentiment I still carry today, because police are special people. From an early age I wished for no other occupation than that of a police officer.

Second, the bad, annoying times during that period of training, when you were subject to penalties such as jogging around the radio mast in the back yard of the Depot with a .303 rifle held above your head for the infraction of talking while on parade, and who can forget the hand in the white glove moving across the wall of your room searching for dust during room inspections.

Both of these examples are from a bygone era, and thank God for that. Character building and instilling discipline? I don't think so. Mindless petty bastardisation, and at the end of the day that is all it was, no more, no less, instilling only fear and loathing.

On to Moorooka, and upon arrival at that police station I found myself in the office of the officer in charge, Senior Sergeant Charles Moses McNaught (one of the force's characters I am told), standing to attention before his desk. The senior sergeant did not acknowledge me as he was otherwise engaged talking to a workmate on the telephone. The conversation then went as follows:

Bainbridge: "Constable Bainbridge reporting for duty, Senior."

No acknowledgment.

McNaught to mate on telephone: "Yes, we are short of staff here at Moorooka, and you should see what they have sent me."

I was touched, such a generous and heartfelt welcome. Words fail me. Senior, you were a prince among men.

Moorooka in those days was a busy southside suburban police station with varied police duties, and every Sunday morning at eight I would "mop out" the police station with Senior Sergeant McNaught in his pyjamas and dressing gown supervising me.

"You missed a spot there," he would exclaim.

The police station and the residence being the only buildings, I then went on to wash two motor cars, a Mini Minor and Falcon sedan. After fatigues, one would change back into uniform, after splashing yourself with water from the wash basin to try and freshen up. No showers and no hot water.

What a relief when five months later I was transferred with my family to Warwick. On arrival there I found that that the station employed a "cleaner".

## Warwick Police Station

Warwick for both myself and my family has many fond memories. A pleasant country town, with a staff of 30 people, including a district inspector and a senior sergeant. This station was very social and the staff exceptional. The district inspector upon my arrival in August 1966 was a William McKenzie McNaught, brother of my former officer in charge at Moorooka. Yes, you guessed it — he had also read the Dale Carnegie book on How to Win Friends and Influence People.

Police inspectors came and went at Warwick. It seems to be a town where they saw out the last 12-18 months of their service. In those days the Warwick station workload was constant, with traffic accidents on the main Brisbane to Sydney Highway and also the Cunningham Highway a problem. You worked night work by yourself (midnight to 8am) attending serious traffic accidents with the fog rolling in, plus domestics by yourself. It was at Warwick that

I became interested in the Queensland Police Union, probably due to the influence of men such as Mervyn Callaghan and Ron Eddington, of whom I was in total awe, both men being brilliant speakers who could move the emotions of members at a union meeting.

Constables today would find it hard to believe some of the rules and regulations applying to the employment of their predecessors in those days, eg having to apply for permission to marry, and I saw a number of officers forced to resign for the "crime" of living with their partner.

Have not times changed?

In 1970 at the urging of the Police Minister, Max Hodges, Raymond Whitrod was imported into Queensland as the new Police Commissioner. A decent man by all accounts, but he had no concept of dealing with staff, and quickly got police officers offside by publicly denigrating their educational standards to the media.

I have never understood over the years why governments in Queensland, both Labor and conservative, have this "cultural cringe" and are of the belief that if you import someone, they must be better than the "home-grown" product. So it was with Commissioner Whitrod. (Later with the Victorians, who came into Police Headquarters with an arrogance that had to be seen to be believed.)

Commissioner Whitrod further caused an uproar with his famous 10-year plan. In essence, it was quite simple: If you had been at a particular station for a period of 10 years or more, then you may be subjected to "an unapplied for transfer". At the time I had been unsuccessfully applying for a transfer to a number of one-officer stations in North Queensland, when suddenly I received an unapplied transfer to Burleigh Heads on the Gold Coast.

I immediately arranged a meeting with one of the very senior police administrators, Alfred Martens, who at that time was in charge of all transfers throughout the State.

I explained the following to Martens. I had not applied for the transfer and had only been stationed at Warwick for seven and a half years, well under the prescribed 10-year period. I had only purchased my residence in Warwick approximately four years earlier and this unapplied transfer would cause great hardship to my family.

Martens replied, "We (the Police Service) do not employ your wife and family, we are transferring you, not your family. You have been applying for vacancies in the Police Gazette, so it would appear that you are not happy in your present position".

To the contrary I advised Martens, I was only selecting one-officer stations with a police residence attached. "You will go on transfer," advised Martens.

To give the reader an idea of this man, I recount a personal experience of further dealings I had a number of years later driving him to work. Martens had to be collected from his residence at Carina and driven into the city (all commissioned officers were driven to and from work in those days, a practice later discontinued). To collect Martens, one would park 100 metres up the road from his residence, and as you saw him coming down the front steps, you would drive down to his house, stop the vehicle, rush around and open the front passenger door, saluting him as he entered the vehicle with a grunt.

Many a poor constable would park outside his residence a few minutes early, to be met by sarcastic abuse. One had to come to a stop at the residence as he came out the front gate.

It was an attitude I encountered from Martens that motivated me to "ramp up" my Police Union activities. The Police Service had in those days a number of senior officers with the charm and compassion of Martens, but fortunately they were in the minority.

## Burleigh Heads Police Station

I arrived at Burleigh Heads in March 1973, which was then under the control of Sergeant First Class Bill Blankensee, a fine officer in charge who was a compassionate leader. With a staff of six plus the officer in charge you were expected to work two shifts (8am until midnight). While at Burleigh I made the acquaintance of a fellow officer, John Wilson, "Words" to his friends. John was a decent and compassionate man and I am proud to call him a friend to this day.

However, a senior family illness necessitated that I go to Brisbane, a place I once vowed never to return to having tasted the easy relaxed style of country policing. How did one get to Brisbane?

## Mobile Patrols

I was fortunate that Brisbane Mobile Patrols, quartered at the old police barracks, Petrie Terrace had just been formed and they were having trouble obtaining staff. Union President Ron Eddington informed me to apply. "Mate, the place is known as the salt mines; apply and you will have no trouble getting there." I took Ron's advice and within a month I was in Brisbane at Mobile Patrols. I could never understand the bad press Mobiles received; the place was humming and staff stuck together. Solid coppers such as Neil Linde, Frank Burke, John McDonald and many others made it a pleasure to go to work. The staff played hard and worked hard.

Mobiles were one of the few good ideas Commissioner Whitrod came up with, a motorised version of the beat in Brisbane suburbs with overlapping patrols. In theory an "instant response team", and so I stayed at Mobiles from late 1973 until 1982, apart from a 12-month period at the police operations centre.

## Beenleigh

With just over 16 years' service I was promoted and transferred to Beenleigh station, which was then under the control of Senior Sergeant Bill Sheehan, a decent human being who was both fair and firm. Beenleigh was a very busy station on the southern outskirts of Brisbane, having the main highway to the Gold Coast under its control.

In those times the suburb of Eagleby formed part of the Beenleigh Police Division and was a problem area, and with its history, no wonder. For the short period Gough Whitlam was Prime Minister he released money to the States for housing, but as with all things Gough did, the deal had strings attached. The housing had to be public housing. As a result, land in whole streets was purchased and overnight house frames shot up and modern ghettos were created. No supporting infrastructure and no decent transport. Stand back. It had been created by the bureaucrats at the Queensland Housing Commission, and it was up to the Beenleigh police to referee the problem. Eagleby was a real- life drama, and in its day would have given Big Brother a run for its money.

I had by this time been voted on to the Queensland Police Union Executive, winning three elections and serving from 1979 to 1985, and had found it rewarding and an interesting position. Life was never dull on the executive, which was professionally run in those days by General Secretary Mervyn Callaghan, Assistant General Secretary Tom Mahon and part-time President Col Chant.

During my time on the Union Executive I was paid the princely sum of $20 per fortnightly meeting. We met monthly with Commissioner Terence Murray Lewis in deputation, and I found him to be fair and a reasonable person. That is, as fair and reasonable as one can be with the usual government interference that goes with the job.

Make no mistake, it continues today.

Without debating the rights and wrongs of Commissioner Lewis' stewardship, I have recently pondered what happened to our judges and civil libertarians, who appeared to be missing in action with regard to "pre-trial publicity" in the Lewis trial. It, the "pre-trial publicity", I am happy to report, has been located by Judge Botting in the Denis Ferguson proceedings.

## Beware of The Sharks

I have for some time now explained to some of our young people in the service that every 10 years or so the "powers that be", led by the newspapers, "our moral guardians" (yes – the very same newspapers who took paid advertising from the owners of illegal brothels/escort services), require a victim to feed to the sharks, in order to show that all is well and above board. Don't stub your toe and don't exhibit any human failures in your dealings with the dregs of society.

## Mundingburra

In 1995 I found myself at Logan Police Station and back on the Queensland Police Union as Vice-President. In late 1995 a series of events would occur that would later cause major disruption to the Union and grab the news headlines.

No conspiracies, the facts were simply as follows.

In late 1995 a young policewoman forced to work alone in the Nerang area, her partner going sick and no overtime being approved, was violently assaulted and injured. In the past all attempts to increase staffing thoughout the State had met with negative results. The Police Union had no joy in dealing with Police Minister Paul Braddy.

The attack on the young policewoman was the last straw. The executive decided "to draw a line in the sand" and formulate a plan to expose the staff shortage to the public of Queensland. It was then announced that a by-election was to be conducted in the Townsville suburb of Mundingburra. A young Michael Barnes, the then Metropolitan North Regional Representative and now the current Police Union General Secretary, and myself, would travel to Mundingburra to publicise the staff shortage to the public via the media.

## The Memorandum of Understanding

(See deal with residents –Wolfdene – re dam Wayne Goss.)

The history of the Memorandum of Understanding is well documented. Our Memorandum Of Understanding was to obtain better conditions for our members.

Prior to the Police Union's MOU with the Borbidge Opposition, conservation groups in Queensland had a 37-page MOU with the Goss Government: The National Farmers Federation also had a similar MOU with the Federal Government and Opposition. Interest groups are no strangers to making demands on political parties on behalf of their members.

To quote a local journalist, "The significance of such groups is particularly acute at the time when their leverage is greatest at elections". It made commonsense for the Queensland Police Union employees to travel to Mundingburra and obtain maximum exposure with the press over the shortage of staff, which had resulted in some of their members being injured.

Obviously, as the Police Union's MOU did not appear on the front page of the Courier Mail newspaper, it was "a conspiracy". If not a "conspiracy"then it was, at the very least,a "secret deal". I would ask you, when was the last time you read chapter and verse the demands of any welfare, sporting associations, pro-choice, anti-abortion groups, etc, which were made to both Government and Opposition around election time. Is it seriously suggested that the people in these groups are involved in secret, corrupt deals? I think not.

Michael Barnes and I drove around Mundingburra the week prior to the by-election towing the billboard, and obtaining good coverage with respect to shortage of staff, and then returned to Brisbane. The seat was won by Frank Tanti, a Liberal, and the Goss Government fell. The Police Union was savagely attacked as being the reason the Government lost office. The MOU then became public knowledge. The then Police Minister, Russell Cooper, sent a copy of the MOU to the Criminal Justice Commission Chairperson, Frank Clair, to refute the claims of secret and improper deals.

However, a Commission of Inquiry was to be held under the chairmanship of Mr Kenneth Carruthers QC.

The Criminal Justice Commission had set up what became known as the "Carruthers Inquiry". How impartial was this inquiry? You be the judge.

In an interview I gave to the ABC's talk-back host, Anna Reynolds, I accused the Criminal Justice Commission of bias and "out to smash and destroy the cares of the Police Union Executive for its members". Then following a raid by the CJC at Police Union Headquarters, North Quay (yes they had warrants), Mr Frank Clair, the Chairman, made the following statement to Anna Reynolds, that there was "no question that the Police Union involvement in Mundingburra was a political activity".

Could these remarks perhaps show bias on the part of the chairman of the CJC? This comment was given while the inquiry was in progress. "No, no bias," said Kenneth Carruthers QC. So on went the inquiry.

The Police Union was under attack, and the fledging Borbidge-led Liberal National Party Government was caught in this chain of events. The Police Union was under no misapprehension that the CJC wanted the 'head" of President Gary Wilkinson, a career police officer who bled blue, for breaching Section 155 of The Electoral Act.

But wait a minute! Did I mention that the CJC had in their office received legal advice that there had in fact been NO breach of The Electoral Act.

So what, the inquiry rolled on.

I continued on as Vice-President of the QPU until I contested the position of General Secretary and was elected by the membership and took up that position on the 1 July, 1996. After winning that election I had to resign as a member of the Queensland Police Service in which I had served for 30 and a half years.

The Union was then under the control of Gary Wilkinson as its full-time President. I have always believed that each of us has our own style of leadership and so it was with Gary Wilkinson. He adopted a policy of "take no prisoners", and was in a hurry to right the wrongs and see that our members were well paid and enjoyed reasonable work conditions.

## Anecdotal Information

(Supplied by colleague, friend and fellow political animal Bill Feldman)

Mervyn John Bainbridge, Merv to his mates, was one of the last great characters in the job, a charismatic storyteller who gave the phrase "Never let the facts get in the way of a good story" its true meaning.

I first met Merv in 1977 when I was performing beat duty in the city and he worked in Mobile Patrols. I was in my first weeks on the job and this crusty old senior constable with the wicked sense of humour and a glint in eye, sucking on a cigarette like there was no tomorrow, seemed like the font of all knowledge.

I was at that time the new kid on the block, a bunny, a cadet, not a probationary like the real boys. I was not to be trusted – I was one of Whitrod's "Boys from Brazil". Trained for three to four years at the new Police Academy at Oxley, I was about to race up the promotion system like a monkey up a trapeze and take all their jobs while they wasted their lives on the road.

An example of the distrust was shown first-hand in one of my first arrests, a drunk sailor (enlisted man) in a consulate vehicle who had run up the rear end of an ambulance at the intersection of Queen and Edward streets, pushing the ambulance on to the pedestrian crossing and injuring several persons. (There was NO Mall there in those days and you could drive the length of Queen Street.)

As I arrived back at city station, drunk sailor in tow, I was seeking inspirational advice from my duty sergeant as to my suggested course of action, bearing in mind that I had an RAN sailor in Uniform who was the driver of a consulate vehicle. His reply filled me with a dread I have never experienced since. "You're the smart arse son, work it out for yourself."

Had it not been for a certain senior constable in the Breath Room with an arrest of his own, I am sure the drunken sailor and I would still be there today. Merv helped me through the rigors of my first arrest and assisted with the preparation of my charge sheets and other paperwork, which I know impacted on his own time.

But this was the unique character of the man until his untimely death, always prepared to help, guide, mentor and train, often to his own detriment.

In those days we were also both great political animals and both on the left side of politics, which often put us on the wrong side of most of our senior officers.

Queensland in those days was known as God's Country and Joh Bjelke-Petersen ran his empire with a firm hand and a gerrymander.

Merv and I also stood shoulder-to-shoulder in some of the street march protests of that era as well – we still remember some of the later Labor luminaries of the '90s at that time being arrested for street offences along with a future Brisbane Lord Mayor.

I renewed my acquaintance with Merv when he was promoted to sergeant and transferred to Beenleigh in 1982. I had been transferred to Woodridge Station a year earlier in 1981.

It was the time of the energy disputes – union versus government – and our political allegiances put us at odds with our employers' directions with respect to legitimate union activity and strikes.

At Merv's insistence I became more active in the Police Union, becoming a secretary in the Woodridge branch in 1982. I formed a good friendship with a younger up-and-coming detective at the time, Gary Wilkinson.

Merv made nightwork a blast, having a late-night BBQ breakfast with all the boys and girls from the surrounding stations arriving for the final morning debrief and breakfast – and, of course, Merv holding court and the attention of every constable on shift with some amazing old war stories that I can't tell – only to protect the innocent and not so innocent. Everyone used to delight in the irreverent references to the hierarchy at the time and their failings as constables and supervisors and their not so illustrious rise to their positions of power – and as I said before – never letting the truth spoil a good story.

Merv also took another mate, Axel Pfuhl, under his wing at Beenleigh as well as mentoring him on union activity. Axel has also been engaged ever since with helping those around him. Anyone that worked with Merv knows his genuine concern for his junior staff and the need to keep them safe. Even before there was workplace health and safety legislation there was Merv Bainbridge – like a general looking after his troops.

Merv epitomised the meaning of what I term "Police Culture" – a genuine love for the job (treating it like a vocation and a calling) and a love and respect for each and everyone in the job, deserved or not. An attack on any member of the QPS was like a personal assault on Merv's character himself – this was what made him such a great advocate to have on your side. He genuinely put himself in your shoes and walked the mile in them.

Police culture was vehemently attacked by the Fitzgerald Inquiry and the CJC as a breeding ground for corruption, and the cadet system of education and induction as systematic, institutionalised corruption. I think this was what put Merv at odds with the CJC and later the CMC. Police culture is none of those things at all.

Later Merv Bainbridge, Gary Wilkinson and Axel Pfuhl would all rise to the executive level of the Queensland Police Union. I had another direction coming. With the old Beenleigh Woodridge team of Bainbridge/Wilkinson/Pfuhl all on the executive of the Union, there seemed to be a distinctive Logan connection.

## The Fish Dinner

Hot on the heels of the Mundingburra campaign that saw the Goss Labor Government fall and the subsequent attack on Merv's "other love" (as described by his wife, and true love, Barbara), the Queensland Police Union of Employees, by the CJC in the form of the Carruthers Inquiry, Merv suffered the indignation of being expelled from the Labor Party because he took a stand for the police. His family suffered through his exclusion as a means of punishing Merv, but he stood resolute and showed none of the pain, knowing that those responsible would get their own in the end.

You could really stand Merv at the gates of hell and he would not back down. Seeing what Labor had become, the way they could turn on their own and seeing first-hand their hatred for policing in general, it bought stark reality home to me as well. I hated seeing Merv and his family suffer – just because Merv stood up for his mates – his fellow officers who needed help. Merv seemed the centrepoint of their focus as to why they lost the Mundingburra by-election.

Merv later used his smarts, cunning, nous and wily way with words to cajole me into standing for Pauline Hanson's One Nation in 1997. Wilkinson and Bainbridge double-teamed me with my love of politics and my hatred for what the Labor Machine had become over a fish dinner and a few beers on Caxton Street, much to the bemusement of my son and wife. One Nation had all the earmarks of Old Labor and I could see it winning the heartland of the party – which it did.

Merv became my campaign manager – a job he used to do for a former Police Minister in the southern fringe of Brisbane – and the rest was history. Merv assisted with my election to the Legislative Assembly in the former seat of Caboolture. It is just a pity the gig did not last longer: one more seat for One Nation in the 1998 election and the political landscape would be a lot different today. It was at least refreshing to see Labor squirm for three years. A lot was achieved for police in those three years. Having a political ear so close was always a very handy thing: Police officers know more than they should; they just need a voice to air it. Merv was very attuned to that scenario.

I think Merv got some satisfaction during this period and saw a little payback with a few Labor luminaries exiting from Queensland Parliament.

At the time of writing Bill Feldman is a police officer stationed in North Queensland and is the Queensland Police Union Employees Central Region Representative.

The following paragraphs were added by Barbara Bainbridge – widow of the late Mervyn John Bainbridge, following his death.

> Merv loved his job with the Police Union. He always said he was having the time of his life. He never forgot his friends and NEVER forgot his enemies. Particularly after the Carruthers Inquiry. He enjoyed touring the State and meeting many friends he had served with in the past, no doubt telling his famous "war stories" along the way.
>
> He resigned from the Police Union in the year 2002. He was made a Life Member and this entitled him to attend their annual conference (which he loved going to). There he met up with many of his friends, past and present.

Merv remained on the board of the Queensland Police Credit Union for almost 10 years and this also kept him in touch with his much loved police family. He resigned only a few days before his death, which occurred on 13 May, 2009 at 9.00 am. Our daughter and I were with him and saw him pass peacefully.

His funeral showed how much he was loved and respected by the attendance of more than 500 friends and relatives.

He will be missed by many, but none will feel the absence of this unique man like myself and his children, Kym, Terri and Christian.

# Roslyn Mary Peters nee Kelleher

The first eight female police officers were sworn in on 31 March, 1965. They attained powers of arrest at this time, but a uniform did not become available until 30 June, 1965. The first women to wear a police uniform were Brenda Wilson, Roslyn Kelleher and Sandra Patterson when they were inducted on 30 June, 1965. However, both Wilson and Patterson resigned from the Department, leaving Constable Roslyn Kelleher, PW11, the only uniformed policewoman in the State of Queensland at that time. Roslyn was to meet and marry Constable Tony Peters on 28 October, 1967, and was forced to submit her resignation as the State Public Service Act stipulated that married women could not serve in the Public Service and the Queensland Police Force.

The Act was amended in 1969 to allow the employment of married women in the Public Service but this change did not apply to the Police Department. The high rate of resignation of female police officers due to marriage prompted Police Commissioner Ray Whitrod to seek an end to the marriage bar. Police Minister Max Hodges put the amendment to the Queensland Cabinet and Parliament in October 1971. The amendment allowed for the reappointment of women upon application to the Police Commissioner, but serving policewomen who wanted to marry still had to resign or were automatically dismissed.

The first married woman to rejoin as a police officer was Diane Lindsay. She was first sworn in on 24 April, 1969, met her intended husband, Ian, and resigned to marry on 12 March, 1972 and was credited with past service.

It is thought that sometime in the 1980s policewomen were allowed to marry and remain as serving officers, but marriage applications at the time could be declined or approved at the whim of Police Commissioner Terry Lewis.

The first female uniform issued in June 1965 was worn for the first time at the official swearing-in of probationaries held at the parade ground, Police Academy, Oxley on 30 June, 1965.

Roslyn's experience as a police officer was a huge benefit to her husband, Tony, during his period as officer in charge of Emu Park Police Division, a one-officer station, and during Tony's absence on duty she acted as the Emu Park de-facto police officer. Roslyn's one regret in life is that she was forced to resign from the Queensland Police Force through marriage, and some 45 years later still speaks with enthusiasm about the career she thoroughly enjoyed.

**Laurie Pointing**

# Roslyn Mary Peters nee Kelleher

I was born Roslyn Mary Kelleher on 13 February, 1938, the eldest child of Alice Maud and Terence Kelleher. I have one sister, Margaret, and two brothers, Terrence and John.

My father was a hard-working man employed as a builders' laborer at Wilson & Harts Sawmill in Maryborough. My mother was a stay-at-home mum who looked after and reared the children.

I was educated at St Mary's Convent in Maryborough to junior level.

After leaving school at age 15 I worked for Woolworths until I gained a clerical position at the Maryborough Base Hospital. I worked in many different positions at the hospital, first on the switchboard and assisting with patients' accounts.

I then went to X-ray and Pathology where I assisted in both areas. I then reverted to the reception area in the Outpatient and Emergency Department and from there I left to join the Queensland Police Force.

I entered the Petrie Terrace Police Depot on 5 April, 1965 with approximately 97 male and four female probationaries. The females were – Glenice Bell, Brenda Wilson, Sandra Patterson and myself. From memory Frank Clifford was the senior sergeant (later Assistant Commissioner) in charge of training at the Police Depot and Constable Tom Molloy was the drill instructor.

Tom was an Irishman and a former merchant seaman with a reputation as a man who could make or break a probationary constable within the first few weeks of his/her training. While I found him to be very strict I developed a good working rapport with him and was never once disciplined.

Glenice left about one month into the course, but Brenda, Sandra and myself were sworn in on 30 June, 1965 and I was allotted Registered No. PW11.

We were inducted on the parade grounds at the Petrie Terrace Police Barracks and I believe the Commissioner of Police at the time was Frank Bischof.

That meant I was police woman number 11. In those days there was a distinction between male and female and females placed the letters PW before their registered number when signing correspondence. That has now changed and males and females are all referred to as one.

After our induction we three females were transferred to Roma Street Police Station. Some three to six months after we were sworn in Brenda Wilson resigned and some short time later Sandra Patterson also resigned, which left me the only uniformed policewoman in Queensland.

I performed general duties at Roma Street, Traffic Branch and with the Criminal Investigation Branch detectives in Consorting. Because I was recently sworn in and not known I also performed duty with the Licensing Branch and over a period was involved in quite a number of Licensing Branch raids.

I can recall going to a country town on an SP betting raid and there were 18 detectives and me. We stopped at a park to partake of morning tea and as we were not travelling in recognisable police vehicles nobody knew who we were.

A lady with a little girl approached us and said, "Are you people from the Apex?" Someone replied, "No". She replied, "Thank God for that; I just come down to pinch some sand for my daughter's sand pit". One of our crew remarked, "I wonder what she would say if she knew we were 19 coppers".

Another interesting job for me was taking a young girl on escort to Roma and she was a witness in a carnal knowledge case. During the escort I was accompanied by Sergeant Trevor Blackwell and we left Brisbane by train and from memory travelled through the night before reaching Roma early next morning.

The girl was aged about 16 and was an inmate of the Holy Cross Home at Woolloowin where she had been admitted by the Children's Court for being in need of "Care and Control/or Care and Protection".

Entering the witness box she gave her evidence and the presiding District Court judge remarked that her evidence was different from what she gave in the Magistrate's Court. He then said, "I am going to adjourn to think about it".

This young girl then said to me "What am I going to do?" I said to her, "When you get back in the witness box, just speak the truth and you can't get into trouble". We went back into court and the judge said to her, "Has any person in authority, including police officers, told you what to say?"

The girl replied, "Yes". The judge said "Who?", to which the girl replied "Roslyn". The prosecutor then informed the judge that Roslyn was Constable Kelleher. The judge then said, "And what did Constable Kelleher tell you to say?" and the girl replied, "If you speak the truth you can't get into trouble". That was a relief for me.

While stationed at Roma Street Police Station, the roster clerk, Les Howard, introduced me to Constable Tony Peters who had just arrived back from a tour of duty in Cyprus. I told Sergeant Howard I was not interested in anyone, however, Tony and I started keeping company and then we became engaged. Our engagement made headlines in the Courier Mail newspaper with the heading "Two Constables become engaged", with a write-up about our engagement.

Tony and I married on 28 October, 1967 and as a result I was forced to resign as married policewomen were not acceptable in the police force back then.

At the time of our marriage Tony was a constable first class (one stripe) and early in the year 1968 was transferred to Killarney Police Division, a two-man station, as the second police officer. A sergeant second class was the officer in-charge. Today police divisions like Killarney are referred to as "Two-officer stations".

We were there for about three years and it was not a happy time. The sergeant was a very selfish man who treated his constable like a second-class citizen and his wife had a very high opinion of herself and on the occasions when she introduced me to other people would say "Oh, meet Roslyn. She is the constable's wife".

In April 1971 Tony was successful in being appointed the officer in charge of Emu Park Police Division, a one-man station in the Rockhampton Police District and not that far from Yeppoon.

Having had experience as a police officer was a big plus as the police officer's wife at Emu Park, manning the telephone and answering inquiries in Tony's absence. On many occasions I was able to refer the person's complaint or inquiry to other police establishments, enabling them to have their complaint satisfactorily finalised before Tony returned from the urgent job he was investigating, such as serious or fatal road accidents.

During flood periods at this location I would be up all night manning the telephone while Tony was absent on flood or other serious duty. If there was an accident on the Emu Park Road the casualties would be brought to our police residence and laid on the lounge-room floor until the ambulance arrived from Yeppoon.

Tony was a diabetic and on one occasion went for days with little sleep while searching and dragging Cooramin Creek for a missing female. He had just returned home and was taking his medication and partaking of a meal when he received a telephone call from a female regarding a prowler.

On investigation it was established that there was no prowler, but this woman was at the home of a well-known doctor and maintained that she was renting the premises. It was established that this woman was wearing a lace dress with no under garments and appeared to be somewhat unstable.

Next morning the doctor telephoned and said to me, "Ros, do you know if there is anyone at my house?" I replied "Yes," and told him the story.

Tony accompanied the doctor to his residence and this woman, who was unknown to the doctor, was still there. She had set the dining-room table with the best of everything and had consumed all the doctor's alcohol. This unfortunate lady was suffering from mental problems and was admitted to hospital for treatment.

Superintendent Frank Clifford was the senior police officer for the Rockhampton Police District during our period at Emu Park and one day when he called at the police station he said to me, "Police wives in one-man stations, in addition to rearing their families, do much for the Police Department and the community and should be paid an allowance".

While at Emu Park our four sons, Clinton, Bradley, Roderick and Gregory, were born and our daughter, Maree, was born after we left Emu Park and returned to Brisbane.

After approximately five years at Emu Park, Tony transferred to Ashgrove and we moved back into our own residence. For the remaining years of his police career Tony served at Ashgrove, City Station and Mobile Patrols before retiring on 24 January, 1994 with the rank of sergeant first class.

Sadly in the year 2004 we lost Roderick and in 2007 Tony passed away aged 68.

I have never regretted serving one day as a police officer or one day as a police officer's wife. If I were young again I would again pursue a career in the

Queensland Police Service, however, today I would not have to resign from a career that I enjoyed once I married.

Once we had settled back in our own home in Brisbane from Emu Park and the children had reached a manageable age, I obtained my security officer's licence and worked undercover for Target for many years. I also performed security work on crowd control at football matches, concerts and many other functions where the public gathered in mass for some form of entertainment. At the time of writing I work on security at the front door of Target at Chermside.

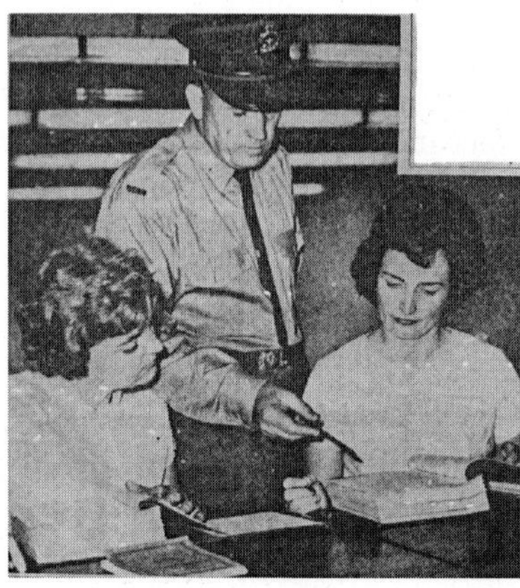

First classes for the latest batch of four probationary policewomen who entered the Petrie Terrace police training barracks today. Here is Sergeant D Bodenham an instructor from the police educational section, with two of the trainees – Brenda Wilson, left, and Roslyn Kelleher. They will do the same study and physical courses as male constables.

Constable Roslyn Mary Kelleher. Policewoman number 11' following her induction on 30th June, 1965.

y Western Publishers Pty. Ltd.,
es Street, Toowoomba.

SUBSCRIPTIONS (PAYABLE IN ADVANCE) TO THE "WESTERN STAR" ARE:
BOTH PAPERS — £2/10/-; FRIDAY ONLY — £1/10/-; TUESDAY ONLY — £1.

Y IN QUEENSLAND

ern Star

MITCHELL NEWS

. Friday morning)

19th Year of Publication

**K. J. Simons & Co.**

Home handy to town, suit large family, Combustion stove, H.W.S. .. £1975 (189)

Two bedroomed home with S/O., Combustion stove, H.W.S. .. .. .. .. £3,000 (185)

Large High home, concreted underneath, in excellent position .. .. .. .. £3,500 (182)

RIDAY, OCTOBER 15, 1965

(Registered at G.P.O., Brisbane, for Transmission by Post as a Newspaper.)

## own Clerk sends letter to Mayor

**Roma's Town Clerk, Mr. Frank S. Smith, resigned from his position at last Wednes- week's Council meeting and was given a to re-consider his decision, wrote a letter e Mayor, Ald. K. A. McGrath, this week.**

The letter reads: "I refer to my resigna- dated October 2, 1965, and more par- arly to a motion carried at a Council ing held on the sixth instant, which gave seven days to re-consider my decision. I , therefore, formally to advise that I have ved at a decision and this will be announc- o Aldermen present at the next ordinary ting of the Council to be held on October 1965. — (Signed) Francis S. Smith.

GH SCHOOL IN TROUBLE

## day out for the spinners

**ma State High School lost to Railways first innings on Sunday after getting o a good start, with fast scoring in an even time.**

G. Sabine dis-
ry strong leg
e falling l.b.w.
Brien for 28.
on also scored
the fast attack,
bowled by P.
12.
ice of High's
und great diffi-
lling Railway's
Brian Fogarty,
could be the
ol coaches will
edy early, as
gures of 5 for
ol leg spinner,
showed good
pture four Rail-
ts for only 15
1st innings

R. Harms, b. Brinin .. 18
G. Thompson, not out .. 13
J. Gillam, b. Perkins .. 3
R. Eddy, c. and b. Perkins .. .. .. .. .. .. 0
K. Kearsey, b. Eske .. 1
P. Stevens, b. Eske .. 0
T. Lunney, b. Perkins 1
Sundries .. .. .. .. .. 9

Total .. .. .. .. .. 137

Bowling: K. Brinin 2/25; M. Langton 1/37; K. Killorn 0/23; G. Sabine 0/27; F. Eske 4/15; C. Perkins 3/1.

**High School, 1st innings**

G. Sabine, l.b.w., b. O'Brien .. .. .. .. .. .. 28
C. Perkins, b. O'Brien 0
M. Langton, b. Thrupp 12
M. Legg, run out .. .. 0
K. Feeney, c. Fogarty 0
F. Eske, stpd. Lunney 3

## LATEST FASHION

The latest fashion in police-women's summer uniform is worn for the first time in the State by Const. Roslyn Kelleher, who is on escort duty at Roma. The uniform is coloured green and is of a lightweight material. According to Const. Kelleher, it is very comfortable. Const. Kelleher, who was a clerk at a Maryborough (Q.) hospital, joined the Police Force in June. She has been in Roma on escort duty in connection with a district court case.

## LITTLE PARIS TO

*Western Star* – Roma – Friday, October 15, 1965. The latest fashion in police- women's summer uniform is worn for the first time in the State by Constable Roslyn Kelleher, who is on escort duty at Roma. The uniform is coloured green and is of lightweight material. According to Constable Kelleher, it is very comfortable. Constable Kelleher, who was a clerk at a Maryborough (Q) hospital, joined the Police Force in June. She has been in Roma on escort duty in connection with a District Court case. The above article refers to the photograph in the *Roma Western Star* – October, 15, 1965.

**A Maryborough woman, Constable Roslyn Kelleher, one of the first three Queensland policewomen in uniform, has found her new life full of interest.**

Constable Kelleher, who formerly was on the Maryborough Hospitals Board office staff, said yesterday that she had never regretted changing her job.

A woman did not lose any of her femininity by doing the work.

Any woman with good stamina and who liked people, and who mixed well with people should find the work interesting, she said.

Yesterday, Constable Kelleher looked feminine and well groomed in her summer uniform of mint green terylene, made with a tailored bodice, rolled collar and revers, and inverted pleat in the centre back.

The uniform is buttoned through with regulation police buttons, has a trim tailored skirt and is cut with two side inset pockets. It has a concealed front closing from waist to hem.

Her cap is the same style as that worn by male officers, except that those worn by women have a chrome band across the front.

She wore flat-heeled brown tie shoes, nylon stockings, brown leather bag (casual size), and brown leather gloves.

Constable Kelleher joined the force on April 5, 1965, and after having completed three months' training, was sworn in on June 30, 1965.

She then was transfered to the Roma Street station, Brisbane.

**DIRECTING TRAFFIC**

Her official duties since have included directing traffic in Brisbane. One of her duty points had been the "five-way" corner at Kelvin Grove.

She also has done general duties and rounds, assisted with women prisoners, done rounds of sound lounges and hotel lounges.

She has assisted in taking mental cases from the Brisbane General Hospital to Goodna, and travelled to Roma with a woman on trial.

Her official visit to Maryborough has been to escort a woman defendant on a wilful murder charge.

Constable Kelleher said that women police did exactly the same routine work as male officers. They could make an arrest.

She carries her official notebook at all times.

She said that policewomen could issue on the spot tickets for traffic breaches.

"It's not all arresting, though. You try to help people as much as you can," she said.

Constable Kelleher said she had found the public "easy to handle," and ready to accept the policewoman's authority.

—"JENNIFER."

*Maryborough Cronicle*, Thursday, April 21, 1966. Photograph – Happy In Job

A Maryborough woman, Constable Roslyn Kelleher, one of the first three Queensland policewomen in uniform, has found her new life full of interest.

Constable Kelleher, who was formerly on the Maryborough Base Hospital office staff, said yesterday that she never regretted changing her job.

"A woman did not lose any of her femininity by doing the work.

Any woman with good stamina and who liked people and who mixed well with people should find the work interesting," she said.

Yesterday, Constable Kelleher looked feminine and well groomed in her summer uniform of mint-green terylene, made with tailored bodice, rolled collar and revers, and inverted pleat in the centre back.

The uniform is buttoned through with regulation police buttons, has a trim, tailored skirt with inset pockets. It has a concealed front closing from waist to hem.

Her cap is the same style as that worn by male officers, except those worn by women have a chrome band across the front.

She wore flat-heeled brown tie shoes, nylon stockings, brown leather bag (casual size) and brown leather gloves.

Constable Kelleher joined the force on April 5, 1965, and after having completed three months training, was sworn in on June 30, 1965.

She then was transferred to the Roma Street Station, Brisbane.

## DIRECTING TRAFFIC

Her official duties since have included directing traffic in Brisbane. One of her duty points has been the "five-ways" corner at Kelvin Grove.

She has also done general duties and rounds, assisting with women prisoners, done rounds of sound lounges and hotel lounges.

She has assisted in taking mental cases from the Brisbane General Hospital to Goodna, and travelled to Roma with a woman on trial.

Her official visit to Maryborough has been to escort a woman defendant on a wilful murder charge.

Constable Kelleher said that women police did exactly the same routine work as male officers. They could make an arrest.

She carries her official notebook at all times.

She said that policewomen could issue on the spot tickets for traffic breaches.

"It's not all arresting though. You try to help people as much as you can," she said.

Constable Kelleher said she had found the public "easy to handle", and ready to accept the policewomen's authority.

*Maryborough Cronicle – Thursday, April 21, 1966*

Constable Roslyn Kelleher — the first policewoman Rockhampton has seen — is pictured at right discussing an entry in her police book with Constable Warren Hansen of the Rockhampton Traffic Branch.

Constable Kelleher is wearing the official policewomen's winter uniform.

It includes a semi-fitted tailored jacket, fastened with silver police buttons, and slender skirt, both in the same khaki fabric which is used for uniforms worn by policemen. The blouse is more feminine — it is in cream silk terylene, with full-length cuffed sleeves, flap pockets and military shoulders. Her police cap is exactly the same as those worn by male police officers, apart from a chrome band, which is fastened above the peaked leather brim at the front.



**then look again!**

**Constable Roslyn Kelleher has had to become used to people turning for a second glimpse of her all over again, after a year of complete acceptance in Brisbane.**

**She has spent the last three days on duty in Rockhampton, and has caught the public eye because she is the first policewoman to be seen in the city.**

Constable Kelleher has been with the Queensland Police Force nearly a year, and is quite used to acceptance by policewoman-conscious Brisbane people.

She is one of the first three uniformed policewomen to become members of the Force at a swearing-in ceremony in Brisbane last June, and is proud of her uniform.

The swearing-in ceremony came after a three-month training course — the same one followed by male constables before they officially join the Force.

The Queensland Police Force has for some time included policewomen who wear civilian clothes, and there are nine in this section in Brisbane. But the uniformed policewoman is definitely a newcomer, and there are only four in Queensland. All are stationed in Brisbane.

Constable Kelleher said that a few more women who will become uniformed police, are being trained now at the Petrie Terrace depot.

She said uniformed women constables are given the same general duties as the male constables, and have the same powers. The only difference between them is that policewomen receive less pay than men.

Her general duties have included quite a lot of escort work (to Rockhampton, Maryborough, Roma and in the Brisbane area), court orderly work, accidents and traffic (she has been on point duty at busy Brisbane intersections).

Because she is attached to Brisbane's Roma Street police station she also works with that station's Juvenile Delinquency Squad. She said being a policewoman has sharpened her powers of observation and she takes her community responsibilities more seriously.

Constable Keleher came to Rockhampton on escort duty, but during her stay has been rostered on general duties with the Rockhampton police.

She finds Rockhampton an interesting city, and the people very friendly.

But because she is a woman in police uniform, she has been attracting quite a lot of attention, and most people turn for a second glance as she carries out her duties.

Before her application to join the Force was accepted in April last year, Roslyn Kelleher was a clerk at the Maryborough Base Hospital.

She said none of her family or friends in Maryborough expressed surprise when she left to become a policewoman — she had been talking about it for years.

Constable Kelleher said that when she is off duty and out of uniform, and meets people who ask where she is employed, she replies: "I'm in the Police Force." Their immediate reaction is: "Oh, in the office section."

When they discover she is a uniformed policewoman, they show surprise, then interest.

"And that," says the constable, "is what is marvellous about my job—it is always interesting and full of variety."

Rockhampton: *The Morning Bulletin*, May 13, 1966.

**FEATURE PAGE**

Constable Roslyn Kelleher – the first policewoman Rockhampton has seen – is pictured at right discussing an entry in her police book with Constable Warren Hansen of the Rockhampton Traffic Branch.

Constable Kelleher is wearing the official policewomen's winter uniform.

It includes a semi-fitted tailored jacket, fastened with silver police buttons, and slender skirt, both in the same khaki fabric that is used for uniforms worn by policemen. The blouse is more feminine – it is in cream silk terylene, with full-length cuffed sleeves, flap pockets and military shoulders. Her police cap is exactly the same as those worn by male police officers, apart from a chrome band, which is fastened above the peaked leather brim at the front.

A policewoman, people say – then look again!

Constable Roslyn Kelleher has had to become used to people turning for a second glimpse of her all over again, after a year of complete acceptance in Brisbane.

She has spent the past three days on duty in Rockhampton, and has caught the public eye because she is the first policewoman to be seen in the city.

Constable Kelleher has been with the Queensland Police Force nearly a year, and is quite used to acceptance by policewomen conscious Brisbane people.

She is one of the first three uniformed policewomen to become members of the Force at a swearing-in ceremony in Brisbane last June, and is proud of her uniform.

The swearing-in ceremony came after a three-month training course – the same one followed by male constables before they officially join the Force.

The Queensland Police Force has for some time included policewomen who wear civilian clothes, and there are nine in this section in Brisbane. But the uniformed policewoman is definitely a newcomer, and there are only four in Queensland. All are stationed in Brisbane.

Constable Kelleher said that a few more women who will become uniformed police are being trained now at the Petrie Terrace depot.

She said uniformed women constables are given the same general duties as the male constables, and have the same powers. The only diference between them is that policewomen receive less pay than men.

Her general duties have included quite a lot of escort work (to Rockhampton, Maryborough, Roma and in the Brisbane area), court orderly work, accidents and traffic (she has been on point duty at busy Brisbane intersections).

Because she is attached to Brisbane's Roma Street Police Station she also works with that station's Juvenile Delinquency Squad. She said being a policewoman has sharpened her powers of observations and she takes her community responsibilities more seriously.

Constable Kelleher came to Rockhampton on escort duty, but during her stay has been rostered on general duties with the Rockhampton police.

She finds Rockhampton an interesting city, and the people very friendly.

But because she is a woman in police uniform she has been attracting quite a lot of attention, and most people turn for a second glance as she carries out her duties.

Before her application to join the Force was accepted in April last year, Roslyn Kelleher was a clerk at the Maryborough Base Hospital.

She said none of her family or friends in Maryborough expressed surprise when she left to become a policewoman – she has been talking about it for years.

Constable Kelleher said that when she is off duty and out of uniform, and meets people who ask where she is employed, she replies: "I'm in the Police Force." Their immediate reaction is: "Oh, in the office section."

When they discover she is a uniformed policewoman they show surprise, then interest.

"And that," says the constable, "is what is marvellous about my job – it is always interesting and full of variety."

MYER McWHIRTERS Allan & Stark
Chermside • Coorparoo • Toowoomba

Now! Lowest ever prices on Hoover!

For the fli

TWO CONSTABLES HAVE BECOME ENGAGED

CONSTABLE PETERS.

CONSTABLE KELLEHER.

**ONE of the first three women sworn in as uniformed members of the Police Force announced her engagement—to a policeman.**

She is **Constable Roslyn Kelleher**, of New Farm and formerly of Maryborough, who joined the Police Force in April, 1965, and was sworn in on June 30 of that year. Since then she has done general police duties including school crossings, Coroner's Court and working with juvenile delinquents.

Her fiance is **Constable 1-c. Tony Peters**, of Ferny Grove, who is attached to Windsor Police Station. Constable Peters spent 12 months in Cyprus with the Australian contingent and returned to Brisbane last July. He was posted to Roma Street where he met his fiancee.

Constabl Kelleher is wearing a solitaire diamond ring set in yellow gold. The wedding date has not yet been fixed.

**Two constables have become engaged**.

One of the first three women sworn in as uniformed members of the Police Force announced her engagement – to a policeman.

She is Constable Roslyn Kelleher, of New Farm and formerly of Maryborough, who joined the Police Force in April 1965, and was sworn in on June 30 of that year. Since then she has done general police duties, including school crossings, Coroner's Court and working with juvenile delinquents.

Her fiancé is Constable 1-c Tony Peters, of Ferny Grove, who is attached to Windsor Police Station. Constable Peters spent 12 months in Cyprus with the Australian contingent and returned to Brisbane last July. He was posted to Roma Street where he met his fiancée.

Constable Kelleher is wearing a solitaire diamond ring set in yellow gold. The wedding date has not yet been set.

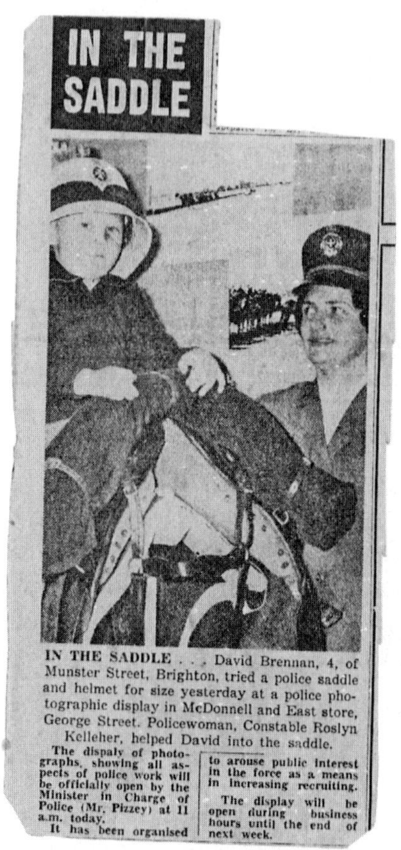

**IN THE SADDLE**

**IN THE SADDLE** . . . David Brennan, 4, of Munster Street, Brighton, tried a police saddle and helmet for size yesterday at a police photographic display in McDonnell and East store, George Street. Policewoman, Constable Roslyn Kelleher, helped David into the saddle.

The dispaly of photographs, showing all aspects of police work will be officially open by the Minister in Charge of Police (Mr. Pizzey) at 11 a.m. today.

It has been organised to arouse public interest in the force as a means in increasing recruiting.

The display will be open during business hours until the end of next week.

In the saddle… David Brennan, 4, of Munster Street, Brighton, tried a police saddle and helmet for size yesterday at a police photographic display in the McDonnell and East store, George Street. Policewoman Constable Roslyn Kelleher helped David into the saddle.

The display of photographs, showing all aspects of police work, will be officially opened by the Minister in charge of Police (Mr Pizzy) at 11am today. It has been organised to arouse public interest in the Force as a means of increasing recruiting. The display will be open during business hours until the end of next week.

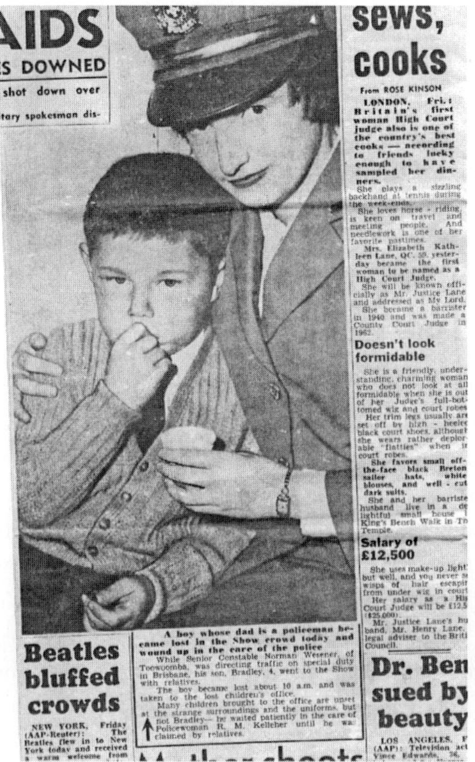

AIDS

ES DOWNED

shot down over

itary spokesman dis-

**sews, cooks**

From ROSE KINSON

**LONDON, Fri.: Britain's first woman High Court judge also is one of the country's best cooks — according to friends lucky enough to have sampled her dinners.**

She plays a sizzling backhand at tennis during the week-ends.

She loves horse - riding, is keen on travel and meeting people. And needlework is one of her favorite pastimes.

**Mrs. Elizabeth Kathleen Lane, QC, 50, yesterday became the first woman to be named as a High Court Judge.**

She will be known officially as Mr. Justice Lane and addressed as My Lord.

She became a barrister in 1940 and was made a County Court Judge in 1962.

**Doesn't look formidable**

She is a friendly, understanding, charming woman who does not look at all formidable when she is out of her Judge's full-bottomed wig and court robes

Her trim legs usually are set off by high - heeled black court shoes, although she wears rather deplorable "flatties" when in court robes.

**She favors small off-the-face black Breton sailor hats, white blouses, and well - cut dark suits.**

She and her barriste husband live in a de lightful small house King's Bench Walk in Th Temple.

**Salary of £12,500**

She uses make-up light but well, and you never s wisps of hair escapi from under wig in court

Her salary as a Hi Court Judge will be £12,5 ($25,000).

Mr. Justice Lane's hu band, Mr. Henry Lane, legal adviser to the Brit Council.

**A boy whose dad is a policeman became lost in the Show crowd today and wound up in the care of the police**

While Senior Constable Norman Wesener, of Toowoomba, was directing traffic on special duty in Brisbane, his son, Bradley, 4, went to the Show with relatives.

The boy became lost about 10 a.m. and was taken to the lost children's office.

Many children brought to the office are upset at the strange surroundings and the uniforms, but not Bradley— he waited patiently in the care of Policewoman R. M. Kelleher until he was claimed by relatives.

**Beatles bluffed crowds**

NEW YORK, Friday (AAP-Reuter): The Beatles flew in to New York today and received a warm welcome from

**Dr. Ben sued by beauty**

LOS ANGELES, F (AAP): Television act Vince Edwards, 36,

Exhibition Grounds. Photo of young Bradley Wesener.

A boy whose dad is a policeman became lost in the show crowd today and wound up in the care of the police.

While Senior Constable Norman Wesener, of Toowoomba, was directing traffic on special duty in Brisbane, his son, Bradley, 4, went to the Show with relatives.

The boy became lost about 10am and was taken to the lost children's office.

Many children brought to the office are upset at the strange surroundings and the uniform, but not Bradley – he waited patiently in the care of policewoman R M Kelleher until he was claimed by relatives.

# Alan Beattie (Abe) Duncan

Abe Duncan was born on 31 May, 1915 and entered the Police Depot at Petrie Terrace, Brisbane to commence his training as a probationary constable on 3 August, 1936, and at the time of writing this remarkable man is still functioning quite well and celebrated his 97th birthday on 31 May, 2012. It is interesting to note that Abe commenced his police training 16 days before I was born. I commenced my Criminal Investigation Branch career at the CI Branch, Brisbane almost on the same date that Abe received his promotion to sub-inspector of police. I quickly gleaned that Sub-Inspector Duncan was one of the few senior officers in those days who fostered good working relations between commissioned rank and non-commissioned officers, and he went to great lengths to encourage junior officers in their day-to-day activities and to assist them wherever possible. When I took up duty at the Criminal Investigation Branch, Biloela (a one-officer CI Branch office) during September 1970, Abe was the inspector of police in charge of the Rockhampton Police District and was quick to pick up the telephone and welcome me to the district. I served as a member of the Queensland Police Service for just on 35 years and during that period and my retirement years I have heard many positive reports regarding the ability and competence of this highly respected retired Assistant Commissioner of Police, Alan Beattie (Abe) Duncan.

Had Abe been appointed Commissioner of Police for the State of Queensland during the late 1960s and early 1970s he would have done much to enhance the reputation of the Police Service during that period. He was awarded the Queen's Police Medal on 1 January, 1974 and the Queensland Police Service Medal on 19 April ,2010.

In his story Mr Duncan mentions a character named Edward Eugene Ebzery, who was well known in police circles many years ago. I had never met this gentleman as he was past his prime when I joined the Police Service, however, I believe that during his lifetime Eugene Ebzery held the record for the most convictions for the then offence of "being found drunk in a public place". Ebzery from all accounts possessed a humorous wit and at times the presiding stipendiary magistrate found him to be rather amusing.

It is said that on one occasion the magistrate said to him "And what brings you to court this time, Mr Ebzery?" to which he replied, "Two constables, Your Worship". "Drunk again I see," replied the magistrate. "Yes, Your Worship, both of them," was Ebzery's curt reply. On another occasion the magistrate said to him prior to handing down his decision, "I am considering sentencing you to a term of imprisonment. What do you have to say for yourself?" Ebzery replied, "I would like another chance, Your Worship, I have a job to go to. It's called ringbarking. You know, ringbarking trees". After some consideration the magistrate replied, "All right then, one more chance". As the defendant was leaving the courtroom the magistrate remarked, "By the way, Mr Ebzery, where is this job?" Ebzery replied, "A place called One Tree Hill, Your Worship".

My thanks to retired Assistant Commissioner Greg Early for his efforts in obtaining the following story from Mr Abe Duncan.

Alan Beattie Duncan passed to eternal life on the 21 June, 2012.

**Laurie Pointing**

# Alan Beattie (Abe) Duncan

I was born at Kilcoy on 31 May, 1915 in the Kilcoy Hospital and I was brought up in and around the Kilcoy district for most of my early life. I'll explain why I am known as Abe. My initials are AB and in my youth I was usually called AB, but in later years that was changed to Abe. I prefer Abe to Alan.

I first went to school at Hazledean, the correct name of which was then the Stanley River State School, which was about seven miles south of Kilcoy on the way to Somerset Dam. I walked about three or four miles to school in those days, and then when I was in my final year before scholarship I walked three or four miles the other way to the Kilcoy State School, where I was successful in passing the scholarship examination in 1928.

From there my parents sent me to Brisbane Grammar School where I boarded for two and a half years to the end of 1930, after which I passed the Junior university examination, but because of the Depression days and the lack of funds they were unable to send me on to Senior and I was forced to come back home and live with my parents. My father was then a teamster – he had a bullock team – and I did a little bit of assisting on my grandparents' dairy farm.

It was a sacrifice for my parents to send me to a boarding school and I still don't know how they managed it. Of course the fees weren't very high in those days, but by the same token I was very grateful for the fact that they were able to send me just the same. I'm sorry in this respect that they weren't able to send me on to Senior, because in later years I met many of my school friends who did go on to Senior who showed no greater brilliance than I did and yet were able to become specialists, doctors, lawyers and all sorts of things that I would have dearly loved to have had the opportunity of becoming.

I was always a keen sportsman and represented Kilcoy in cricket and football. I continued playing cricket after I joined the Police Force and one of my proudest moments was in the 1937/38 season, while playing for the police team in the Warehouse Competition, when I gained a double hat-trick (four successive wickets) as a fast/medium opening bowler.

Why did I join the Queensland Police Force? I longed in my teens to try to get a government job that would guarantee me work satisfaction and security, and anything that came along in the papers I would apply for without much success. I tried to become a school teacher. I'd put in an application for the police cadets when that first came out around about 1934. They only selected very few at that stage and I was unsuccessful in getting employment beyond a very small period in which I obtained an office job in Kilcoy around about 1935. My employer died and I was out of a job again, but then when police qualifying examinations were set for the first time in 1936, I sat for them in the Kilcoy courthouse. I think that was on my 21st birthday, together with Frank Thrupp, who later went through the Police Force and became a superintendent. I was called up on 1/8/1936 in the first call-up after the examination.

Policemen in the making. A study in concentration at the police depot yesterday, when the theoretical examination of recruits for the force was in progress. *Courier Mail.*

At this time I was working in a gang on Ferling's property at Sheep Station Creek. We were grubbing small bushes and ringbarking trees. I recall riding my pushbike to Kilcoy and getting a ride in a utility truck to Brisbane so that I could attend the Commissioner's Office, which was then in the Treasury Building (now the Treasury Casino) on Saturday, 1/8/1936. I was successful in getting through the medical part of it. I was allowed to go home and get some clothes so that I could return to Brisbane and go into the Police Depot as a recruit on Monday, 3 August, 1936.

The period of my probationary training at Petrie Terrace (3-8-1936 to 26-10-36) was in the days before the brick Police Depot, which was built in 1939. Probationaries would rise at 6am and clean out the stables of approximately 12 police horses, which assisted the Mounted Police; we would put the horse manure into a large brick kiln, which was later emptied by Chinese market gardeners; after breakfast a fellow probationary, Mal O'Mara, and myself would stock up the wood heap using crosscut saws and axes. The wood was used for the wood stoves there at the time; probationaries did all the manual work that was required at the Depot.

In those days Sergeant Digger Walsh lived in a house on the premises and Inspector Charlie Perrin also lived in a little wooden house alongside the wooden barracks. Inspector Perrin was one of the lecturers as was Sergeant First Class Tom Walsh. Probationaries were given lectures in the afternoon on the Criminal Code, Vagrants, Gaming and Other Offences Act, etc. We had rifle drill with .303 rifles, wrestling and boxing as well as other physical training, all performed at the Depot. The wooden barracks were on top with a large classroom underneath.

The older probationaries would play tricks on the new recruits, such as sending them out with a bucket to find the cows to milk or climbing up a tree and rattling the branches so that the leaves would fall off so that they could be swept up.

I was sworn in at the Police Depot with Ted Chandler, Stew Walker, Mal O'Mara, Keith Hall and Ted Osborne. We were sworn-in by Cec Carrol, who was the Commissioner of Police at the time. Carrol is the second-longest serving Police Commissioner after Commissioner Seymour in the history of the Queensland Police Service.

The date of my swearing-in was on 27 October, 1936 and I was allotted Registered No. 3496.

I was pretty light in those days and having come from the country I was selected, not of my own wish, to go into the Mounted Police, which I did as soon as I was sworn in. I did this somewhat reluctantly. I served with the

Mounted Police, who were then based at Petrie Terrace, until 1938. Our job then was grooming the horses, taking part in parades and crowd control, attending to governmental escorts and all those sorts of things. That to me wasn't really attractive and I applied for a country transfer. On 9 July, 1938 I was posted to Bollon, which is in the south-western corner of Queensland in the Roma Police District.

That was a two-man station where I served under Sergeant Jim Elstob. Jim was a very good sergeant. He was comparatively junior, but he was quite a student and he maintained strict disciplinarian procedures even at a small place like Bollon. He used every opportunity to help me with my studies. I lost no time either in studying laws associated with the Police Force because I hadn't done much actual police work before I went out to Bollon. I've got to thank Jim for quite a lot of the knowledge that I acquired, even though I applied for and was appointed a junior plain-clothes constable on 11 March, 1939 at the CI Branch, Brisbane, after only having served about eight months in the country, but I might say that while at Bollon I learnt a lot there in clerk of petty sessions work and all sorts of work associated with government duties at a two-man police station.

There was a special intake of, I think, 20 plain-clothes constables into the CI Branch and I was fortunate to be selected with such a small amount of service. Another thing that had some bearing on my selection was an arrest I made while at Bollon. I had some difficulty one day with the arrest of a well-known character of the west, who was generally known as The Desert Lair. I attempted to arrest The Desert Lair on a charge of disorderly conduct. I was unable to handle him and I did call on a member of the public in the name of the King to assist me in arresting him. Then there was an offence, an indictable offence, under the Criminal Code, and if any person when called on in the King's or Queen's name to assist a police officer did not do so he could be charged with an indictable offence, and it so happened that the person I did call on didn't assist me. He was later charged and was committed for trial and that may well have had some bearing on the fact that I wasn't too proud to try and administer the law as I saw it. That law of course has been omitted from the statutes, although I don't know why this was done.

After 12 months in the CI Branch in Brisbane I was transferred as a plain-clothes constable to the CI Branch in Rockhampton. I received further assistance there from Detective Sergeant Jack O'Malley, who was the only other member of the CI Branch then at Rockhampton, and the two of us handled the situation well there until I was transferred in 1941 to Cairns as a detective on probation, which appointment was confirmed after six months.

While I was at Cairns Japan had come into the war and we had a lot of extraneous duties associated with the war. After serving there until 1943 I was transferred to the mobile police section under Inspector Bill Garvey at Atherton. When I went to Atherton there were thousands and thousands of troops and civilian employees there all over the tableland. There were large numbers of police at Mareeba, Atherton and a lot of other places.

While I was in Cairns I had gone to Rockhampton and got married and my wife then accompanied me to Atherton.

In 1943 I was transferred back to Brisbane as a detective constable and I served under various detective sergeants in Brisbane. Norm Bauer was one of those with whom I first served. He later became Commissioner. I worked with Bill Cronau who was a well known thief catcher. I was the junior partner of course for many years until in later years they used to assign a junior partner with me. I was successful in obtaining second class sergeant rank after about 13 years' service, but I had to fight for that.

I was the first as far as I'm aware to win a successful appeal in the police appeals court when I won on proof of efficiency rather than seniority. I was successful in appealing the promotion of five other detectives and generally I then retained that seniority for the rest of my service. This stood me in good stead for the rest of my career, although it did not win me any popularity contest I might say because a lot of people thought I had taken advantage of the Police Act and Rules, but I only went in those days by rule 27, which proved among other things that seniority was only to be taken into account when all other things were equal, and I was able to prove greater experience in all the other factors associated with my appeal.

Generally speaking in those days the seniority factor played a very prominent part, and if I had waited for my turn to come around strictly on seniority I probably would have had to wait another two years to get promoted.

The vote was two to one. The union representative and the magistrate found in my favour. The dissenting member, of course, was the Commissioner's representative.

(At this time members got to second class sergeant rank with between 15 and 17 years' service.)

As a detective sergeant second Class I was in charge of the Company squad that investigated frauds and all those associated matters. I had various stints on the Burglary squad, the Homicide squad and served on the various squads at the CI Branch.

I went right through the ranks and eventually got to detective senior sergeant, still at the CIB in Brisbane, and about that time I was appointed the chief prosecutor in the Brisbane Number 1 Magistrate's Court. My job then was to conduct daily prosecutions of the cases to be heard in the lower court and I fulfilled that duty with one, two or more members under my control for a couple of years. It was while in this position that I believe I did a very satisfactory job. I had a good understanding with most of the magistrates. I had a good and friendly association with a lot of solicitors, a lot of barristers and made many friends among the legal staff, some of whom, then as probably junior solicitors or barristers, later became QCs or even judges.

Some of these were Sir Edward Williams, Des Sturgess, who later became a prominent QC, and Bill Elson Green. Bill was one of my former friends and as a matter of fact he appeared for me in my police appeal.

In those days there was no Prosecutions Corps and you built up your expertise by just doing the job. What helped me was that over the years I had been in and out of the witness box on many occasions. I had had plenty of experience in the giving of evidence both in Brisbane and in outside places where I had to travel on many occasions, and I felt that stood me in good stead when it came to handling prosecutions and the matter of knowing what evidence was admissible, what wasn't admissible, the cross-examination of witnesses and all those sorts of side issues. I used to handle the criminal matters – summary trials and committal proceedings.

I well remember a humorous incident. Edward Eugene Ebzery appeared before Magistrate Warwick McKenna one morning. Mr McKenna wasn't noted for his good looks, but he was a very fair magistrate. On this particular morning Ebzery appeared before him I think on a charge of drunkenness or some minor offence, and Mr McKenna had told him only the previous week that if he appeared before him again he faced a jail sentence. On this particular morning after pleading guilty, Ebzery made a long appeal not to be sent to jail, made all sorts of promises that he would go out of town and he would get work and so on. It had no effect on Mr McKenna who sentenced Ebzery to one month's imprisonment and forthwith Ebzery came out with these remarks and I remember them to this day: "I hope all your fowls die. You've got a head on you like a Mongolian racing duck." Those of us who were in court could hardly resist laughing straight out and some of us had to beat a hasty retreat from the courtroom, and I think it took the magistrate rather by surprise because he quickly said: "Get that man out of here," and as he went out of court I detected a sly grin on the mouth of the magistrate because I think he too probably appreciated the humour of Ebzery's remark. He certainly didn't send him away for contempt of court.

Well I was always a sportsman. I used to play cricket and football before I joined the police and while in the Mounted Police Nobby Clark, who was captain of the police cricket team in the Warehouse Competition, got me to play with the police team and I recall that (I think) it was early in 1937 or '38 while playing one day in a competition game against a team called Strand and Imperial at Tingalpa I got four wickets with successive balls – in other words a double hat-trick – and I recall the Sunday paper the following day came out with some sort of a headline about me. It was one of the things of which I was very proud because even now, no matter what grade of cricket, I can't recall anybody having secured four wickets with successive balls.

In 1967 I think it was – after being appointed a commissioned officer – I became greatly interested in the affairs of commissioned officers. They had no registered union and I was appointed secretary of a group. I saw the necessity for an application to become an affiliated union and I was one of the prime movers, together with assistance from Merv Callagan, who was the general secretary of the Police Union, in doing the spadework and having a motion put before the Industrial Court with the result that eventually the police commissioned officers' union was registered. I think it still maintains its original title today.

After being appointed to commissioned rank, I was transferred to the Commissioner's office, then occupied by Commissioner Frank Bischof, and I fulfilled the role of what was then generally known as the troubleshooter. I had taken over from Inspector Harry Reinke and one of the things associated with the troubleshooter's job was investigating any more or less minor offences against police rules and regulations, not only in the city area, but throughout the State, and as such I had many trips to different areas investigating matters. For example, a watch-house keeper may well have not supplied a prisoner with meals or there was an over-claim or something for a meal that was never supplied. These sorts of things plus other things such as assault, the application of too much pressure when arresting people, and together with other matters that come under the notice of the administration. I believe I carried that out satisfactorily, and another one of the duties I had was not the setting of the police exam papers, but I had the marking of them for two or three years from all ranks up to commissioned rank, and that was a job that I enjoyed. Having always passed my own exams with fairly satisfactory results I felt that I was in a position to do this marking, and I think I gave a satisfactory performance over the years too.

I was doing that job more or less then until 1969 when in the meantime Mr Norm Bauer had become Commissioner. He transferred me to Rockhampton as officer in charge of the Rockhampton Police District. Now in the first stages of my transfer to Rockhampton I was disappointed in the sense that I thought well I'll be out of Brisbane and now I'll be more or less forgotten. My prospects of further progress in the service had not been helped at all. I had a talk to Mr Bauer and he reassured me that he felt that I needed this additional experience as a district officer and I had to agree with him that I had not had the experience of a district officer. It wasn't very long before I was very thankful to him for transferring me out to Rockhampton because while I was there I was able to carry out satisfactorily the duties associated with a district officer and I was there until early in 1971 when through the process of reorganisation Mr Bauer had retired and an appointment from outside, Mr Ray Whitrod, was made Commissioner. I was one of three Assistant Commissioners appointed to take up duty in March 1971 in Brisbane under Commissioner Whitrod. He appointed Assistant Commissioner Val Barlow in charge of Administration, Assistant Commissioner Les Hughes as Assistant Commissioner in charge of Traffic and myself as Assistant Commissioner in charge of Crime. Hughie Low was Chief Superintendent at the time and I don't think the ranks of Deputy Commissioner and Commissioner's Inspector then existed.

We served in those positions more or less in an experimental situation for some 12 months or more and Whitrod was feeling his way too. He had come there not so much under a cloud, because he had excellent theoretical qualifications, but a lot of members of the police, myself included, had some doubts that he would prove to be a success because he hadn't had the overall general experience that a lot of us senior officers had had. For example, he'd been in charge of the Commonwealth police, which had provided a lot of escorts for Governor-Generals and important politicians, overseas trips and all those sorts of things over the years and then he had had a short time as Commissioner in charge of the Papua New Guinea Police.

Well, he had a big hurdle to overcome to take charge of the Queensland Police, because as it turned out before long, it was quite obvious he had a very minute knowledge of some things associated with the Queensland Police in the sense that his geography was way out, way astray, he didn't know the men and he had a very poor knowledge of Queensland law. For example, it took him a lot of trouble to work out the difference between some of our simple offences and our indictable offences, etc. and on many occasions he came to us with queries about things that to us were really simplistic sorts of things. Over the years he effected various changes, some of which were no doubt thought to be good, others were of a doubtful nature, but in any case after about 12 months, one of his thoughts was on the traffic situation – or anyhow this is what he told me.

He took me away from the Crime portfolio and put me on what he called country traffic and as such he had me travelling for quite a while to various country districts to try and improve the situation in so far as preventing deaths on country roads and this sort of thing. Well, to my mind it was a very important portfolio of course, but my background was all to do with crime and I was a little disappointed about being taken off the crime situation, and it subsequently proved to me that it was one of the things he should never have done because I do firmly believe that if he had left me on the crime situation certain things might never have occurred or may well have turned out for the better.

I firmly believe in the initial stages he was right behind me in my appointment as Assistant Commissioner because he made two unsuccessful attempts while he was in Canberra to come to Brisbane to try and induce me to join the Commonwealth police, and that was way back in 1960, so he had some knowledge of my general ability and I have no doubt that he was one of those in favour of having me appointed as Assistant Commissioner. I do think, however, that after some time in Queensland – finding out that I was never afraid to express my opinion on different things, several of which were not entirely in agreement with his own view – there may have been some things that may have antagonised him to some extent. I never intended to be argumentative, but I've always put things as I saw them and I felt that if there was room for discussion – no matter who it was – there was always that room for discussion.

Whitrod had his own ideas about different things and somehow he seemed to have the idea that if anyone had disagreed with him they may well have been plotting against him. Maybe he did get that idea to some extent, but I don't know. In any case, those last three or four years under Whitrod were not entirely as satisfactory to me as they should have been.

In the 1974 Imperial Honours list I was awarded the Queen's Police Medal. I think that was the last year in which these awards were awarded as they were abolished by the Whitlam Government and they were discontinued.

Another factor that I like to be associated with, and this occurred many years after I retired, was the Fitzgerald Inquiry in which a lot of mention was made of police irregularities, police misconduct and so forth. In his book The Tangled Web, Mr Des Sturgess QC referred to me as a person whose integrity was always absolutely correct and I'm very grateful to Mr Sturgess for doing that. That's one of the things of which I am very proud.

It was a book in which police misconduct received quite a mention, together with quite a lot about the subsequent trial of former Commissioner Terry

Lewis. So I was very proud of Mr Sturgess for making those remarks and I treasure them greatly.

I was associated in the investigation of several murder cases. Unfortunately I don't think I was responsible for the arrest of any case that received a lot of prominence, but I do recall one of the disappointments of my service and life has been the fact that the murder of Betty Thomson Shanks in 1952 at The Grange in Brisbane was never solved. Ted Chandler advanced a theory about a possibility that existed at the time and I believe that was never properly followed up. Anybody that wants to read the details of what his theory was should read chapter nine of Ted Chandler's book, What Price Protection?, published in 1988.

A few years ago I participated in a review by Channel Nine and their investigating team of unsolved murders in Queensland, one of which was the Betty Shanks murder. I did comment on this theory at that stage and I believe that it was followed up.

During my service I received several commendations and favorable records that were awarded or recommended by commissioned officers for work performed in the solving of various crimes, and I was successful, without elaborating in any detail, because most successful detectives over the years have received their just rewards in relation to commendations and favourable records.

There was no official training system in my days and over the years I endeavoured to assist people who were sitting for police examinations by conducting unofficial classes in law and police duties. Wherever I served I tried to contribute to the success of people in their various examinations. When I first went to the CI Branch, as I said previously, I worked with senior men. Later on, when I became more experienced, junior men were appointed to work with me and I was able to assist and supervise them. Some of the officers who worked with me and who, in my opinion, were successful detectives were Tony Murphy and Terry Lewis. Now, I know that Terry later fell into disfavor, but I'm only talking now as I knew them when they were junior members of the CI Branch as investigators. They were top detectives. I'd like that to go down because both of them received unfavorable mentions at different inquiries, particularly the Fitzgerald Inquiry, in later years.

In my book the top of them all and most generally accepted as being the top detective of all time was Bill Cronau. Now Bill, who died in his 90s, was a senior man when I went to the CI Branch, and over the years his successful investigation in all types of crimes was outstanding. There are other detectives with whom I was associated whose names I'd like to mention, one of which was Stan Hambrecht. He generally never ever received a lot of prominence, but as an investigator he was a top man. Another who is still with us and who was in the top bracket of successful investigators was Jim Hamilton, who later resigned and went to the Commonwealth police and who later led a military branch of some sort in Cyprus.

I would like to add some comments about the last four years of my service. While I was happy and satisfied with my own performance in my 38 years and nine months in the Queensland Police Force, I was to a great extent disappointed with events within the last four years. That is when I was Assistant Commissioner under Ray Whitrod. I was certainly not disappointed with my own performance, but I was most unhappy at times with the performance of the Commissioner. Several senior officers were also unhappy with his stewardship, and while there are now few survivors, there are still some who can confirm my view.

When Whitrod took over as Commissioner there was some resentment within the senior ranks, first because he was an outsider and second because of his lack of real worldly experience. All of us were prepared to give him a fair go and co-operate in the hope and wish that he would prove successful but, like me, most of the senior officers were disappointed. Quite early he displayed a poor knowledge of the laws of the State, the geography of the State and the men and women serving under him. He was self-opinionated and at times took the view that anyone who didn't agree with his viewpoint was working against him. He relied for his success to a great extent on his co-operation with the media and they reciprocated to the extent that even now I doubt that any of them would say anything of an adverse nature against him. He made many wrong decisions and in my view became an expert at placing square pegs in round holes.

He liked to take the credit for things for which he was not totally responsible, and two cases in point were the opening of the Oxley Police Academy and the establishment of the Police Breathalyser Unit. I think that deep down he knew his limitations and was well aware of the superior ability of several of his senior officers, but he was at all times careful to cover this up. It was very difficult to get to see him on a matter of urgency and at times he got his priorities all wrong.

An example of this follows: I recall once that there was an intruder in a house out in the western suburbs. He was firing shots everywhere and generally the surrounding people were in terror. We got everything in motion. We sent the riot squad out there and I thought, well I'd better tell the boss because he doesn't like it if the press sometimes contact him before his officers do. So I went to his aide, Senior Constable Ken Hoggett, who was looking after his office, and I said to Ken that I wanted to see the Commissioner on a matter of urgency. "Right," he said, "I'll check." He went straight into his office. He came out and he said, "He's busy writing his newsletter; can you call back at 2 o'clock tomorrow afternoon?"

You can imagine my disappointment. If that's the attitude of a Police Commissioner when his number one Assistant Commissioner has to tell him something on a matter of urgency? That displays to my mind lack of knowledge of priorities and I couldn't understand it at times. I was bitterly disappointed and at times he seemed to encourage the wrong people to have access to his office. You would see people going into his office at various times and you'd wonder what were they going in there for?

He liked to dominate discussions and, on the rare occasions he did take notice of another viewpoint, at some later stage he'd take the credit for it. I did clash with him in particular on an occasion in 1974. It was the occasion when the floods were on, late January 1974. Whitrod had gone down to the Gold Coast for the day by car and at this time the floods were receding. People were out in their cars everywhere trying to see where the flood heights had been, etc and he experienced great difficulty in getting back from the Gold Coast. It'd taken him, I think, some four hours to get back through the traffic.

I happened to be at the police communications office when he walked in, sweaty, dishevelled and obviously in a bad mood and he said, "What's going on with the traffic out there?" I said, "I know it's a bit unruly, but what can we do about it? People are out looking at everything". He said, "Why haven't you done something about it? This doesn't show much for your administration," or words to that effect. Well, this did upset me and I said, straight away, "Don't talk to me about my administration. Fifteen people died under your administration and you know they never should have died".

My statement upset him terrifically and he immediately said, "Oh, let's get out of here," because this was in the presence of at least half-a-dozen people on the staff. "Let's get out of here. What's this, what's going on?" So he led me to another room and he said, "What do you mean?" I said, "You know what I mean," and I related to him then about the Whiskey Au Go Go fire that had occurred the previous year and for which the two offenders, as I believed he was well aware, should never have been out of jail to commit the offence. From that day onwards I don't think that Whitrod thought that I deserved much more official accreditation because he became more distant from then on, but it is a fact in my view that there should have been some inquiry into the administration associated with the Whiskey Au Go Go fire.

I believe that that inquiry would have found whether administration was deficient in some way or other because those two men who were found to have committed the offence should have been in their right place behind bars at the time of the offence. Well that was the sort of thing that brought this to a head. That was the one instance in which I definitely clashed with Whitrod and I know he never forgave me for it because from then on, until I retired in May 1975, there wasn't a lot of conversation between us, barely any more than was necessary. We did pass the time of day and so on, but he didn't attend my official send-off presided over by the Deputy Premier of the State, Sir Gordon Chalk. He sent along some inept excuse as to why he couldn't attend.

Another thing that I remember him by and which I'll never forget, was that after I retired, in March 1976, my wife, Iris, died after a long period of ill-health. Whitrod was aware of her ill health because she had to cancel several engagements at different times because of not being able to attend. Anyhow, it was a funeral well attended by serving officers and retired officers. There was no recognition from Whitrod of her death. No recognition by way of a card or anything of that nature, no phone message and within a week after her funeral I went across to the Indooroopilly Bowls Club on the morning of the official opening of the interstate police bowls carnival. I was then, and had been previously, a member, but had been the patron of that club until I handed over to Whitrod in 1974 and, as such, he was waiting at the entrance to the club to welcome the Police Pipe Band this particular morning.

I walked past him to enter the club. I stopped, passed the time of day, spoke to him; still no word from him in the course of our few words of conversation about my wife's death and then, thinking possibly that somewhere along the line he hadn't heard of my wife's death, I said to him quite courteously "I suppose you heard, Mr Whitrod that I lost my wife last week". His words, and I remember them to this day were. "Yes, I know". He then said, "I've got to go now" and off he walked to meet the band.

That's my last conversation with Whitrod. I'll never forget his words to me until my dying day. I can never imagine a less compassionate reply than I received from him that morning and that to me indicates the type of man that we had been dealing with all those years. I can forgive him, but never forget what he said, and I'll always remember too a somewhat jocular remark that Norm Bauer passed to me. Norm Bauer, the previous Commissioner, said: "He's a show pony. He's never pulled a plough."

I mentioned previously the Whisky Au Go Go case. I believe that one of the offenders, John Andrew Stuart, was committing offences all the time. He'd only needed a little bit of observation by the observation squad and they would have found him committing offences and would have put him behind bars. Instead of this he was confiding in one or more members of the Crime Intelligence Unit, Whitrod's own particular section, pretending to pass on valuable information.

My knowledge of the various ranks was very limited when I first joined and I did aim of course to get as far as I could because I was always ambitious, but I suppose I had no real positive ambition at the time. My main thought was to get a good secure positive job where I'd be able to contribute something to the community, and I feel that through the whole of my service, 38 years and nine months, until I retired on 31 May, 1975, I performed entirely to my own satisfaction.

I'd like to be remembered as an honest, sincere, hard-working, conscientious, dedicated police officer who always did his job to the best of his skill and ability. I think that sums it up in a few words. Another thing I would like to say is that I have always spoken my mind and I have no fears in what I say.

# Albert Thomas (Tom) Pointing

My brother, Albert Thomas (Tom) Pointing, and I came from a large country family. Tom was the seventh child: I was the 10th. We both joined the Queensland Police Force. Tom in September 1945, 13 years before me.

When Tom left the dairy farm I was only nine years of age and we saw very little of each other until he retired to his property at Imbil, south of Gympie. Being a keen horseman I visited his property on weekends whenever possible to ride my horses and assist Tom attending his cattle. I am pleased to say that by the time of his unexpected death at 70 we had developed a very close brotherly relationship.

Being a country boy who left school at 13, Tom did very well in life, rising as he did from police cadet to regional superintendent of police. Besides being a fingerprint expert, a very capable detective and police administrator, he also earnt a reputation as a boxer and footballer. Most of all he was a family man through and through. I have every reason to be proud of my brother and his many achievements.

We begin his story with an Ipswich police report dated 28 May, 1945 wherein Constable Seary assesses Tom and our family in response to Tom's application to become a police cadet.

**Laurie Pointing**

Ipswich District

Ipswich Station

28 May, 1945.

Relative to:- Inquiries re Albert Thomas Pointing, of Pine Mountain, Ipswich who has made application to join the Queensland Police Force as a Cadet.

Ipswich District Ref No 188 M 98

Sir,

I have to report the result of inquiries concerning the above-mentioned applicant. I find that Pointing was born at Lowood, 28 May 1928, and attended school at Fernvale, Esk and Colinton. Last attendance at school was at Colinton to September 1941. Since leaving school the applicant has been working on farming properties at Colinton with his parents, and also at Pine Mountain.

He has been at Pine Mountain for approximately two and a half years, and from my inquiries in that locality the lad bears an excellent character.

The parents, Albert Edward Pointing, father, and Ethel Mary Pointing, mother, were married in Ipswich, January 15, 1916, and have since that date worked farming properties at Fairney View, from there to Reid's place at Wivenhoe Pocket, then to Mt Beppo working half/shares, then to Lowood. From Lowood they went to work half/shares basis a farm owned by Mr Harding, and on leaving Colinton where Mr Harding's farm was situated they came to Pine Mountain.

As stated previously in this report they have been at Pine Mountain now for approximately two and a half years, and during that time they have become well liked and respected people in the district. Inquiries as far as can be pursued in the Ipswich Division reveal that both the applicant and his parents bear good character. As a result I would consider that the applicant is a fit type of youth to be admitted to the Queensland Police Force as a cadet.

LE Seary

Constable No #3780

Upon leaving school in 1941 Tom helped his parents on farms at Colinton, in the Brisbane Valley and Pine Mountain. He also worked on neighbouring farms at those locations and was employed on droving trips walking cattle to Churchill saleyards at Ipswich prior to sale day.

Tom's father urged him to seek a government job because he could see no future on the land for the youth of the day. Tom made application to sit for the railway porter's examination, but missed the opportunity when he developed mumps.

Some seven miles from Tom's home, George Westerway operated a mixed farm. George taught his son, Bill Westerway, and Tom the fundamentals of boxing. He also taught Tom to play the guitar. Family members remember Tom riding his pushbike the seven miles over dirt roads with his guitar strapped to his back for weekly guitar and boxing lessons.

There are grounds to believe that George Westerway, a friend of the Ipswich police inspector, encouraged Tom to join the police as a cadet. However, on a neighbouring farm lived the McKenna family and one of their sons, Jim, was a policeman stationed at Ipswich. Tom gave him the credit for his entry into the Service. Jim eventually became the District Inspector at Redcliffe and at the time of writing is still alive and alert in his 96$^{th}$ year.

Tom was admitted to the Queensland Police Service (it was then called a "Force") as a cadet on 3 September, 1945. Sworn in on 18 June, 1948, he was attached to Woolloongabba Station. The following year he filled a vacancy in the Fingerprint Bureau where he remained for five years and gained the classification of "Fingerprint Expert".

During this period Tom gained a reputation as a boxer and rugby league player. (In those days a member had to apply to the Commissioner for permission to be involved in these sports.) Tom is to be remembered for a boxing contest with Denis Flannery, who also represented Australia as a rugby league player. Tom lost the fight on points, but was runner-up in the Golden Gloves boxing competition. He fought as a welterweight and was trained by Percy Jamieson.

Having completed his fingerprint training Tom wanted to use this expertise in conjunction with general investigative police work. He applied for and was successful in gaining a position as plain-clothes constable in the Toowoomba Criminal Investigation Branch. He was posted there in 1954 in the dual capacity of an investigator and fingerprint expert for the whole district.

A tough rugby league forward, Tom played A grade with Southern Suburbs in Brisbane and for the police team. Upon his posting to Toowoomba, he played 54 A grade games for the All Whites and helped them to premiership wins in the Bulimba Cup. He twice won the Des McGovern Perpetual Trophy. In his story Beneath the Southern Cross, Mick Moloney bemoaned the fact that he was denied a permanent A grade position with the All Whites "because…a big policeman, Tom Pointing, kept me out".

Attached to the Criminal Investigation Branch, Toowoomba as a plain-clothes constable, as well as normal criminal investigation duties, Tom also carried out the role of fingerprint expert for the Toowoomba police district. In the 1950s and 1960s the Dalby police district did not exist, and while there were detectives stationed at that centre, Tom was responsible for carrying out fingerprint examinations in that division.

In 1961 Tom transferred as a detective senior constable to Charleville. At that stage there was only one detective stationed in that district, which included the police division of Cunnamulla, which had no detective. In May 1965 his office was upgraded and Tom was promoted to detective sergeant second class and remained at Charleville.

(During his Charleville tour of duty he was involved in a protracted murder investigation known as the "Bulloo Downs" murder. More of that later.)

As a result of a serious illness diagnosed in one of his children Tom was transferred on that rank to the Gympie Criminal Investigation Branch in February 1966 to be close to professional medical treatment required by his son. In those days there were no detectives stationed in the northern suburbs of the Sunshine Coast. At Gympie the Criminal Investigation Branch consisted of two detectives to carry out criminal investigations as far south as Noosa, and Tom's subordinate was the late Detective Senior Constable Arthur Springer, a veteran of World War II.

Promoted to detective sergeant first class in charge of the Bundaberg CI Branch, Tom remained at Bundaberg until August 1976 when he moved on transfer to CI Branch Headquarters, Brisbane with the rank of detective senior sergeant.

In August 1976 Tom was appointed to commissioned rank and as an inspector he took charge of the Crime Intelligence Squad. From there he worked in the Internal Investigations Unit before being posted as officer in charge of the Wynnum Police District.

Promoted to detective superintendent in charge of the Internal Investigations Unit (1981-82), Tom was also the representative of the Queensland Police Department on the Royal Commission of Inquiry into Drug Trafficking headed by Mr Justice Stewart. In 1982 Tom's final posting was to the North Coast Region where he was based at Gympie as the regional superintendent. He retired on 2 July, 1986.

Bulloo Downs Murder, Thargomindah. Campsite. L-R: Detective Sergeant Tom Pointing; Constable 1/c Lyle Pratt; Unknown; Unknown; Unknown; Ken Volk; Tracker Tommy Swan; Inspector Bill McNaught. *Queensland Police Museum.*

That same year the reputation that Tom had built up over the many years was highlighted when he was presented with the Queen's Police Medal for Distinguished Service.

The fact that Tom was awarded three official Favorable Records and four Official Commendations for outstanding police work bespeaks the fact he was an exemplary policeman. Details of these seven awards are abbreviated to point form.

- January 1957 – Awarded a Favorable Record regarding the arrest and conviction of two men for breaking and entering the National Bank of Australia and stealing money and a pistol.
- May 1958 – Officially Commended regarding the arrest of two men on charges of rape.
- April 1960 – Awarded a Favourable Record regarding the arrest of two men for breaking, entering and stealing.
- May 1960 – Officially Commended for the arrest of three men on charges of robbery with actual violence.

- February 1964 – Awarded a Favorable Record for the arrest of four men on charges of rape.
- November 1964 – Officially Commended for the arrest of a man on charges of stealing wool and illegally marking sheep.
- October 1971 – Officially Commended for the arrest of two men on charges of breaking, entering and stealing.

It is to be understood, of course, that other police officers involved in these cases also received appropriate recognition.

Ross Beer is a retired inspector of police and when transferred to Charleville police station as a junior constable in mid-1963, Tom was the detective sergeant attached to the Charleville police division. Ross has this to say regarding Tom:

> I joined the Queensland Police Force in early 1959 as a cadet and harbored a desire to follow in my father's footsteps with a career in the Criminal Investigation Branch.
>
> Having served in "hands on" positions as a cadet at the CI Branch photographic section, and senior sergeants' clerk, I was eventually sworn in during 1962 and transferred as a junior constable to Charleville, my initial country posting, in mid-1963.
>
> It was here that I first met Tom Pointing, who was the sole detective for the entire Charleville police district. This was a vast area in the south-west of Queensland, which extended to the New South Wales, South Australian and Northern Territory borders.
>
> With permission from successive district inspectors, Jack Holliday and William McKenzie McNaught, I was able to accompany Tom on several occasions on investigations. He was a tremendous mentor and I learnt much from his vast experience.
>
> Tom was always most helpful and willing to assist other young police officers throughout the district, several of whom went on to have successful careers as members of the Criminal Investigation Branch in various locations throughout the State.
>
> Largely due to Tom's encouragement I was appointed a plain-clothes constable at Brisbane CI Branch in April 1964. In May 1965 I was selected as one of five Queensland Police Officers to form a contingent of "Forty Australian police from every State and Territory within the Commonwealth," to be seconded to

the then Australian (now Federal) Commonwealth Police for inclusion in a United Nations Peacekeeping Police Force (160 members) on the troubled island of Cyprus in the Mediterranean.

This force comprised Australian, Austrian, Danish, New Zealand and Swedish police, plus a contingent of 500 military peacekeepers from numerous nations.

I consider that Tom Pointing substantially contributed with his mentoring to my selection for that consignment. I served in Cyprus for 12 months and then returned to the CI Branch, Brisbane in August 1966 and immediately served at Caloundra and Nambour for several months.

Tom by this stage was the detective sergeant in charge of the Gympie CI Branch and we shared a common boundary as the Gympie district in those days came as far south as Noosa, north of Eumundi. Again Tom assisted in several investigations and we shared a stipendiary magistrate, the late and great Ted Loane.

I could continue to embellish on Tom's capabilities, but I can say he played a major role in my criminal investigative career where I served in numerous places and roles at all rank, including the rank of commissioned officer. Not only that - Tom's mentoring of numerous young police officers over the years enabled them to rise through the ranks and contribute greatly to the success of the Queensland Police Service.

Tom maintained a unique fitness regime throughout his life and was a fine specimen of manhood. In his recreation hours he would demolish old tractor tyres with a heavy sledge hammer, thus reducing the tyre to a heap of cotton and rubber waste. TRY IT SOMETIME!!

Granville Patrick Pearce is a retired chief superintendent of police, now living in retirement at Bundaberg and first worked with Tom as a junior plain clothes constable at the Criminal Investigation Branch, Bundaberg and this is what Grannie has to say:

"I first met Tom Pointing at Bundaberg. Tom took charge of the CI Branch not long after I commenced duty at Bundaberg Police Station. I arrived at Bundaberg in 1969 and after a short stint in general duties I was assigned to uniform inquiries.

Tom replaced Jack Jesson as the officer in charge of the CI Branch. He had four detectives under his control and they were Frank Swindells, Trevor Menary, Kevin O'Brien and Bob Minns.

During my time in uniform inquiries I worked with Ron Creevey, Warren Kemp and Graham Clarke. Later, Ron Rooke replaced Graham Clarke and during that period we managed to locate and arrest quite a number of offenders. Prior to Tom's arrival all arrests were referred to the CI Branch staff and uniform personnel were excluded. Under Tom's leadership this changed and he directed detectives to assist uniform staff to arrest offenders and assist with the preparation of court briefs of evidence. There was a standard instruction not to take arrest from uniform members.

Tom fostered a close working relation between uniform and CI Branch staff. He particularly worked well with the Traffic Branch boys, who had a good knowledge of who was who around town and what vehicles they were in possession of. The Traffic boys also knew who was driving the streets late at night when offences were being committed.

I managed to get seconded to the CI Branch after Frank Swindells left on transfer and I continued to relieve for a very long period. Tom recommended that I should be appointed to the position vacated by Swindells, but Trevor MacIntosh was given the position. Tom then persuaded me to apply for the CI Branch in Brisbane, which I did and I was subsequently transferred there.

I had only been in Brisbane for 10 months when Tom telephoned and said that Kevin O'Brien was leaving and he would like me to come back to Bundaberg. I applied and was transferred back to the CI Branch, Bundaberg.

This helped my career no end. Tom was a really good mentor. He was articulate and his interrogation techniques were superb. We all learnt quickly from Tom. He had a completely new team of detectives: John Banham, Max Moloney, Gordon Watson and myself.

Under Tom's guidance the CI Branch worked well, with a high percentage of offences being cleared. The main attributes we found in Tom's leadership were that he was honest and a straight shooter. He had great ability as an investigator and was able to pull the team together. He certainly taught us many skills during his period as the officer in charge. Some of his key words were "Hasten slowly" and "Do your homework well, put yourself in a better position than the person you are interrogating".

> I was fortunate to have served under Tom's guidance. In my view he certainly would have attained the rank of Assistant Commissioner, however, he chose to retire to his beloved farm at Imbil, south of Gympie.

Tom married Kathleen Maureen Dowling, who grew up in the Brisbane suburb of Corinda, on 26 August, 1950. There were five children to the union, namely, Sharon Cecilia, Gary Thomas, Richard James, Julie Maree and Christopher Gerald.

Sadly, Gary died on 6 September, 2003 at the age of 47 following complications after undergoing open-heart surgery. His mother, Kath, passed to eternal life on 15 May, 2010 aged 83.

Patrick Cornelius (Pat) O'Brien commenced his distinguished police career as a police cadet with the Queensland Police Service on 19 February, 1945. He commenced duty at the Fingerprint Bureau, Brisbane during June 1948 as a constable of police and retired as the senior technical officer in charge of that bureau on 13 May, 1983. It is without question that during his career Pat was one of our most competent and valued fingerprint experts.

Pat and Tom formed a friendship during their cadet days and that continued until Tom's untimely death on 21 March, 1999. Pat has this to say about their friendship:

> I first met Tom about 1946 when we were both cadets and we became great mates and remained that way until his unfortunate passing. He was the fittest 70 year-old man I have ever known. We used to go to dances at the Corinda Library Hall when we were cadets and probationaries. I introduced Tom to his future wife, Kath Dowling, at one of the dances.
>
> When I was sworn in with Tom on 18 June, 1948, I was transferred to the Fingerprint Bureau, where I had been attached as a cadet. Tom went to Woolloongabba Police Station. In 1949 there was a vacancy at the Fingerprint Bureau and the officer in charge asked the staff if they knew any officer that may be interested. I approached Tom and he was interested: I mentioned this to the officer in charge and Tom was interviewed and transferred to the Bureau.
>
> He remained at the Fingerprint Bureau until 1954 where he became a very competent fingerprint expert. He then decided he was interested in transferring to the CI Branch and was transferred as a plain-clothes constable to the Toowoomba Criminal Investigation Branch. Among his duties at Toowoomba was undertaking the role of the fingerprint expert for the Toowoomba Police District.

The Fingerprint Bureau in Queensland was established in 1904 and the Police Department decided at the Centenary of the Bureau in 2004 to create an Honour Roll of all fingerprint experts during that 100-year period. Tom is number 15 on that Honour Roll and I am number 14 in a list of some 88 fingerprint experts throughout the history of the Bureau.

Tom was a tough rugby league forward and played A grade with Southern Suburbs, which was based at Davies Park, West End. He was a member of that team when it won the premiership in Brisbane. He was also a good fighter and was runner-up in the Golden Gloves boxing competition.

When we both retired, Tom and Kath would stay at our residence at Tugun with my wife (Ursula, who I also met at a Corinda dance) and I and we would attend the Gold Coast retired police annual function at Twin Towns. When the Gympie retired police held their annual function, Ursula and I would stay with Tom and Kath at their property at Imbil for a few days.

Tom was a civil, courteous, genial, modest, capable and efficient officer, and I doubt if there was a more sympathetic and tactful person in the Police Force. He was an active and assiduous worker in every phase of his life. He carried out his duties fearlessly and impartially and displayed all the attributes that made him an ideal "detective".

Tom was a friend to everyone, a quiet, reserved gentleman, traits that no doubt he had maintained all his life. His friendship was valued and I only heard genuine praise and admiration of this very popular man.

If we had more people like Tom and parents of the calibre of Tom and Kath Pointing, it would be a better world to live in.

The first chapter of this book deals with police work in the first decade of the 20th century. We conclude this final chapter with an interesting murder case resolved by Tom in the year 1965, arising out of the discovery of three human skulls found on Bulloo Downs Station near Thargomindah. Roy Boatswain (also known as Bill Conroy) was charged:

> "That on or about the 21st day of May, 1964 at Bulloo Downs Station near Thargomindah in the State of Queensland, wilfully murdered one Maxwell Henry Ricketts."

The story illustrates Tom's tenacity as a detective and begins on 9 June, 1965 when Arthur O'Shea, the manager of Bulloo Downs Station, found a human skull about 36 miles from the homestead. He was in the company of Bernard Sopeer, a rabbit dealer.

They reported the find to the Thargomindah police and Sergeant Ted Warner and Constable Lyle Pratt made initial investigations. They were joined by the Charleville detective, Tom Pointing, who took charge of the case.

A police search-party camp was established at the site where the skull was found. Within three-quarters of a mile of the first find, two more skulls were recovered as well as other bones. Harry Harrison, a journalist/photographer who was accompanying the investigators, was appointed the official photographer for the police at the scene of the crime.

Clothing and other exhibits, including a mobile rabbit chiller, were found within miles of the scene. Because of the vast area to be searched and the thick growth of lignum bush, a light search aircraft was used to advantage. Some five miles south of the mobile chiller was found a Land Rover and a trailer hidden in lignum bush nine feet high. Clothing, crockery and a double mattress were found about the vehicle.

An examination of the skulls and bones by Doctor Tongue of the Department of Microbiology and Pathology determined that all were of European origin: The first a male aged 40-50, the others a female about 40 years and a child.

From information obtained from Arthur O'Shea, the station manager, police established that from 1963 to mid 1964 two men named Bill Conroy and Max Ricketts were trapping rabbits in the vicinity where the skulls were found and they camped at a nearby spot named Robber's Roost. They supplied rabbits to Bernard Sopeer who ran a rabbit depot near the homestead. Ricketts had a woman and child (thought to be his wife and son) at the camp. Conroy was by himself.

O'Shea told Detective Sergeant Pointing that the manager of the rabbit depot, Bernard Sopeer, visited Broken Hill in May 1965 where he spoke to Rex Jenkins who trapped rabbits in the same area as used by Conroy and Ricketts in 1964, but by then the pair had left the area. While trapping Jenkins found a human skull, but did nothing about it.

Recounting events, Sopeer said that in September 1963 Bill Conroy asked him for a land allocation to trap rabbits for supply to Sopeer. Conroy delivered his first load of rabbits on 21st September, 1963.

Not long afterwards Conroy was joined by Max Rickett's who was accompanied by a woman and child. All of them camped together at Robber's

Roost. Ricketts was driving an old Chevrolet with a wooden trailer. He later replaced the car with a Land Rover.

Conroy and Ricketts operated a partnership and by agreement Ricketts took responsibility for all financial matters and for the delivery of the rabbits to the depot.

In June 1964 Conroy asked Sopeer to be paid in full for all the rabbits he supplied. He explained that he had an argument with Ricketts about financial arrangements the night before and Ricketts had chased him into the bush with a stick in his hand. Conroy claimed he had hidden all night and on returning to camp next morning found that Ricketts and his family had packed up and left.

Conroy further informed Sopeer that Ricketts had not collected the rabbit traps he had set. Also, Ricketts had deliberately damaged Conroy's car, which took two days to repair. Sopeer paid Conroy the money due to him. When the depot keeper awoke next morning Conroy had left, presumably to go to Thargomindah.

Investigations by Tom and other police in Queensland, New South Wales and Victoria identified the three victims as:

Maxwell Henry Ricketts

Marie Philomena Brown

Cecil John Brown (son of Marie and Maxwell Ricketts)

Inquiries established that "Bill Conroy" was an alias used by a New South Wales criminal named Roy Boatswain. Boatswain was found to be in a Brisbane prison for an offence of unlawfully using a motor vehicle. Upon his release on 12 July 1965 he was met by Detective Sergeant Pointing, Detective Sergeant Chalmers and Detective Senior Constable McCosker of the Brisbane Homicide Squad.

Boatswain admitted to having an affair with Marie Brown and claimed that Ricketts was aware of the fact. He stoutly denied shooting the woman and child, claiming this was Ricketts' doing.

According to Boatswain he was in the mobile chiller with the engine running and when he stepped down from the doorway of the chiller, he saw Ricketts coming around the corner of the chiller with a .303 rifle in his hands. He ran away from Ricketts, who fired a shot that missed, whereupon Ricketts threw the rifle at him. Boatswain grabbed the weapon, blew sand out of the barrel and chamber, and from a pouch of ammunition on his belt he loaded the .303 rifle. Ricketts allegedly ran back to the camp and again came towards

Boatswain carrying a .22 rifle. Ricketts fired another shot, which again went astray, and Boatswain fired a shot over Rickett's head. Boatswain admitted he reloaded and fired a shot that hit Ricketts in the chest. He reloaded and fired a second shot into Ricketts' chest and he fell to the ground.

According to Boatswain he shot Ricketts because when he called out to the woman she did not answer and he thought that Ricketts had shot her and the boy. He claimed he did not intend to kill Ricketts with the first shot, but did so when he fired the second and third shots. After shooting Ricketts, Boatswain claimed that he ran to the camp where he discovered the bodies of both Marie Brown and her son Cecil on the ground near Ricketts' old Chevrolet vehicle. They were both dead.

Boatswain said that after the shooting he drank rum and became intoxicated. As darkness approached he loaded the three bodies on to the Land Rover and drove some miles to a small sand hill where he buried them in a shallow grave. Returning to the camp he loaded the property of the deceased on to the Land Rover and then drove about five miles to hide the vehicle and trailer in a lignum swamp before walking back to camp.

In the absence of sustainable evidence that Boatswain had killed the woman and child, he was charged only with the wilful murder of Ricketts. On 2 October, 1965 at the Circuit Court, Roma he was found guilty of manslaughter and sentenced to seven years' imprisonment with hard labour.

If in fact Boatswain was having an affair with Marie Brown this may have contributed to the death of this unfortunate woman and child.

Tom enjoyed a unique niche in Queensland policing in that he was the first qualified fingerprint expert to be appointed a field staff detective. This happy combination of skills added to his value to the Department.

But Tom was more than just a good policeman. A considerate husband, a caring father, a loyal brother and friend, most of all he was a successful human being and a good bloke.

# About the Author

Laurie Pointing is a retired senior Queensland police officer with a country background. As a police officer he served in many locations throughout the State of Queensland, both as a uniformed officer, member of the Criminal Investigation Branch, Stock Investigation squad, police prosecutor and administrator.

In retirement Laurie spends time travelling through the outback, reading and writing poetry. He is a lover of country music and the sport of cricket. He is a proud Queenslander.

This is his third book. Laurie's first publication, His Saddle Hangs There Idle, was published in 2004, and his second, When I Left The Dairy Farm, in 2007.